D1467074

STRONGER

THE JACOB PETERS STORY

BY GARY PETERS

PRAIRIE MUSE BOOKS INC

©4/3/2021 by Gary Peters. All rights reserved.
This is a true account.
Names, characters, places, and incidents
are the product of the author's experience.
Any resemblance to other persons is entirely coincidental.
No part of this book may be used in another work, with the
exception of critical reviews, may not be copied in whole or in part,
or stored physically or electronically without having been
purchased from the author or having gained
permission from the author.

STRONGER: THE JACOB PETERS STORY
ISBN 978-1-952911-18-7
Lincoln, Nebraska

That beautiful wonder is my son.
- GARY PETERS

Peters Family – Jacob, Gary, Jerod, Shari, and Dalton

INTRODUCTION

I was blessed to be given three boys—Jacob, Jerod and Dalton. I have raised my boys to focus on giving their best effort in whatever venture they are pursuing. Athletically and academically I expect them to do their very best at all times. Some people have said that I am too demanding, but I don't think that life will take it easy on you, so you had better be prepared to fight your own battles and expect to succeed. As a parent I see too many instances where there is no accountability, or where a parent will interfere with a child's situation to manipulate the outcome. How will a child ever learn to deal with life's adversity if a parent is always fixing their problems? People have said that I am too strict, but all three of my boys are known for their work ethic and high standards, without my interference.

I had the opportunity to listen to Andy Means, a respected high school football coach in Nebraska, at the Nebraska Football Coaches Clinic in Lincoln. He summed up my philosophy when he explained that his team only has three rules. They are as follows:

1. Be where you are supposed to be.
2. Be there early.
3. Do the very best you can while you are there.

The simplicity astounded me. This is exactly what I want my children to strive for every day. This applies to any athletic team at any specific time. Whether it pertains to attendance or how you execute your assignment on any given play. It also pertains to how you live your life in general. Apply this to the classroom or the workplace and it carries the exact same message.

It did not take long for me to copy this information and use it for my own youth football team. We started every practice at the beginning of the season by reciting these three simple rules. After a couple of weeks, every player knew and understood the all-encompassing meaning behind them. We used this for the entire season and, coincidently, went undefeated and won the league championship for the first time in our program's short history.

This is also now the perfect way to communicate my expectations with all three of my children. My boys are typical siblings. Typical in the fact that they are dissimilar, in many ways. They each have their own distinct personality and good and bad qualities. They are truly individual. Most parents that I know that have multiple children of the same sex will agree that each child has their own unique qualities. I love the fact that my boys are not carbon copies. I think that would create a lot of pressure on each successive child if they are always viewed to be a newer version of an older sibling.

Having three boys with differing strengths and weaknesses creates challenges as a parent and provides an opportunity to bond with each child in a different manner. To me, it is important to feel a unique connection with each of my boys. Sometimes we get lost in a herd mentality which only stifles the individual. It is true that we all enjoy some of the same things. However, they all have additional interests which is where the opportunity presents itself. One of the great things about being a family is that we can all have differing interests and opinions, but we can still find comfort in the herd. Regardless of your similarities and differences, those three simple rules will help you succeed.

This is the story of my family's greatest challenge and the journey that we were all a part of.

Pediatric Cancer Action Network

One diagnosis is not rare enough

www.pcanaction.org

One

THE FIRST SIGN OF TROUBLE

JANUARY 14, 2011. Jacob played horribly tonight in a basketball game against Central City. He made stupid mistakes and played totally out of character. He was sloppy with the ball. He got pushed around and just didn't play very smart or hard. After the game I told my wife, Shari, "He will be sick tomorrow". Sometimes a parent can just tell when there is something not quite right with your child, whether it be emotionally or physically. Often it is as simple as a look in the eye or a slight change in routine, but sometimes it can present itself as a bad grade or bad game. Almost every parent I know can read their child this way even though that child may not have presented any other symptoms yet. Sure enough, Jacob woke up Saturday morning heavily congested and feeling horrible. He spent the weekend drinking fluids, resting, and taking Nyquil.

After the weekend, we scheduled an appointment with one of our local physicians. He looked Jacob over and did the standard stuff, listened to his lungs, checked his throat, ears, heart, etc. It appeared that Jacob just had "the crud", so we left with a prescription for antibiotics and cough suppressant just like we had planned. He also wrote Jacob a note for school that said, "No physical activity until Friday". He sat out the rest of the week of basketball practice and started feeling better. The antibiotics seemed to be working.

Friday night he suited up for the Seward JV game with no expectations of playing since he had not practiced all week. He was even told by the head coach to suit up, but he would just sit on the bench. However, in the 2nd quarter the JV Coach told him to check in and he did. His job, as always, was to shut down the other team's biggest player, who had been scoring at will. The teams made one trip up and down the court and approximately one minute after

Jacob entered the game there was a stoppage and he ran to the bench doing a slashing motion across his throat. "I'm done," he told his coach. He couldn't breathe because of the congestion. This was a cause for concern for Shari and I because he never wants to come out of the game. He can't help his team if he's on the sideline. Something wasn't right. We thought that he just wasn't quite well yet and that he just needed more rest and medicine.

Over the weekend his symptoms worsened, so on Monday we called the doctor for another prescription, because he didn't seem to be over the hump yet. This time we didn't go in for another visit. The doctor just prescribed a new antibiotic. With a new prescription in hand, he practiced all week in anticipation of getting to play the next week. He practiced all week and had no complaints. His breathing was not normal, but it appeared to be getting better and did not limit his efforts. He appeared to be getting better.

Over the next weekend his symptoms once again took a turn for the worse once he ran out of antibiotics. On Sunday he woke up and felt worse than he had for the past two weeks. We decided that we would make another appointment to see the doctor first thing Monday morning.

The doctor that Jacob had seen earlier was not available until mid-afternoon, but another doctor was available mid-morning, so Shari scheduled the appointment with the first available. His breathing was so labored that Shari felt if we did not get him in early, that he might be in the Emergency Room by lunch. We had no idea that by 11:00am our lives would be changed forever.

Two

———

OUR LIVES WERE
CHANGED FOREVER

Day 1, Monday, January 31, 2011

On Monday morning we called in for an appointment to see if he had pneumonia or some other infection that we were not treating correctly. At 9:40am we had an appointment with a different doctor. He did all of the same things the first doctor did during his examination, except he checked Jacob's throat for swelling. He spent quite a bit of time feeling a large lump in Jacob's throat that I had not noticed before. The doctor ordered blood tests to check for possible infections and a chest X-ray to check Jacob's lungs for abnormalities. I stayed in the exam room as they took Jacob for X-rays and was never concerned about what they would find.

The doctor came back in to tell us that the blood tests had come back negative for any type of infection, but there was something on the X-ray that concerned him. The doctor told us that he wanted to consult a surgeon who just happens to do his rotation through Aurora on Mondays.

The surgeon came in first and told us that he felt there was a chance that Jacob had lymphoma and that they would have to do a biopsy to know for sure. Jacob was sitting on the end of the examination table and I was in a chair behind him and to his right. The doctor sat in a chair directly across the room from me and I will always remember the confused look on Jacob's face as he turned over his right shoulder to look at me while the doctor was speaking. We were both completely taken aback and neither one of us actually believed what we had

9

just heard. Denial was our first defense.

I called Shari and told her that she should come to the clinic, still not quite comprehending what was unfolding in front of my eyes. Soon after she arrived we were whisked away for a CT scan of Jacob's chest and neck. We sat in the waiting room stunned and confused. We consoled each other by clinging to the fact that we did not have an official diagnosis and hopefully further testing would result in a different diagnosis.

We returned to the exam room and the word came down soon after that. We were to be in Grand Island by 6:30am for a biopsy and stay there for a 2:15pm meeting with an oncologist at the Cancer Treatment Center. There it was, the word "cancer" was spoken for the first time. As we were gathering our things and walking down the hall, a nurse approached us and said that she would be praying for my family. The gravity of the situation really hit home for me then. We were in trouble.

Of course, like any family, we went home devastated. Crying, talking, crying, hugging, crying, and staring at each other in stunned disbelief. We wandered around the living room, occasionally huddling for a group hug, sobbing the entire time. I remember thinking to myself, "What am I supposed to do now?" I can usually find the right words to say or have a suggestion for the right plan of action, but I was at a total loss. Helpless.

By this time, Jacob was having an extremely difficult time breathing. His breaths were sporadic, labored and had a heavy wheezing sound. Eventually we decided to rent a movie that afternoon to pass the time and try to escape the reality we found ourselves struggling to comprehend. As we sat in our living room, I spent more time watching every labored breath Jacob took instead of watching the movie. It was a surreal environment. Maybe this was the denial stage of our grieving, I'm not certain. But it was bizarre.

Jacob's younger brothers came home from school around 4:00pm and their Grandpa Beran showed up at approximately the same time. We tearfully explained what had transpired and what would take place the next day. Grandpa had brought over some barbequed meatballs from Grandma, so we sat down to eat supper and discuss the day's events. After supper we rented another movie to fill the void and again distract ourselves from the reality of the day.

When the movie was over, we talked about going to sleep even though we all knew there would not be a lot of sleeping in our house that night. Jerod and Dalton went to bed around 10:00pm, probably just to escape the crushing weight that enveloped our living room that night. Jacob went downstairs to the family room where he likes to sleep in an attempt to get some rest. His mother and I followed him and sat on the futon with him watching some TV in between statements of disbelief and questions about the future.

One of the first things that I told Jacob in the clinic was that we were not going to waste time asking, "Why me?" We were going to focus all of our energy on getting better as fast as possible. We are going to attack this the same way he would prepare for any other test or competition. He is not the most gifted athlete in any of the sports he plays, but he will outwork anyone any time.

I have no idea how I will convince a 16-year-old not to waste time on self pity. He has lived his life to this point with the singular focus on being the best student/athlete that he can be. That is one of the hardest things to deal with in this whole situation. He has lifted weights diligently since the summer after his 6th grade year. He is a fixture in the weight room and is known for his dedication and tenacity. He doesn't drink pop and he has always done extra work above and beyond the scheduled workouts. We go to the High School gym during the winter so that he can work on his passing mechanics and improve his arm strength and accuracy. About three weeks ago I purchased two different nets and six more footballs for him to practice with. We also purchased some new shoes that he wanted that will help improve his vertical jump and reduce his 40 yard dash time. He even started a program to reward offensive linemen in his class who regularly attend the weight lifting program before school.

Around 1:00am Jacob finally gave us permission to go upstairs and try to get some sleep before our 4:30am wake-up call. We relented, but both his mother and I got up at different times to go downstairs to check and see if he was still breathing, just like we did when he was a newborn. Neither one of us actually slept.

As this day had worn on, we were encompassed by a severe winter storm.

Through the course of the evening we also had to decide what to do with Jerod and Dalton the next day and whether we should leave that night and try to beat the oncoming storm. We decided to stay at home, let the boys all sleep in their own beds and set out early in the morning. School was cancelled the next day so the younger boys could spend the day at Grandma and Grandpa Beran's house.

We did not realize at the time how close we were to losing Jacob. We would later find out find out that we could easily have lost him at any time. The tumor was compressing his trachea and could have crushed it any time. We could have gone downstairs one morning thinking that he had overslept only to find him dead from suffocation. He would have only needed to roll over onto his right side and it would have been quite possible, and maybe probable, that the weight of the tumor would have crushed his trachea. Not being able to yell or otherwise notify us, he would have fought his final battle alone in our basement. This was the first time that he dodged death.

On day one we were all scared and confused and my little boy was in the midst of a bad dream that he could not awake from. On day two the warrior showed up.

Day 2, Tuesday, February 1, 2011

We left the house at 5:15am for a 6:30am appointment. Normally this drive would only take 30 minutes, but with the ongoing storm we thought we should plan on an hour or more. Through 30 mph winds and white-out conditions with wind chills around minus 30 degrees, we slowly made our way to Grand Island. When we got to the hospital we were promptly checked in and taken to a patient room for surgery prep. After putting on his gown and being asked all of the standard questions, we waited impatiently for the procedure to begin.

They are going to do a biopsy of one of his lymph nodes and install an infusion port for future procedures and chemotherapy. After a long wait, we were taken to the pre-op area and informed of all the upcoming procedures and risks involved. This was possibly worse than actually getting the diagnosis initially. We were told that the tumor was compressing the trachea and if Jacob was under general sedation that the tumor might completely close the trachea. I felt like crying, vomiting, passing out, running away screaming and punching something all at the same time. Time was creeping along at an excruciating pace and ripping my guts out in slow motion.

I was losing it, Shari was losing it, Jacob's blood pressure was elevating, but he never flinched. He answered every question directly, and when asked if he needed to sit up more he replied, "I'm good", do you need another blanket, "I'm good", another pillow, "I'm good", any questions, "I'm good". I was in awe of his courage. As they were preparing to wheel him away he said, "I hope that this was all a mistake and what they actually saw was a chicken wing lodged in my chest", a very timely reference to the movie "Tommy Boy". He was very amused and managed a smile as they wheeled him away, his mother and I unsuccessfully trying to hide our emotions with a few uncomfortable chuckles. Now we wait two more hours to see our son again.

After the procedure, the surgeon came in to tell us that everything went extremely well and he was confident that Jacob would be completely cured. For a moment I felt relief, I cried again. Jacob was wheeled in and immediately we could hear that the wheezing had almost stopped. The surgeon had given him a large dose of steroids to shrink the tumor and open Jacob's trachea. He felt great and had no pain. Now I went back to feeling some relief. I could see my son and he was better than when I had left him in the pre-op area. We were now going to wait a couple more hours before our appointment with the oncologist. The nurse was outstanding and allowed us to stay as long as we needed because we had nowhere else to go in between appointments and the conditions outside were horrible. It has always been my experience that they try to get you out of the room and on your way as fast as possible, but she made sure that we were comfortable and not being pushed out the door. Her name was Shawn and she was great.

The oncologist's office was friendly and efficient. They took us straight back to the patient room and proceeded to get all of the vital information. Dr. Ramaekers was prompt and precise in his initial visit and then informed Jacob that he would be doing a bone marrow biopsy before we left the office that day, and soon after, we were in another procedure room.

The bone marrow biopsy was the most pain that Jacob has ever felt—a bit worse than what he was led to believe, but somewhat brief. Basically, in order to extract the bone marrow they use an instrument that resembles a T-handled cork screw and drill a hole in the back of your pelvis by hand. Being young and strong meant that Jacob had excellent bone density which made Dr.

Ramaekers really struggle with every turn of the instrument. Dr. Ramaekers was talking to Jacob the entire time and even told a somewhat off-colored joke that made Jacob laugh.

When the procedure was complete there was one nurse drawing blood and one nurse discussing prescriptions and after-care with my wife. It was very efficient. Now we were on our way home, feeling a lot better than when we started the day.

Being from a small town is sometimes good. We stopped to pick up Jacob's prescriptions and were greeted by two family friends that work at the local pharmacy. They both have children that are classmates and close friends of Jacob. They recognized the drugs that were prescribed and both wanted to know what was going on and immediately offered their love and support. I was a blubbering idiot trying not to cry in public. Once home and settled in, Jacob informed two friends of the situation and promptly spent the rest of the night responding to countless text messages and facebook posts. We received phone calls and text messages from friends and family and Jacob received a call from his varsity football coach, which he said was the hardest to hold back the tears.

He was a rock all day long and took on this challenge as I believe few kids his age would. On day two the warrior showed up.

Day 3, Wednesday, February 2, 2011

I am not a morning person. I hate getting out of bed, especially on a cold winter's morning. Now I hate it even more. Reality slaps me in the face when the alarm goes off. It's almost like for a split second I believe that it was all a bad dream, but then immediately realize this is as real as it gets. I can hear Shari crying in the shower. My phone shows two missed calls and a text message from a lifelong friend. It's time to start another day in this new world.

Standing in the shower I start to cry again. Now that we have told people what is happening, the phone calls and messages of support are coming and for some reason other peoples' support of my family makes me cry.

I don't cry.

I cried when Jerod had his cancer scare two years ago. Before that I cried after losing in the state football semi-finals in 1985. Crying has always been a sign of weakness and loss of control. I don't lose control, and weakness can be exploited by other people. You are vulnerable in those situations and I am never vulnerable.

I went to the gas station to fill up before today's trip to the imaging center in Grand Island. I called my lifelong friend that had tried twice and left a text message. I know that I can talk to him without breaking down. Approximately three seconds into the conversation I lose it again, sobbing into my cell phone while sitting in my truck with the gas pump running. I look around and wonder if everyone is looking at the cancer patient's dad and feeling sorry for him. Our friend Pam from the pharmacy pulls up beside me to offer her support again and then asks the question that we agreed never to ask again after day one, "why Jacob?" Now I'm standing outside my truck sobbing for everyone to see while trying to thank her for her support and the gas is still pumping. When I get back into my truck and dry my eyes I think, "You just cried twice while filling your tank with gas." When will I be able to function in public without breaking down in front of everyone?

Now we are at the imaging center for the PET scan, which is the scan of Jacob's entire body looking for signs of cancer anywhere else in his body. The phone is ringing, the texts and emails are coming and the support is overwhelming. We will be here all morning and then back to the hospital for another CT scan of Jacob's abdomen. The CT scan from Monday only looked at his neck and chest. He wants to call college football coaches that he has spoken with to let them know that he probably will not be able to attend their camps this summer but he still plans on playing football in the future. When he called coach Baldus at NU, I cried when I heard him say, "Yesterday I was diagnosed with lymphoma", that was the first time I heard those words come from Jacob. Hearing Jacob say those words was powerful and heartbreaking.

Today is National Signing Day for high school seniors and ESPN has all-day coverage of the top recruits in the country. This is one of Jacob's favorite things in the world. Every year he states that he is going to be sick on this day so that he can stay home from school and watch the coverage.

School was cancelled again today because of the snowstorm and frigid temps. In a normal year he would be at home today watching every minute and getting updates on his cell phone while curled up on the futon downstairs. Today he is lying in a mobile scanner and will be drinking a barium solution when he gets out to prepare for his CT scan this afternoon. Is that ironic or just unfortunate?

We stopped by to see Grandma and Grandpa Peters this afternoon. The roads are in good shape and the weather has improved. They were both very happy to see Jacob and both said that seeing him in person made them feel much better about the situation. A little love from Grandma and Grandpa is good medicine too.

As I spoke on the phone this evening with Nancy Larson who lost her son Tyler to cancer last year, I realized that Jacob is probably mad at the cancer. He uses disrespect and underestimation as motivation to improve athletically. I think that he views the cancer as disrupting and disrespecting his efforts to improve and make himself the best possible. If this is his way of looking at it, I have no doubt that he will overcome. Many times he has been overlooked or told that he is too short, or not fast enough. This only serves to strengthen his resolve and work even harder and he has yet to fail at something that he truly wants to do.

His varsity football coach often speaks of perseverance and overcoming adversity, and these will be key words in his personal motivation to win this battle. His work ethic is his ultimate weapon. One example that I can give was from 6th grade during our youth football season. We had a good team that year and Jacob was our quarterback. We lost our first game that season in week #2 against Fillmore Central. They had a very fast and athletic running back/safety that caused us a lot of problems. He was very good. After the game we went home and later that evening Jacob came out of his room and told me that he has to work harder because, "I was not the best player on the field today". He went back in his room visibly upset. I waited for a while thinking he would calm down, then went into his room to talk to him. I opened the door and found him doing push-ups on the floor of his bedroom. He was doing the extra work to make himself better. A week later we played our last flag football game of the season and lost in the championship game of the tournament. This team had been together for five years and this was the last flag football game they would ever play together. The team was made up entirely of his best friends and they were amazing. Parents from other teams used to come over to our games to watch these boys play. They were supposed to go out as champions. He was inconsolable after the game. As we stood at the end of the field the only words that he could say were, "It wasn't supposed to end this way".

Tonight a few friends stopped in to see Jacob and it was good to hear all of the laughing and yelling that accompanies a basement full of teenagers. Jacob really enjoyed and appreciated the brief time downstairs. He has also been deeply touched by some of the responses he has received by text and Facebook. I think that having the opportunity to put their feelings in print and send them electronically makes it easier to say what they really mean. It can be extremely difficult to express your feelings in person, especially for a 16-year-old boy. He was particularly touched by Parker Davis' new Facebook status which simply said, "I have a new motivation in life… JP3" and a text that he received from his lifelong friend, Ben McQuiston, in which Ben said that he wished he was as strong as Jacob.

Day 4, Thursday, February 3, 2011

School is back in session after a two-day closure due to the weather. We got up this morning and tried to get Jerod and Dalton ready for school just like they had every day prior to this week. We talked with both of them last night about what was happening and that we will do everything we can to keep their lives as normal as possible, but there will definitely be some changes. They are both very understanding and willing to help and that makes me feel good about what kind of adults my children will become. It was nice to see Dalton in his normal routine, feeding the dog, packing his bag and waiting for the bus earlier than he should. It was also nice to see Jerod's routine of staying in bed as long as possible, taking too long to eat his breakfast and grumble about why school has to start so early. This was an especially grumbly morning because he has a basketball game tonight so he had to dress up for school today.

Around 9:00am Mike Larson stopped by the house. Mike, Nancy, and their youngest son Riley lost their oldest, Tyler, to cancer in 2010. Tyler faced obstacles his entire life and cancer was his final battle. Tyler was a kid that everyone loved. He was a manager for the varsity football team and a very important part of their championships. The entire football team wears the initials TL on their helmet for every game this year and Jacob was extremely proud to be able to wear that sticker. Tyler was so popular that he was even voted Prom King his senior year. Tyler was and is an inspiration to a lot of people.

Mike wanted to let us know that we could call at anytime day or night. We have gotten that comment from countless friends and family, but this offer carries more weight. They fought a battle that probably had little to no chance of victory and they did it with the dignity and class that you only hear about. Mike and I sat in my living room and cried. It was very hard for both of us.

He has some of the same personality problems that I do. He owns his own business and can fix any problem or do any job without anyone's assistance. We are both tough and we don't need help. That's great when heavy lifting needs to be done, but it is a problem when that control is removed and you are truly helpless.

We talked about how Jacob's diagnosis has also affected their family because it took them back to when they were fighting Tyler's battle. Another reason that it affected their family is Riley, their youngest son, is in the 8th grade. Jacob is a sophomore, Jerod is in 7th grade, and Dalton is in 6th grade. These boys literally see each other every day. Riley is a passionate lifter just like Jacob and Jerod. I assume that Riley looks up to Jacob as an athlete and hopefully as a leader. So if it can happen to Jacob and Tyler, can it happen to Riley?

Any 8th grader in that situation has to be a little freaked out, plus he just went through this and now it strikes again. This has to bring back a lot of bad memories that are not too distant. However, Riley was one of the first kids to offer assistance to Jerod and Dalton. He told them that they could talk to him any time and he would be available for them. He messaged Jacob on facebook to tell him that his Dad wanted to talk to me and would be stopping by to visit soon. Maturity at that level for an 8th grader is rare. Tyler's cancer changed Riley as well.

Before Mike left he tearfully handed me an envelope with a check for $200 from Team Tyler. Team Tyler is a foundation established to help families dealing with cancer. It included a letter with a brief description of Tyler, his cancer and what they wanted people to know. Needless to say I lost it again. The outpouring of support is one of the most difficult things for me to deal with. Mike, Nancy and Riley will be close to my heart for the rest of my life. As I was trying to stay strong I told Mike that we feel fortunate. And we do. We are being told that Jacob has a very curable form of cancer and that gives us great hope—and some people with cancer don't have much hope. He immediately jumped in and stated "there is always hope. Always".

He was right. I need to understand that. His message will stay with me forever. Stay positive don't say "if" this works, say "when".

At 10:00am we had a meeting at the high school with the principal, counselor and curriculum coordinator. We discussed Jacob's situation and possible scenarios for the continuation of his classes. He is done with P.E. for the rest of the semester and could end up dropping Sports Nutrition, Sociology and Spanish II. We are going to concentrate our energy on trying to keep him going in Advanced Geometry and Biology and they will allow him to do most of his work in English and Global Studies at home. They even offered to Skype his classes to him at the house or record the classes and send them home. If his schedule becomes irregular, he has the option of going to the conference room in the guidance office and having a one-on-one session with his teacher during their planning period. They also stated that he could continue to complete his work this summer if he does not complete it by the end of the regular school year. Finally, they said the teachers can also come to our home if needed to help him along. He has permission to park his truck in a special location to reduce the amount of walking and he will also be able to come and go based on how he feels. The administration has been extremely willing to accommodate his needs and I am sure that they will follow through on their promises.

When we had finished our meeting at the high school we walked across the street to meet with the middle school Principal and Counselor to discuss Jerod and Dalton. We told them how the week had unfolded and what was actually happening so that they would have accurate information. Shari and I asked them both to keep an eye on Jerod and Dalton and let us know if they see any changes. As parents, we are very concerned that our boys find as many support resources as possible. I personally have no idea how they are going to process this, but hopefully the professionals at the school will be able to help us along the way. The counselor has been a friend of our family basically from its beginning and she has watched our boys grow. I have a lot of faith in her abilities to see beyond the shell of a middle school boy.

We had another appointment to do more lab work at the Cancer Center at 2:30pm, after which we had a 3:30pm appointment with Dr. Ramaekers. He informed us that the results from the bone marrow biopsy were negative and they found no leukemia or lymphoma in his bone marrow. Furthermore the PETscan and 2nd CT scan revealed that the cancer was limited to the one tumor in his chest. He also told Jacob that this episode would make him a better man when it was all over. He stated that this would make him a man and when he emerges on the other end of this he will no longer be a boy.

We left the Cancer Center feeling better about our situation. We were in good spirits after receiving some good news. I warned Shari and Jacob that sooner or later the news will change and we need to be prepared for some bumps in the road.

Jerod had a basketball game tonight. He usually plays on the "B" team which would follow the "C" team's game. The "C" game was to start at 4:00pm, so we knew if we hurried we would make it in time for the start of his game. We dropped Jacob off at home and went to the gym. I had been having reservations all day about attending this game. I did not want to be a distraction taking the attention away from the boys playing the game. Once we entered the gym I knew that we would draw a sizable crowd offering support and wishing the best for Jacob.

Don't get me wrong, I appreciate every single person that has reached out to my family and me. This was not about escaping the reality, this was about not distracting people away from those players. I feel that if these boys have spent the time and energy to practice week after week, we owe them our attention and support.

When we walked through the doors I spotted an old friend and asked him if we could watch from the security room on the 2nd floor. He unlocked the room and Shari and I got to watch the game in peace and the boys had the full attention of their families and friends. We missed the "C" game as we thought we would, but we got to watch all of the "B" game and Jerod saw us sitting upstairs. It was important to us also to make sure that Jerod knew we were there to support him and his teammates. We stayed to watch the first half of the "A" game, then exited early to avoid the crowd afterwards.

We went straight home after the game and Jacob had several friends show up to hang out with him. Soon the doorbell rang and it was the Corporate Human Resources Manager from the company Shari works for. She had tears in her eyes when she came in and we figured she was just here to show support for Shari. Shortly after she was seated she announced that the Contact Center that employs Shari will be closing permanently. Shari would be losing her job.

What do you do in a moment like that?

She chose to laugh. What else can you do? There is no control over this situation either. Immediately, she realized that this was secondary. Jacob's problems were our only concern. The closing will take place no earlier than two months from now and no later than four months. Shari will have a small severance coming and some paid time off accumulated, but that's it. She will survive a change in occupation and we will maintain our focus on the task at hand. We will not soon forget this week's activities no matter how hard we might try.

There were quite a few kids in the basement when two senior boys showed up. Austin Smith and Kyle McCarthy were two young men that Jacob revered. They were tough, hard-nosed players that were also avid lifters. Austin was called "the most violent runner" the Aurora coaches had ever coached. Kyle was a three-year starter at middle linebacker and was feared by everyone on the team for his hard hitting. Before Jacob's sophomore season he felt that almost all of the seniors hated him. He thought that they saw him as a cocky little sophomore who was just full of himself. He desperately wanted to earn their respect.

During the season, Jacob was the scout team quarterback. This means that he gets to run the opposing team's offense all week against the #1 defense. Austin and Kyle were both on the #1 defense, of course. He would come home and tell us, "I got lit up by Austin today", or "McCarthy wrecked my life on one hit." I would always ask, "What did you do?" Every time he would say that he just got back up and ran the next play. It was his job to get punished that way and he knew it. He also knew that if he was going to gain their respect, he would have to take their punishment. This is the way the system works. You have to pay your dues and Jacob was willing to pay that price, whatever it might be.

I believe that their visit tonight is proof that Jacob earned that respect. When they left I thanked them for coming over and I told them that they had no idea how much their visit meant to Jacob. I hope they know how much Jacob admired them and desired their approval and acceptance.

At times, Jacob's sense of humor is uncomfortable at best. At one point in the evening while he was lying on the futon, the girls were sitting on the couch above him chatting like they always do. The volume started to rise as multiple conversations were being carried on at the same time and Jacob yelled, "Girls, all this noise is giving me cancer". The room fell silent as he alone chuckled. It was times like that that he had amused only himself and that was good enough. I can see the smile and satisfaction on his face as he chuckled while everyone else stared in disbelief.

Day 5, Friday, February 4, 2011

As a fundraiser for our Youth Football Program we are hosting some of the senior football players from the Nebraska Cornhuskers for a benefit basketball game. This is something the seniors do every year to help make some money and it really is a great outreach program for the football team to the rest of the state.

This event will be held on February 8. Today is February 4, and I have not spent any time working on this event for five straight days. I am the chairman of the Aurora Youth Sports Committee and head coach of the football team and I have been organizing this event for the last few weeks. At 10:00am today Shari and I are meeting with Vonda Tubbs, a family friend and fellow committee member to turn over control of the event to her. We obviously don't have time to concern ourselves with organizing a fundraiser right now, but this was my pet project. I love this football team because it is my own. We started the program seven years ago when Jacob was in 4th grade. Any child in 4th, 5th or 6th grade is eligible to play with a few restrictions. All three of my boys have participated for all three years that they were eligible and Jacob and Jerod have both helped me coach after their eligibility was complete. Dalton's team was fortunate enough to win the league championship this past fall and he is fiercely proud of that accomplishment. I love it because of the kids that I get to coach and most selfishly because I just love to coach football.

I would like to say that it's all about the kids, but I would be lying if I said that it wasn't a bit self-serving. I sent an email to everyone on the team notifying them that the event would go on as planned and that I was committed to making this a fun and exciting evening for the kids and hopefully raise a lot of money for the future of Aurora Football. I also told Vonda that Jerod and Dalton would be in attendance. I wouldn't speak for Shari and Jacob, but I did not think that I would be ready to be out there in front of hundreds of people yet. I'm not ready to face everyone yet and I need to be strong for Jacob now. He does not need to see me break down in front of the entire audience.

At 2:37pm we got the call from Dr. Ramaekers with the official diagnosis. Jacob has T-cell Lymphoblastic Lymphoma. This is a Non-Hodgkins Lymphoma and is extremely aggressive. He is turning us over to Dr. Bruce Gordon at the University of Nebraska Medical Center in Omaha. Dr. Ramaekers said that this is more of a pediatric cancer than an adult cancer and that Dr. Gordon will provide the best treatment option. Jacob really likes and respects Dr. Ramaekers and was visibly disappointed with the news. We immediately started packing and made arrangements for Jerod and Dalton to spend the night at a friend's house. We got the call from Dr. Gordon's office at around 4:30pm with directions on where to go and off we went.

We arrived at the Clarkson Tower of the Med Center and went to the admissions desk. We were expecting only a consultation with Dr. Gordon tonight, but we were informed that Jacob would be checking in and staying overnight at the hospital. We were totally surprised by this and our stress levels immediately climbed. We thought we would be checking into a hotel later and setting up an appointment for therapy to start tomorrow.

After a long walk to Jacob's room, I was taken down to the desk where I could make reservations for Shari and I to stay in the Nebraska House. This is a hotel-type set of rooms for family to stay temporarily. I told the woman behind the counter that we would only need the room for one night and she said she would go ahead and reserve it for two nights.

This was a bad omen.

Dr. Gordon came to Jacob's room shortly after my return. We went through every detail of what had transpired over the past three weeks. He then proceeded to explain at length the basis of chemotherapy and the differences between adult and pediatric expectations. He described a research study that Jacob is eligible to take part in if he is interested. The study would require him to take one additional drug that may or may not make him better. The only major drawback is that he will have to submit to another bone marrow biopsy. Remember, the previous one was the most painful experience of his life. He was also informed that the chemotherapy could make him sterile and not able to father a child later in life. We were offered the opportunity to wait a couple of days before starting treatment if we were interested in waiting until we could get him to a sperm bank. This is not something that we had considered at all. We knew that chemotherapy could make him sterile, but never considered a sperm bank. We decided that he can take on that challenge later in life and that we did not want to slow this process down for that purpose. There are too many variables that have to be in place before reproduction even becomes an issue. If he does not live through this process he won't have any children either, so let's get started now.

We also decided that participating in the study with the possibility of helping someone else is definitely something that he should do. We were told that he will be under anesthesia for this bone marrow biopsy and won't feel a thing and that they would do the procedure at the same time they are doing his spinal tap. I told him that even if he had to endure some short term pain the long term knowledge accumulated would be worth it. Another lesson he has learned from football is that personal sacrifice is the only path to the team's success. He will learn that he has now joined another team.

Dr. Gordon was very thorough, but ultimately could not answer Jacob's burning question, "When will I be able to play football?" This is the only subject that makes him upset. He broke down for the first time since we got home from the clinic late Monday morning after the initial doctor's appointment. He is not worried about his long term plans. He's 16. He really only cares about getting out of shape and not being able to play football this fall. We continue to reinforce the fact that if he does not take care of this situation in the proper manner, that he will jeopardize more than just next year's football season. This will be the most difficult part of his emotional recovery and it concerns his mother and me.

Later in the evening the nurse asked Jacob what he does to reduce stress. He stated that he really doesn't have that much stress, but that is probably because he lifts three days a week and has either practice or games every night after school. His stress relief is physical exertion and that will be taken away for awhile. I told him he will have to find a way to redirect, but that will not come easy. Nothing will be easy for the foreseeable future.

Phase one of Jacob's chemotherapy protocol is called "Induction". We are scheduled to stay in the hospital for four to five days for this first treatment and then return every Friday for outpatient treatment for the next four weeks. We sit here now at 1:00am. Jacob has returned from his latest CT scan, pounding the keys on his blackberry and watching SportsCenter. Another day will bring another battle and new challenges and so the next phase begins.

Three

PHASE 1
INDUCTION BEGINS

DAY 6, SATURDAY, FEBRUARY 5, 2011

The first thing on the agenda today will be a spinal tap and the second bone marrow biopsy this morning. Dr. Gordon came in around 8:30am to discuss the procedure and give us an idea of what to expect today.

We walked to the prep area where they will do the procedure and Jacob was in good spirits. They immediately told him that they would not put him completely under because there was still a chance that the tumor could compress his trachea. He instantly tensed up and got extremely nervous due to his prior experience with the bone marrow biopsy in Grand Island. The doctors assured him that he will not feel a thing and they will have him on drugs, so that he won't even remember the procedure.

Shari and I were taken to the waiting room and we told his nurse that they probably only have this one chance to get it right, because if this hurts anywhere near as badly as the first one, he would probably be leaving the study we had just signed up for. This bone marrow biopsy was only necessary because of the study and this study will probably require more procedures at a later date.

Dr. Gordon came to the waiting room personally to tell us they were finished and took us back to see Jacob. What we saw we will not soon forget. Jacob was as high as a kite. He was smiling from ear to ear and pointing at me while twirling his finger in the air he repeatedly stated, "I wanna fight you". His mannerisms were that of a toddler. He said that he couldn't feel his lips, he giggles uncontrollably and makes totally random squealing noises. He is totally entertaining himself as well as everyone in the recovery area. Soon the effects of the drugs started to disappear and he is now experiencing dizziness, vertigo and nausea and he really needs to use the restroom. We walked with the nurse as she wheeled him back to his room and helped get him situated. He tried to relieve himself while sitting on the edge of the bed, but not much came out. He laid back down, but soon was asking to try again. The nurse told us that he was not supposed to get out of bed or stand up on his own for a while, so he sat on the bed for a while with no results. Finally I told him to stand up and I would support him while he did his business. I stood beside him and wrapped my arms around his chest and under one of his arms. This simple change in position started the flow. He amazed himself by how long it took to completely finish and proceeded to carry on for quite a while about how great he felt once he finished. I don't care why he feels better. We will take what we can get.

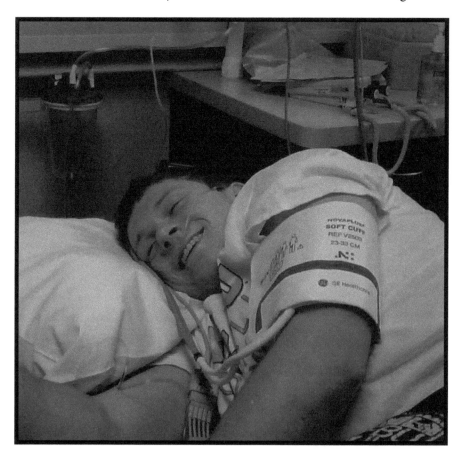

This afternoon Dr. Gordon returned to talk about the individual chemotherapy drugs and their possible side effects. He is confident that if Jacob communicates how he's feeling that the side effects should be minimal. We asked about our future schedule and he said that after this initial hospitalization we will need to be back once weekly for the next four weeks. He did not allude to what we would be doing after that because we need to concentrate on getting through this first stage. At around 5:00pm the nurse entered to start Jacob's first round of chemotherapy. It is a relief that we are officially starting to aggressively attack this disease.

Rod Perry and his family stopped by for a visit at the exact time that Shari's parents, Glen and Patsy, arrived with Jerod and Dalton. We had a nice visit with the Perry's. Jacob looks up to Rod's boys, Brandon and Chase. They treat him like a little brother and I really think he enjoys that. Rod's wife Kristi is at the Med Center having just undergone a heart transplant a couple of days ago. She was not in good condition and was very fortunate to get a donor heart in a fairly short amount of time. Shari and I were told about Kristi's condition by Rod the same night in Central City where Jacob showed the first signs of being sick. Now here we are basically in the same hospital in Omaha, three weeks later, she has a new heart and Jacob is starting chemotherapy. They will forever be linked by their individual struggles. Rod brought his Mom and Dad over after supper and we had a wonderful visit. They have known me and my sons since birth and they are great people. Jacob even admitted after they left that he enjoyed their visit and thought it was very nice of them to stop in.

Glen and Patsy left to spend the night at Shari's brother Pat's house in Omaha. Jerod and Dalton stayed with us and will spend the night at the Nebraska House. It is 9:10pm and the family is watching the "Hulk". Shari is lying in bed beside Jacob and he has one arm hanging off the bed. I told him to move over and get more comfortable and he said that he doesn't want to touch his mother because "friction makes heat and heat gives you cancer"!

That is my son.

DAY 7, SUNDAY, FEBRUARY 6, 2011

Today is all about monitoring. They are watching several items to make sure that the chemotherapy is not removing the tumor too quickly. If we move too fast—especially in this first week—the chemotherapy can damage some of his other vital organs. So far, everything is moving along on schedule. Jacob waited too long early this morning to let the nurse know that he had nausea and paid the price. Everyone has said that he needs to communicate right away because they have plenty of drugs for that. He received two doses of additional drugs to make him feel better and the major side effect of both drugs is drowsiness. It's 2:00pm and he has slept most of the day, getting up only to use the restroom and inhale of couple of doughnuts. I'm glad to see him resting. If nothing else, it will make his stay here feel shorter.

Glen and Patsy took Jerod and Dalton home around 12:30pm. I feel bad for them because their lives have been turned upside down also and they are healthy. We will soon be home and they will be able to sleep in their own beds and wake up at home. I think we are all looking forward to that.

We started watching the Super Bowl, then shortly after it started we figured out that we have a wireless internet connection in Jacob's room. Until now I have been the only one on my computer and all that I have been working on is this journal. That will soon change. Once Jacob learned that we had a wireless connection he commandeered my computer for better access to Facebook and ESPN. I managed to keep possession long enough to patch together a rough copy of Jacob's sophomore highlight video. He asked this past Friday—before we knew we would be going to Omaha—if he could have a highlight video because a lot of his friends from football camps were asking for one. I called the guy who has done Jacob's videos before and he said he would have time on Saturday, but that didn't work out. So I decided to take it on myself. Once I finished editing the final sample, I showed Jacob and Shari. Shari cried through the whole thing and Jacob could not understand why. He honestly did not understand the sadness she felt watching her son do what he loves the most as he lays in a hospital bed beside her uncertain if and when he will play again. We all understand that the prognosis is for him to return to "normal", not return to play football. We have not gotten anyone to give us a straight answer yet about what lies ahead, but I think that is because they honestly don't know. We are hopeful but guarded.

Support from other people makes me cry. I don't know why someone show-ing support and wishing us well makes me so emotional, but it is what I strug-gle with the most. My mindset now is to help Jacob fight this with positive forward energy. I want him to see me with great confidence and strength so that he can feed off of that. Our strongest common thread is competitiveness. He has seen me compete while coaching his teams and Jerod and Dalton's teams. I think he feeds off of that energy and attitude. He has seen me cry more this past week than he has in his entire life. Shari and I have both told him that it is OK to cry and let out your sadness and that it is unhealthy to keep it inside. He has cried on Day One and Day Five, but not in between and not since. The only time he gets emotional is when someone sends him an honest and open-hearted message or we start talking about the sports he will be missing. I have basically the same reaction. Any time I get a heartfelt message reaching out to my family I struggle. I appreciate greatly anyone who shows concern for Shari and I, but anything concerning my boys puts me over the top. I hope that my feelings are so strong for the right reasons, but I'm concerned that they aren't. Sometimes I think that I get emotional because of our level of exposure to other people right now. We are naked in the middle of the playground. Maybe people feel bad for me because I'm vulnerable right now and that makes me scared? Maybe I only want people to see my family as strong and this exposes a weakness? I have thought about it a lot and I have not figured it out yet.

When Rod stopped by the other day he told me that he had the same problem and that makes me feel better. Rod does not have the same problem that I do emotionally. He has an open heart to everyone and is willing to be the first on the scene to help at all times. I would rather come in after emotions have calmed and help pick up the pieces from behind the scenes. So when Rod tells me he feels the same way it makes me more confident that I am feeling these emotions for the right reasons. I am a hard-hearted SOB sometimes, but mainly with adults. Compassion is sometimes hard to come by in my world, especially if the result of your misfortune should have been obvious and avoided. I have always had a soft heart for children as most people do. I can't even watch TV dramas or movies that deal with children's injuries or illnesses. I fear that the worst of the emotions are yet to come. We have a lot of public events in our life and I'm sure that someone will say or do something extremely caring and nice and the flood gates will open again. I am not ashamed to cry in public anymore, but I also don't want to sadden other people by seeing me cry. I don't want pity, maybe that's the problem. My pride clouds the difference between charity and pity.

We updated Jacob's Care Page online. We had not made any updates since before we left for Omaha because we did not think we had internet access. After our technical revelation, we have been checking it often. It is really nice to be able to see who is checking the page and reading messages left for our family. We are alone in this room and can feel isolated, but Care Pages closes that gap and makes us all feel better.

Day 8, Monday, February 7, 2011

Jacob had a great night of sleep last night. The alarms on his IV tower went off five times during the night and he doesn't remember a thing. He never woke up and was very comfortable. I have been sleeping in his room in case he needs assistance getting to the restroom. I heard every alarm and went down the hall to alert the nurse each time. Jacob never stirred.

He spent most of the day on my laptop and texting on his cell phone at the same time. Occasionally he would set the laptop down and Shari and I would grab it to check his Care Page, but soon after he would let us know that he could use it when we were done. He misses his friends a great deal and Facebook is his best connection to those people. He even told us today that he missed being in school. That has never happened. He has not been hungry at all today. We're not sure if he really has no appetite or if he is just scared to gain weight because he has been told weight gain is a side effect of the steroids.

Dr. Gordon stopped in to check on Jacob today. At the end of this conversation he returned to the subject of sperm donation. He said that if we were interested in having Jacob make a donation, we could make arrangements through the nurse and it was not too late. Since he has only had one dose of chemotherapy the odds are he could still donate healthy sperm. After he left, Jacob, Shari and I had that discussion. Jacob is losing some of his teenage borders. He had an open and honest discussion about sperm donation with his mother and I. Not many kids could or would do that. Dr. Ramaekers was right, this journey will make him a man. We all thought it was a good idea. We did not want to wait when the original offer was made Friday night because ultimately we did not want to wait two more days before starting treatment. Now we have started the treatment and it makes more sense to try. Jacob understands that someday he might want to have children and this might be the only way to have them biologically. We also discussed that most people ultimately want to have their own kids and the inability to do so may cause the perfect relationship to end. We discussed the pressure that sterility can place on a marriage and that he might have a hard time finding a woman that does not care if she can get pregnant. It was not a very long discussion before we all agreed that sperm donation was the right thing to do. It gives him options later in life.

Day 9, Tuesday, February 8, 2011

Jacob had another good night last night. Dr. Lowas visited this morning and said that everything has been going well as far as his labs go. Jacob walked to the Nebraska House and took a shower in our room. The water pressure is better and he needed to get away for little while. Now he also knows where his Mom goes to sleep at night. Any time we leave the Oncology floor he needs to wear a mask. When we were coming back he asked if he would always have to wear a mask in public. He said he felt like a freak when he wears it. The truth is that he will have to wear a mask whenever his counts get too low and he's not able to fight off infections. That is our biggest concern at this point. We are planning to take some additional actions at home to help prevent an infection. Once we go home, anytime he runs a fever we have to call the Oncologist's office and most of the time he will have to go to the Emergency Room at St. Francis Medical Center in Grand Island. Most likely he will be admitted to the Med Center if he does get a fever so they can monitor him closely. Dr. Lowas told us of an 18-year-old female patient who didn't want to go to the hospital right away when she got a fever and she died from infection. I think that really hit home with Jacob. I hope it did, he is ultimately in charge of his future.

Around noon the nurse came in to unhook Jacob's IV. For the rest of this stay he will be on oral medication as long as everything goes well. He will get three shots around 4:00pm and then he will be monitored overnight. If all goes well we will be home tomorrow.

Shortly after 4:00pm the nurse gave him his final three shots. We are now just hoping that there are no complications so that he can be released tomorrow morning.

Tonight is the big fundraiser for the Youth Football program. Several Husker senior football players will be coming to Aurora to play in a benefit basketball game against the youth football coaches. We turned the entire operation over to Vonda Tubbs last Friday. We have not spent a lot of time thinking about the fundraiser lately because of all the madness around us, but tonight our thoughts wandered home a lot. At 6:00pm I started watching the clock wondering if everything was arriving as planned. At 6:30pm I envisioned people showing up for the pre-game meal and wondered if we would have a good turnout. My friend Dave sent a picture from his cell phone with a note "great turnout". I felt more emotion than I thought I would with that note. At 7:30pm I looked at the clock and imagined the Huskers being announced as they ran onto the floor. At 7:33pm I got another picture from Dave showing the crowd. The stands were packed. We had sold quite a few tickets for the event, but the weather was extremely cold and I was not sure how many people would actually attend and support this event. We got a couple score updates during the game, then after the game Dave sent me a picture that made me cry. A few of the coaches and all of the Huskers got together to pose for a picture. In the center was Dale Broekemeier holding Jacob's individual picture from this past football season. It had a nice black and white border that was autographed by the Huskers that had played that night. It's moments like that that they touch me the most.

Day 10, Wednesday, February 9, 2011

Today we get to go home. Jacob has been unhooked for a while now and he is feeling good. I went down to the pharmacy to pick up some of his meds and stopped by the gift shop on my way back. I remember as a child that when my Dad was in the hospital we would always come home with some kind of souvenir. I don't remember anything specifically, but I do remember the act. I found a completely tacky cookie jar that looks like a tree stump with a moose sitting beside it. The lid to the jar is the top of the tree stump and the handle is a squirrel. Jacob was less than excited about it even though I filled it with Reese's Peanut Butter Cups and chocolate Riesens, two of his favorites. He was craving a Baconator from Wendy's, so we stopped in Lincoln on the way home. The ride went smoothly and he rested in the back seat the whole way. We got home around mid-afternoon and he immediately settled in to his favorite spot—the futon in the basement family room. He had his PS3, Netflix and DirecTV all on our 62" big screen TV. Everything was better in the world. The table was covered with Get Well cards from family and friends, but one stuck out from all the rest. The long, thin red card with a big white "N" on the front was open and lying on top of all the rest. This was the card signed by the Husker Football Coaching Staff. It might be his most valuable possession now.

After we got him settled in I went to the local pharmacy to pick up all of his meds. Half way to the pharmacy I realized that I had forgotten the written prescriptions at the house, so I turned around. In the short time that I was gone, someone had hung a "Welcome Back Jacob" banner from our garage door. It was signed by a bunch of students earlier that afternoon. I made my way back to the pharmacy with tears in my eyes and returned with a bucket load of pills. We pulled Jacob reluctantly back outside and he was surprised by the banner and happy that his fellow students had been thinking of him.

Several classmates came over that night to welcome Jacob home and it really helped his spirits. This was the moment that he was waiting for. He had mentioned several times that he just wanted to go home and be surrounded by his friends. Shari and I stayed upstairs giving his friends instructions on hand sanitizer and staying away if they had any sign of illness. We also took this time to catch up on what Jerod and Dalton had been doing. Jerod and Dalton were both very happy to be home with the rest of the family beginning to return to their normal routine. The visitors were all gone by 9:30pm and we all went downstairs as a family for a few moments together. It was good to be home.

DAY 11, THURSDAY, FEBRUARY 10, 2011

Today is all about getting organized. I went to the office for a while to pay some bills and Shari started organizing the house. Medications, paperwork, schedules, phone numbers, laundry, meals and the other boys' activities all require attention. We ordered some Purell stations for around the house, so that everyone has easy access to hand sanitizer. We placed those in appropriate locations around the house and started making arrangements for improving the cleanliness of the house and the air quality. One of my best subcontractors is Jerry's Sheetmetal in Grand Island. I called Monte and asked if they could add a better filtration system to our furnace and he stated that he would also give us an air purifier for Jacob's room at no charge. This is a $1,000 unit and he offered it without my request or inquiry. This kind of generosity is hard for me to accept, but as I told a good friend of mine in an email, "There is no place in our lives for my silly pride now".

Jerod had a basketball game in Grand Island at 4:30pm. Shari and I went alone and Shari's mom came over to stay with Jacob and Dalton. It was good to watch Jerod play. He is not a naturally talented basketball player, but he plays with great intensity and determination. He is a menace on defense and even though he is undersized, his coach announced to the team that Jerod was the team's best low post defender. He usually defends the opposing team's biggest player and is a constant disruption and sets crushing screens for his teammates. It is nice to see him assert himself physically. He has always been the one that has lacked focus and we are seeing him mature right before our eyes. After the game he rode home with Shari and I. We drove through Dairy Queen for the traditional post-game meal and went home talking about his game. We are very conscious of Jerod and Dalton's need for attention during this time also.

Dalton had wrestling practice from 6:00-7:15pm, so we went straight to the gym to pick him up on our way home from Jerod's game. Dalton is frustrated because there is nobody his size to wrestle in his age group. He decided that he wants to practice with the 7th and 8th Graders instead. It's good to deal with traditional problems for awhile.

Day 12, Friday, February 11, 2011

We returned to Omaha today for chemotherapy treatment #2 at the Med Center. First thing on the agenda is to have some lab work done. This is a surprisingly simple process which took approximately five minutes to complete. We now have approximately 2½ hours until his next appointment. Since the port in his chest has been accessed they frown on leaving the premises, so we went to see our friend Kristi Perry. Her heart transplant was done nine days ago and she is going home today. We had a nice visit with Rod and Kristi before more staff came in to continue checking her out, so we wished them well and went to our waiting room. As we walked into the waiting room we saw the husband of another high school classmate of mine sitting in the chairs. Kim has thyroid cancer and was in town for a scheduled check-up with her doctor. It is always good to see a familiar face, however we are seeing too many from our hometown here at the hospital.

Our meeting with Dr. Lowas went well. Everything is proceeding as planned and Jacob has been feeling well. She reluctantly gave Jacob permission to attend the basketball game on Thursday night. Jacob had already made up his mind that he would attend the game with or without her permission, but Shari and I felt better with her permission. After the check-up, Jacob was scheduled for another spinal tap with a second chemotherapy injection directly into his spinal fluid. Jacob was a bit apprehensive about the procedure because of how bad he felt after the first spinal tap. Everyone assured him that they would be using a different anesthesia this time and he would have no after effects. Luckily, they were right. He felt great after the procedure and even said it was the best he had felt in a month while lying in the bed. We then had a somewhat long wait at the treatment center before he was taken back for IV treatment #2. Once we were back into one of the treatment rooms things moved rather quickly. His nurse Linda was an avid Husker Football fan and hit it off with

Jacob immediately. We talked about football and all of his other activities and it made the time pass quickly.

After he was released we went straight to Grisanti's Italian Restaurant. Jacob was not allowed to eat or drink after midnight because of the spinal tap and it was now 4:30pm. He had been craving a ½ pound Baconator from Wendy's all day, then as we were ready to leave he changed to Grisanti's. Luckily we found a Grisanti's on an easy route out of town. When you eat at this restaurant there is always a loaf of garlic bread on a plate being warmed by a candle in the center of the table. We usually eat at least one loaf before the meal arrives. Today was no exception. We ordered fried mozzarella and calamari, two of his favorite appetizers and he ate almost all of it. His meal started with a bowl of minestrone and he then ordered manicotti marinara for his entrée and told me to order veal parmigiana so that he could steal from my plate also. While waiting for his main course he also had a couple bites of his mother's salad and countless refills of strawberry lemonade. It was good to see him eat like normal.

The drive home was thankfully uneventful and we spent the rest of the evening lounging in the basement.

Day 13, Saturday, February 12, 2011

This morning Jerod has a basketball game in Central City. Shari is staying home with Jacob and organizing the house. Dalton went along with me to watch the game. As usual, Jerod played well. His effort is outstanding which is all that I really ever ask from my kids and he delivers. After his game we stayed to watch the 8th grade team play. Riley Larson, the boy who lost his older brother to cancer last year, plays on the 8th grade team. He has offered to make himself available to both Jerod and Dalton if they ever wanted to talk about handling this as little brothers. His parents are a wealth of information and have been more than helpful through this process. I wanted to watch his game as a small sign of appreciation for his efforts.

After the games were over we went to Dairy Queen for the traditional postgame meal. As much as I would like to believe that Dalton went to the game to support his brother, I know the real reason was to get Dairy Queen.

Later in the afternoon Jacob had four friends stop by for a visit. He was feeling "fine" all day, though he was a little fatigued. He has mentioned many times that he really wants to spend time with his friends while he is at home, so we have not restricted that activity yet. However, it didn't take long for the volume in the basement to get out of control. Around 6:00pm he asked for everyone to leave because he had gotten a headache. We knew then that we had made a mistake, if it was bad enough to ask everyone to leave, then he was hurting pretty bad. He spent the rest of the night in the basement with the lights off trying to get over his headache and the onset of nausea from the chemotherapy. He did not sleep well at all.

Day 14, Sunday, February 13, 2011

Today has not been a good day for Jacob. The headache from last night has not gone away. We then realized that he is running out of pain medication which he takes for his headaches. He takes Oxycodone for pain because it does not contain Tylenol. Dr. Lowas instructed us not to give him anything with Tylenol because it would mask a fever and if he got a fever we would need to know about it immediately and possibly end up in the emergency room. If he gets any infection while his immune system is compromised it could be fatal, so we are very aware of keeping him healthy. After a call to the Med Center we found out that Oxycodone is a narcotic which can only be prescribed with a written prescription. It cannot be called in to the pharmacy. The doctor on-call at the Med Center told us to increase his caffeine intake and try to keep everything as dark and quiet as possible. We were going to have to ration his pain meds and try to make it on our own for the rest of the day. The mistakes of last night are carrying over into problems today.

Another side effect that he constantly deals with is nausea. We try to keep him comfortable by eating saltine crackers and drinking Sprite, but when it starts to get worse he takes Zofran. One of the side effects of Zofran is headaches which only magnifies his problem. Without the proper medication he is going to have a headache for the rest of the weekend and we don't want to compound the problem by not treating his nausea, so we gave him a dose of Zofran in an effort to make him more comfortable. We are learning that this will be a constant juggling act with multiple side effects and medications all in the air at the same time.

DAY 15, MONDAY, FEBRUARY 14, 2011

We were hoping that today would bring a new prescription of Oxycodone so that we could treat Jacob's headache correctly, but the doctor at the Med Center did not want to have a local doctor write the prescription. They did write a prescription for Vicodin, but that contains Tylenol. I went to the pharmacy and got the Vicodin, but we were apprehensive about using it because of the fever worries. We called the Med Center again and were told that Vicodin was OK, but we would have to monitor his temperature more closely. This is the first time that we have gotten conflicting information and we were thoroughly confused. Shari and I decided to take the safest path and try to handle the headaches for the rest of the week with food and environment instead of medication which meant that school was out of the question today.

I went to the office briefly in the afternoon and Jacob called to ask me to bring home a double quarter pounder with cheese from McDonald's. I gladly complied as this seemed to be a sign that he was feeling better and maybe his headaches were under control. Three hours later he vomited due to all of the grease in his sandwich and the accompanying fries. Of course he did this immediately after taking his nightly medications, so we called the Med Center again to ask for advice. We were told to re-medicate slowly and monitor him for any other problems or changes in behavior. Just as everything appeared to turn the corner we now had another crisis on our hands and I firmly believed that we would be back in the hospital before morning. We got him some more saltine crackers and some Sprite hoping to calm his stomach enough to get some sleep. Things calmed down as the evening progressed and several checks of his temperature revealed that we were not fighting an infection. His body just rejected the double quarter pounder with cheese. Crisis averted.

DAY 16, TUESDAY, FEBRUARY 15, 2011

I got Jacob to come upstairs about mid-morning. I thought maybe a small change of atmosphere might be nice. We watched some TV, I made him a grilled cheese sandwich and we talked a little bit. Shari came home for lunch and Jacob requested that she bring Arby's home with her. We know that he can't handle McDonald's quarter pounders, but thought that a plain roast beef sandwich might be nice. Jacob loves eating Arby's. He would eat there every day if we let him or if he had enough money.

He's been lying in the basement for the last three days and I think he is battling some depression right now. I helped him get started on some homework to distract him and hopefully get him started on his academic comeback. He worked for about twenty minutes then said his head hurt, so we took a break. At 2:00pm Jacob's Advanced Geometry teacher Mr. Titus stopped in to help get caught up on assignments. He stayed for about forty minutes, then Jacob said that was enough. Jacob came back and sat next to me in the living room for about an hour and then we went for a walk. One lap around the neighborhood was all that he could handle, but the temperature was almost 70 degrees and I think the fresh air could only help him feel better. He said that he felt weird being outside because since his initial visit to the clinic we have only been out long enough to transfer in or out of a vehicle. I am hoping that changing his routine and getting him some fresh air will help him sleep better and ease his depression.

Day 17, Wednesday, February 16, 2011

This morning Jacob woke up feeling better. After eating breakfast and taking his morning meds he started to do some of his homework. I think that keeping him upright most of the day and trying to establish a daily routine is helping him feel better during the day and sleep better at night. In the afternoon we took another walk around the neighborhood. The walk only lasted about 10 minutes, but he was tired after one lap.

Day 18, Thursday, February, 17, 2011

Our second straight morning of feeling better led to two trips to school today. He met with a couple teachers at 8:30am until approximately 9:15am. When I arrived to pick him up he was standing in the lobby talking to some friends and smiling from behind his mask. Later that afternoon he went back to school for almost two hours and met with the remainder of his core class teachers.

Tonight is the basketball game that Dr. Lowas gave him permission to attend. He decided that he felt well enough to also attend the JV basketball game at 4:15pm. Tonight is the only chance that he will have to attend a game before the season ends. He will not be able to attend any road games and the last home game is tomorrow night and since he has treatment that day, he probably won't be able to go. He sat behind the bench with Ben McQuiston who was unable to play because of a broken arm. Shari and I noticed that a couple of Jacob's classmates had written his initials and his jersey number on the side of their shoes in a tribute to Jacob. It was good to see him interacting with his teammates and getting into the flow of the game. This is the game that he has looked forward to all season. Grand Island Northwest is a big rival and one of the only teams to beat his class in any sport. Even though this will probably be his last chance to watch his team, I think that watching them win tonight was enough to satisfy him. The varsity also won their game which was really icing on the cake.

In between the JV game and the varsity game we picked up Jerod from his basketball practice. He said that he didn't practice well and wasn't feeling very good, so he was quarantined to his bedroom for the night. We decided to keep him away from the rest of the family until we could get him to the doctor the next day.

Day 19, Friday, February 18, 2011

Shari made an appointment for Jerod as we left Aurora for Jacob's treatment in Omaha. Shari's mom was able to take Jerod to the clinic and he was diagnosed with a bacterial infection. Dr. Sullivan prescribed some antibiotics and said that Jerod needed to be quarantined from Jacob for at least 48 hours, so he packed some things and went to Grandma and Grandpa Beran's house to recuperate.

Treatment #3 went well today. Jacob's stress level was way down from where it was one week ago. We have always heard that when you are receiving chemotherapy that treatment day is usually the day that you feel the best. This has held true with Jacob. He is in good spirits and understands the schedule of the day is much more relaxed. Most of the day is spent waiting. When we get to the Med Center the first item of business is to access his port and draw blood. This time he was not scheduled for another spinal tap, so we got him some nachos and went to the waiting room for his check-up. Dr. Gordon was back this week and met with Jacob to discuss his status. All of Jacob's counts looked good and the only real concern Jacob has is a panic attack that he experienced the other night. Dr. Gordon explained that it is perfectly normal to have these attacks simply because of the stress involved in this fight. Some of the medications that Jacob is on also contribute to the likelihood of panic attacks. Dr. Gordon reinforced what Shari and I have told Jacob, that if he feels like yelling then yell, if he feels like crying then cry. Trying to get a tough teenager to recognize that he can let his emotions out is not an easy task. Most kids his age do everything they can to hide the way that they really feel. Jacob is no different. We have told him that holding these emotions inside is unhealthy and that he needs to let them out. Shari and I explained that you always feel better after you cry and that yelling when you're angry will alleviate the pressure. He has not done it yet, but we hope that we can arrange a visit with a psychologist on one of his next visits to Omaha. I think someone with professional training might be able to ask the right questions and open him up in a way that we as parents cannot. He has been forced to make decisions and process information that no 16-year-old should ever have to.

We left the Med Center and went to the Nebraska Furniture Mart to look at a new bed for Jacob. Even though he enjoys sleeping on his beloved futon, we feel that it would be better if he slept in his bedroom like a normal child. He has always hated his bed and uses that as an excuse to sleep in the family room. We are hoping that since we let him choose this bed himself that he won't be able to use that excuse. It will be easier to control his sleeping environment if it is more private.

We made a return trip to Grisanti's after the mattress shopping experiment with Jacob and what happened next is the stuff of legend. After much debate on what to order he ate the following:

1. The entire Happy Hour Appetizer Menu including:

    Mozzarella Marinara
    Bruschetta Fresco
    Fried Calamari
    Ravioli – when the waitress asked, "beef or cheese"
    he said, "both"

2. Minestrone
3. Manicotti Marinara
4. Strawberry Lemonade (we estimate 8 glasses)

5. At Grisanti's they also have an endless supply of garlic bread resting at the center of the table above a candle that keeps it warm and toasty the entire meal.
6. He ate some of Shari's Shrimp Fettucine Alfredo
7. Sampled some of the House Salad

Granted, Shari and I ate some of the food placed in front of us, but the majority of the load was consumed by Jacob. This has now become the after treatment tradition and if he enjoys it this much we will do this every time.

After Jacob was diagnosed, my construction manager, Jessie, and his wife Brandie mailed a letter to every school on Aurora's basketball schedule asking them to show some sign of support for Jacob as a fellow competitor and athlete. Jerry Buck, the Boys' Varsity Basketball Coach at Holdrege High School, was one of the respondents. He wrote Jacob a letter of encouragement and had it signed by the entire boy's basketball team. Tonight is the last home basketball game of the season and our opponent is Holdrege High School. As expected, Jacob was not feeling well enough to attend tonight's game, but I felt compelled to go to the school to thank Coach Buck for his letter. I spent quite some time debating if I should thank him in person or if I should just let it go. Ultimately I decided that I needed to shake his hand and thank him personally for reaching out to Jacob.

I arrived at the game in the 2nd half and it was a barnburner. The lead changed hands several times and the teams were actually tied at the end of regulation. Multiple overtimes later Holdrege emerged as the winner. I stood just outside the visitor's locker room holding the letter that Coach Buck had sent. I figured this would be the only way that he would know who I was. As he left the gym he walked straight over to me and hugged me. I had tears in my eyes and I had no words. He pulled me in close and said, "I love you man".

Once I composed myself I thanked him and asked if I could say a few words to his team since they had all signed the letter. He got the team's attention and I thanked them for their thoughtfulness. I also congratulated them on their hard fought win, and then told them that there is more to life than winning a basketball game and it was obvious that they understood that. I told them the most important thing is the way you choose to live your life and they should feel fortunate to have a man like Coach Buck showing them the right way. I don't remember leaving the locker room. I think the emotions were overloading my mind, but I did feel better knowing that Coach Buck knew that we appreciated his efforts.

Day 20, Saturday, February 19, 2011

After the mistakes of last weekend, we enter this morning armed with new knowledge and confidence that we can keep Jacob more comfortable. We have enough of the correct medication and understand the miracle of saltine crackers and soda pop. As usual, Jacob spent the entire day on the futon in the basement with the blinds closed and Dalton did a great job of keeping the house quiet. Jacob also has a much better understanding of what his body is telling him. Today was pretty uneventful and that was welcomed by everyone.

Shortly before lunch I delivered Jerod's PS3 and some games to Grandma's house. He was sitting up in one of the bedrooms watching movies. He already looked a lot better and said that he was feeling well. I sat with him for a few minutes and we talked for a while. He is planning on coming home tomorrow.

I told him that we can see the difference only when he is not feeling well. Jacob calls it *sliding*. But otherwise he acts normally.

Sliding is when he can feel himself getting worse. He can't quite explain what feels bad, he just feels lousy overall.

Four

SECOND HALF
OF INDUCTION

DAY 21, SUNDAY, FEBRUARY 20, 2011

Dalton had a wrestling tournament in Utica today. Our neighbors and good friends the Thompsons have offered to take him if Shari or I can't get away. We have waited to make a commitment until we knew how Jacob was feeling this morning. Sunday is basically the pivotal day for the rest of the week. The morning went well and Shari felt that she had everything under control so I rode along with Dalton and the Thompsons to the tournament. Dalton wrestled well. Since he is a big kid, sometimes it is a problem finding someone his size to wrestle at smaller tournaments, but this time there was one kid bigger than Dalton. Unfortunately, that was the only other kid in Dalton's weight class, so they just had to wrestle each other, best two out of three matches. Dalton pinned the kid in the 2nd period in the first two matches, so he got 1st place. As we were getting ready to leave, some of the other parents asked if we would like to stop and eat supper on the way home. Dalton and I had already had some food at the concession stand, but after checking with Shari we agreed to go along. I was uncomfortable through most of the meal because this was the longest period that I had been away from Jacob since that first visit to the Clinic and I was not driving so I was not in control of my own transportation. When I went to Jerod's basketball games I had taken my own vehicle and I knew that I could leave at any time. This was different. Someone else had the keys and that bothered me.

Everything was going well at home and I knew that Shari had it under control, but for whatever reason, I could not relax until we started to drive home from the restaurant. I also felt guilty that I was out having a good time while Shari was home with Jacob and Jerod was still at Grandma's house, but Dalton deserved some time for himself away from everything else that was going on at home.

Jerod came home around 7:30pm tonight and stayed upstairs in the living room for the rest of the evening. It was nice to have the whole family back at home again.

DAY 22, MONDAY, FEBRUARY, 21, 2011

The difference between this week and last week is amazing. Jacob got up this morning feeling better and thinking about going to school in the afternoon. What we have learned in the past week has helped his comfort level immensely. He is also making smart decisions about his activity and knowing the difference between when it's necessary to take meds and when he should just have something to eat or drink. He did a little bit of homework in the afternoon, but did not feel quite well enough to go to school at 2:00pm, so he rested all day. The nausea and headaches appear to be under control for now and he is acting more like his normal self.

At 10:00pm we shut everything off downstairs and got Jacob ready for bed. He has bought into this routine and agrees that it has helped him sleep better through the night. Around 11:00pm he knocked on our bedroom door to let us know that he was having another panic attack. He asked if I would go downstairs and sit with him for a while, so he and I went down to the futon. This is the first time that we have had a serious talk really since we left the hospital on February 9. He asked me if his mother and I thought that he was acting normally. He was concerned that his behavior was changing. One of the things that he is concerned about is that he feels that he is overanalyzing everything and that he has to consider the consequences for even the smallest decisions. We spoke with Dr. Gordon about another panic attack that he had earlier and he said that not only is it normal under the circumstances, but the drugs he is taking will amplify the situation. I told him that we can see the difference only when he is not feeling well—Jacob calls it "sliding"—but otherwise he acts normally. "Sliding" is when he can feel himself getting worse. He can't quite explain what feels bad, he just feels lousy overall. When he doesn't eat or drink often enough or he gets nausea or a headache, he says he can feel himself "slide". We can tell just by looking at him which way he feels, just like what I mentioned the night of the Central City basketball game. We talked for over an hour about what his future might hold and keeping a strong attitude during this fight. I described to him how over the past four years he had always wanted to bench press 200 pounds. That is the first major goal of most young lifters. It is a milestone that brings with it a certain amount of glory and bravado. I explained to him that he never knew exactly when that day would come, but he did know that it would eventually arrive if he kept working hard every day. This is basically the same mindset that he must have in his fight against cancer. Every day that goes by is one day closer to being cancer-free. We do not know exactly what day that will be, but we have been told that he will achieve this someday. Everyone would like to know the exact date so that we could start some sort of countdown calendar, but that's not how this works. There was no countdown to the date when he would bench 200 pounds, but that didn't stop him from committing to that goal.

We talked about how all of the lifting, practices, and special workouts have prepared him mentally as well as physically for this fight. When you compete in sports you must spend many more hours preparing mentally as well as physically for the short moments of glory that the actual contest provides. In our youth football program we talk about how you will typically practice at least five times more than the time spent in an actual game. That amount does not include lifting, film review, camps, and off-season workouts as it does in high school sports. You have to love the preparation as much as you love the competition or the process will not be enjoyable. I tell the kids that you have to learn to love practice and playing a game is the reward. Jacob admitted that he has made himself endure a lot of pain in preparing his body for competition and that now he doesn't really notice the pain after a workout. He is accustomed to it. He says the feeling is almost like an addiction. He craves to feel the strain in his muscles and the burning in his lungs that he has had multiple times per day for the past several years. He has prepared his mind to block out the smaller annoyances in order to attain the long term benefits. This is the mental preparation that will help him get through all of the treatments and all of the "slides" on his way to achieving the ultimate goal.

Day 23, Tuesday, February 22, 2011

It appears that our routine immediately after chemotherapy will be two full days of rest only followed by a day of short intervals of homework then three days of morning and afternoon visits to the school. I think that if we try to move any faster it could prolong the side effects. This seems to be the natural rhythm of his recovery. He is ready to go to school on day four and it doesn't seem to drain him of too much energy when he comes home. His teachers have been great and he seems to be getting back in the groove of some of his classes. He is concerned with keeping his GPA and achieving the Honor Roll and being in the National Honor Society. We have discussed what an accomplishment that would be if he could still maintain all of those academic goals all while overcoming cancer. I think he sees the possibilities for achievement that lie before him and that attaining those lofty goals would make a statement that could impact a lot of people. I think he understands that his story could lift the spirits of other people, not just those with cancer, but any person that faces an obstacle that derails their intended path. When an adult hears his story, they may find more strength because a "kid" summoned the strength. Another teen might find the strength knowing that a peer who had everything he loved ripped away found the strength. Most of all, a younger child may find the strength by looking up to him as a student and an athlete and try to attain the same goals as Jacob.

I truly hope that as he progresses through his treatment that he finds a place in his heart to reach out to other people, especially children. I have witnessed the way younger children admire high school and college students. Jacob got a small taste of that last year during basketball season. Our former high school basketball coach started a program where the high school players went to an elementary school classroom and read a book to the class. Jacob was one of three freshmen assigned to the kindergarten. He had the same class every time he went back to read and they loved every minute of it. He was nervous the first time, but after that I think he had fun being with the kids. He would always come home and talk about the endless random questions he would get once he finished reading and he would laugh like a little kid. I think that seeing an athlete like Jacob walk through the door and share his story and offer his strength and support would have a profound effect on a younger child facing the similar obstacles. The satisfaction of knowing that you may have had a positive impact on a child is one of the greatest feelings one will ever encounter. I hope he learns the full impact of what he can give to someone else.

Tonight Jerod had a basketball game in Hastings. He and I were invited by my construction manager, Jessie McCoy, to meet for dinner and a drink at Bullseye's Bar. We were surprised to see Sean Callahan from Rivals.com at the bar giving a presentation on all of the new recruits for the Husker Football Team. We sat with Jessie and his wife Brandie at a table and watched video highlights on the TV's and listened to Sean breakdown each player. When he was done I went over to his table and introduced myself and told him Jacob's story. He was nice enough to send a get well text from his phone to Jacob. Jacob immediately sent me a text asking me how he should respond to Sean. Jacob follows football recruiting religiously and he knows all about Sean Callahan. He was very excited to receive that text and it was very nice of Sean.

Day 24, Wednesday, February 23, 2011

Going back to school part-time seems to be helping Jacob mentally and emotionally. He is getting something accomplished even though it is not full-time. He has been doing nothing for at last three weeks and he is getting bored, so no matter how much kids complain about homework, in this case it is a good thing.

After the afternoon session at school we went for another walk because the weather was beautiful again. I don't think the walk is as scary now that he is getting his life back into a rhythm. It is a much different rhythm than it was, but a rhythm nonetheless.

The varsity football coaches brought pizza and pasta over to the house at 6:45pm. Jacob has been looking forward to this visit all week. He has the most profound respect for these gentlemen and they teach much more than football to the young men of this community.

As you know, the game of football has huge significance in our family. I relate the lessons that can be learned in football to life lessons. It is amazing how many instances in life can be paralleled with the game of football. The coaches at Aurora teach these same ideals every day. Coach Huebert often talks about, commitment, dedication, perseverance, discipline, unity and overcoming adversity when he speaks to the team. When he says these things he is stating that you should live your life striving toward a goal with these principles in mind. I know each of the members of this staff fairly well and I believe that they are all committed to making young men better in life and then football. In the past couple of years our high school football team has enjoyed great success. In 2008 they went 12-1 and won the first state football championship in school history. In 2009 they went 13-0 and were never truly challenged on their way to a 2nd state title. In 2010 they were ranked #2 all season and were defeated by the #1 ranked Team which went on to win the State Championship. We finished 11-1. Over that two year period they enjoyed a 36-2 overall record with two state titles and in the process compiled a 34-game winning streak. Most experts agree that had our starting quarterback not gotten hurt in the quarterfinals that we would have won that semi-final game and cruised to a 3rd straight championship. Keep in mind that our quarterback was later named the Gatorade Player of the Year for the State of Nebraska and is one of the most prolific and accurate passers in Nebraska history.

All of this is extremely impressive when you look at it from the outside, but when you talk to the coaches they will tell you to a man that the journey is what matters, not the destination. The process of learning and uniting as a team over the course of the season is what they enjoy. The championships are not the priority. This is a great lesson for everyone to learn: enjoy the journey. Whatever you are doing, whatever your stage in life, enjoy the journey. If all that you ever look to is the destination, then you won't truly appreciate the destination if you did not enjoy the path that led you there. Lessons like these from a respected source have a far greater impact on a child than most people realize.

The coaches stayed for about two hours and Jacob thoroughly enjoyed the visit. Most of the discussion revolved around the game of football and stories from the present day and the past, but none of it involved Jacob's future on the Aurora team. These coaches don't care about Jacob's future on the team. These men genuinely care that Jacob fights a successful battle against cancer and lives to be a better person and a better man. If all of that occurs, he will find success in football along that path. I believe that these men had plans to utilize Jacob on the 2011 varsity team and those plans are in jeopardy. But they are not interested in when he will come back, even if that makes their job harder. Not one of them has asked if Jacob will play this year, they only want to know how he is feeling and how is our family dealing with this. It is leadership like this that is lacking in a lot of sports today, especially on the youth level. I have learned a lot on how to coach football and how to be a better man by watching and listening to these five men. They left a nice get well card for Jacob with a personal note from each of them and I am sure that Jacob will cherish that forever.

Day 25, Thursday, February 24, 2011

Chad Johnson came over around 8:00pm to give us some pictures from the night of our football fundraiser. He also brought a list of some simple leg exercises for Jacob to work on while he has nothing else to do. Chad was a decathlete and 400 meter runner at Kansas University and had offered to tutor Jacob this spring in how to get faster. Chad met with Jacob and I this past December and talked about getting together in January to start doing some simple exercises to prepare him for track season. Needless to say, circumstances have changed and Jacob will not be running for the track team this spring. The doctors have told Jacob that he can do some exercising, but it all has to be low or no impact. Chad brought with him a list of simple exercises that Jacob can do from a chair or even lying down as well as a few walking exercises to train his muscles for future running workouts. Last winter we spent quite a bit of time in the high school gym after basketball or track practice changing Jacob's throwing mechanics. This winter we can work on changing his running mechanics.

The exercises Chad listed and demonstrated were all based around training the muscles to act a certain way or "muscle memory". All of these exercises help to strengthen smaller muscles and position his body correctly to run as fast as possible. Simple things that Chad did when he was younger that helped him tremendously. A common quote in coaching is, "You can't coach speed". Chad says that is not entirely true. You have a certain amount of God-given speed, but if you run incorrectly you will never realize all of that potential. If you learn to run correctly you will use all of your natural speed at the highest level possible, thus making yourself faster. It's true that most people will never be sprinters, but that does not mean that proper coaching and technique won't make you faster. Speed is a relative term. What is fast for one person may not be fast for someone else, so you can always coach speed.

Chad's visit was exactly what Jacob needed. He listened intently to every word Chad said. He desperately wants to return to his past life of being an athlete and working out every day. This will give him an outlet and he believes that this will give him a jump start on his road back to being an athlete and also gives him something to occupy his mind. There is a gigantic void in his life right now and these small exercises will help to fill that void.

Day 26, Friday, February 25, 2011

Today is Jacob's 4th chemotherapy treatment in the Induction phase. Another snowstorm blew through eastern Nebraska overnight which made the driving conditions less than ideal. The first 50 miles was pretty normal, but there were several bad spots over the next 50 miles. Countless cars and trucks had slid off the road during the night and crews were starting to remove them.

Everything is going according to plan, however Jacob's blood sugar and blood pressure were pretty high and caused some concern for Dr. Gordon. Jacob has been drinking Mountain Dew to help prevent headaches and it also seems to help with his nausea, but the sugar and caffeine are now causing other problems. We will just have to cut back on his soda pop intake to try to bring these levels down. We don't need to add more medication to his already lengthy list. We will go to the clinic in Aurora tomorrow for a blood draw and blood pressure check. Hopefully, we will see improvement in both areas and avoid more medication.

Dalton had a wrestling meet tonight in Geneva. We got back to Aurora just in time to ride along with the Snyder family who had offered to take Dalton since we were not planning on being back in time. I debated all the way home from Omaha if I should go, or if I should just stay home and help make sure that Jacob was comfortable. I'm glad that I went to the wrestling meet. Dalton had two other boys in his bracket, both of which were significantly heavier. He pinned both kids early in the matches and is wrestling with great effort and determination. He found a way to mentally prepare himself this summer prior to the football season and has competed at that level since that time. He has the size, strength, and talent to succeed, but was always lacking in mental preparation. Now he appears to be unstoppable.

Before his first match, Dalton called me down to the floor to take his sweat-shirt so that it would not get lost or stolen. I noticed some writing on his protective headgear, so I grabbed it to take a closer look. I knew that he had written JP3 on the outside prior to last week's meet, but I was not prepared for what he had written on the inside. "This is for you" was written on the inside of his ear protection not for everyone to see. This was a personal message from Dalton to Jacob and provided him focus and motivation to go out and do his best in every match. So far he is 4-0 and has pinned every kid no later than the second period. I smiled and handed the headgear back to Dalton and returned to my seat at the top of the bleachers fighting back tears the entire way. Later, that night Shari showed Jacob what Dalton had done and he stated, "That's the coolest thing I've ever seen".

Jacob has been doing his Chad Johnson exercises frequently today and really seems to enjoy them. As I was saying goodnight, Jacob stopped me to explain that he had a revelation that night. He stated that the exercises he was doing gave him the tired feeling that he was missing since he has not been allowed to workout. He describes it as an addiction to the pain. He sits on the futon and contracts different muscles in various ways and is trying to find new ways to manipulate his body.

He has also committed himself to eating and drinking better. This week's visit with Dr. Gordon raised some concerns about his blood sugar and blood pressure levels. He has been drinking a lot of soda pop lately and has been craving extremely salty foods. This, in combination with some of the chemotherapy side effects, has raised those levels to the point of concern. Dr. Gordon has ordered an additional blood draw and blood pressure check tomorrow in Aurora to monitor this situation. Jacob spent the evening talking about how he can change his diet and manage his cravings to get this under control. He is now taking a more aggressive approach to the part of his recovery that only he can truly control. The exercises are a tremendous boost to his emotional state and the new diet has him motivated to come out of this treatment protocol ready to get back into top physical condition. It is refreshing to see this attitude return.

As I have stated before, Jacob was always very conscientious about what he put into his body. He had the normal sweet-tooth that most people have, but other than that he was a healthy eater and refused to drink soda pop because it was unhealthy. When we were forced to introduce caffeine into his diet to help control his headaches, it seemed to break his will a little bit. I think that once he started drinking pop his concern for eating healthy disappeared. He had a good week of keeping the side effects under control, but allowed some of his other health to decline. Once again, his mother and I are also learning what we can do to help as we go.

Day 27, Saturday, February 26, 2011

For the next few days, Jacob will need to have lab work done here in Aurora to monitor his blood pressure and blood sugar levels. Today his pressure and sugar levels were back down, but now his sodium level is also low. We will have to keep our eye on that also, but since we have completely changed his diet overnight this should probably be expected.

Another one of Jacob's favorite things is the NFL Scouting Combine. Today it is being televised live on the NFL Network and he is absorbing every second of it. I enjoy watching it almost as much as he does, but I do not soak up all of the information the way he does. The NFL combine is a series of tests developed to help teams derive the athletic abilities of individual players. Watching people run the 40-yard dash or test their vertical jump repeatedly for hours on end would bore most people—even people who claim to be football fans. This is the kind of thing that runs through Jacob's blood. Along with the standard coverage of the testing, they will also demonstrate some tips on how to perform each test at the highest level. Once again, Jacob takes this opportunity to learn new techniques that will help him perform at a higher level.

He told us today that he loves his new bed and he is sleeping better. The last bed that he liked was his blue "racecar" bed that he had when he was really little. He is also staying with the program of getting to bed at a set time and following the same protocol every night to help develop better sleeping habits. We now have learned how to handle his side effects better and with improved sleep his disposition has improved also.

Tonight the varsity basketball team lost in the first round of the district tournament. The season is over. Track practice starts on Monday.

Day 31, Wednesday, March 2, 2011

Today Jacob attended school in the morning and afternoon for a total of just over three hours. This is the longest he has been able to go to school since his diagnosis. After he returned from the afternoon session we walked two laps around our neighborhood which is the most we have walked also. It saddens me to see how quickly he has lost his physical conditioning. I am very pleased that we completed two laps, but six weeks ago this kid could seemingly run forever. In fact, last year during track season he came home one day and told me that he never got tired during their workouts. He complained that his legs would start to fatigue at the end of the workout, but his cardiovascular conditioning was not being tested. He was frustrated during the first part of the season because his legs would get tired toward the end of his 400-meter race, but he was not out of breath. To change this situation he stayed after practice was over to do additional work to try and strengthen his legs. I would stay with him and he was right about his conditioning. At one point he was running 600 meters four times followed by 400 meters four times and finishing with 200 meters four times. This was all being done AFTER he had completed his required team workout.

One day the Middle School Track Team was hosting a meet and there were hundreds of kids showing up and preparing to compete, but Jacob was not done with his workout. He was not deterred and even though there were several times he had to dodge collisions with the younger athletes, he stayed until HE was done. At one point I was standing next to a father of one of the Aurora kids when he leaned over and said sarcastically, "If only that kid had a work ethic".

During our walks we talk a lot and the conversation usually centers around when he will be able to return to his regular workouts and competition. My goal is to keep him positive and concentrating on doing what he needs to do now to get better and staying within the doctor's orders so that he does not create a setback by overworking himself during treatment. We have told the doctors to be very clear in what he can and cannot do, because if they leave him an opening, he will take advantage of it.

Later in the day we went to our friend Bonnie's barber shop and got his head shaved for the first time. He has not lost much of his hair, but it is beginning to fall out in spots. He wants to get his head shaved now that way it was his decision, not a result of the chemotherapy. He has lost control of just about everything else in his life right now, but he can control this.

Day 33, Friday, March 4, 2011

Yesterday Jacob and I went to Omaha for labs and a CT scan as part of the standard protocol. Today we are all back for a visit with a psychologist, another spinal tap, and we met Dr. Beck for the first time at the clinic. This is scheduled as an off week in the Induction phase prior to starting the next phase known as Consolidation. There will be no IV chemotherapy this week, so we are looking forward to a good weekend.

During our first admission to the hospital, our social worker had offered to arrange a visit with a psychologist if we felt Jacob needed to talk to a professional. We have discussed this several times over the past few weeks and both Shari and I think it would be prudent to arrange a consultation. Since Jacob will not be receiving treatment today, we thought it would make sense to take advantage of this time to schedule an appointment. Jacob does not think that it is necessary. He says that he is processing all of the madness just fine. I agree that he appears to be handling the emotional side of things appropriately, but I am not trained to look for subtle hints of larger problems.

The actual visit with the psychologist did not take that long. When Jacob reappeared in the waiting room, he had a mischievous smile on his face and I knew what that meant. His first words were, "That was kinda fun. I was totally messing with her." Apparently she had Jacob draw a house and a tree on a piece of paper and then analyzed the results with him. I don't recall exactly what the tree meant or what her conclusions were, but I do remember what Jacob told me about the house.

Jacob is not an artist. His house was a rudimentary version similar to what a four or five-year-old would draw. He drew a door on the main floor and two windows on the second floor. She then asked him to draw a person standing beside the house. Of course, he drew a stick figure with no eyes, nose or mouth. The psychologist then described what she perceived to see these drawings meant.

First of all, Jacob drew a straight line at the bottom of the house and that meant that he had a solid foundation at home. Then she said that he did not draw any windows on the main floor because he did not like people being able to see how he truly felt inside. She had another reason why Jacob did not draw any facial features on the person standing beside the house, but I can't remember what it was.

When she was finished, Jacob offered the following explanations. He said that even though he did not draw any windows on the main floor, he did draw the stick figure tall enough to look into the second floor windows and he did not draw any facial features on the person because he was just too lazy to put in the extra effort. This was the way the entire consultation unfolded. She would offer a clinical explanation and Jacob would fire back with a simple common sense explanation. He enjoyed the mental jousting immensely. He loves to prove people wrong.

The psychologist followed Jacob into the waiting room and told us, "He's fine", and when we asked if we needed to schedule another session she said, "Only if he starts to have some problems". It was probably a waste of everyone's time, but Shari and I felt much better knowing that he had been seen by a professional and she saw no cause for concern.

Day 35, Sunday, March 6, 2011

Today was a very peaceful day. Since Jacob did not have his normal dose of Vincristine and Daunorubicine yesterday, he is not experiencing any side effects. I think that we have also learned how to counteract the headaches that he normally gets from his spinal taps. We are looking forward to a good week this week.

Dalton's basketball team had a tournament in Grand Island today. Shari stayed home, but I slipped away to watch him play. As we were waiting for the game before us to finish, I noticed that there was a buzz in the crowd. The University of Nebraska's head football coach, Bo Pelini, was standing in the entrance to the gym. Apparently one of his kids was also playing in this tournament. Immediately I thought to myself that I should walk right over and shake his hand and thank him for the card that the Nebraska Football Staff had sent to Jacob. My second thought was to just stay away and leave him alone to enjoy the tournament with his family. I hate it when people intrude on a celebrity when they are just trying to enjoy a private activity with their family. Several times in my life I have seen people approach someone like Coach Pelini and inject themselves into a private conversation. I hate it, and I think it's embarrassing.

This was my dilemma. I did not want to disturb him in this setting, but I wanted him to know how much that card meant to Jacob and that we appreciated their efforts. Jacob is a lot like me when it comes to approaching someone like this. He would love to talk to Coach Pelini at a football camp or a clinic, but not while he's with his family. I found myself in the hallway outside the gym trying to find the courage to approach Coach Pelini because I decided that I probably would never have the chance to thank him in person again. As he left the gym on his way to the parking lot I called his name and asked if he had a minute. Although he did not look thrilled to be beckoned by what he thought was just another "Husker Fan", he was gracious enough to stop and shake my hand. I asked if he remembered signing a card for a young man who was recently diagnosed with cancer and he did remember. I told him how much that card raised Jacob's spirits and that Shari and I truly appreciated them taking the time to send it out. He asked how Jacob was doing and I said "OK", then as he turned to walk away he asked me to give his best to Jacob. The whole encounter probably lasted less than two minutes after I agonized over the decision for at least 30 minutes. As I returned to the gym for Dalton's game I felt good about the decision. Looking back, I had no problem approaching Coach Buck from Holdrege, so my only hang up was the fact that Coach Pelini was a celebrity. In the end, they both sent cards to Jacob that mean a lot to him, so both men deserve a handshake and my personal appreciation.

DAY 36, MONDAY, MARCH 7, 2011

Since he had the week off from treatment, Jacob was feeling well enough to go up to the high school gym tonight for the first time in two months. For the past two winters we have been going up to the school at night to work on his quarterback mechanics. When he gets home from basketball practice he does his homework, eats supper, and then around 9:00pm he would come upstairs and say, "Wanna go throw?" The high school principal assigned me a security code so that I would not have to call someone to let us in all the time. We have spent countless hours alone in this gym working on his footwork, accuracy, arm strength and technique. Last winter I started wearing gloves because my hands would start hurting because he was throwing so hard. I decided last fall to purchase a net for him to throw at and six more footballs identical to the balls that the varsity uses. I also thought that he could take everything up to the gym and workout by himself if I was not available. I can also spend more time critiquing his mechanics if I'm not concentrating on catching a pass that might take my head off.

His determination to improve is amazing. On Mondays, Wednesdays, and Fridays he leaves the house at 6:45am to lift weights, then attends school all day, basketball practice, homework, and when most kids would want to crash and relax, he wants to go work on the little things to get better. They don't lift on Tuesdays and Thursdays so he gets to sleep in until 7:30am.

So much has happened in the past few weeks, it feels like we have been away from this routine for months. I missed the way the gym smells and the squeak of the maple floors, but most of all I have missed this time that I get to spend alone with Jacob doing what he loves. He has a very specific routine that we must follow every night. We have to warm up a certain way. I have to stand in certain places at certain times to simulate where a receiver should be on a certain route, and the night has to end with a perfect pass. The accuracy has to be perfect, the ball has to spin in a perfect spiral, or we don't go home. Tonight he had a much harder time throwing the ball well. His fingers are tingling because of the Vincristine so he can't really grip the ball correctly. I tried to convince him that after all that he has been through that he was throwing the ball extremely well, but he knew that he was struggling and he didn't like it. Even though he was struggling tonight, it still felt good to do something "normal" again. If I am going to keep him focused on the protocol, we are going to have to have some nights like this where he can feel like he's on the road to recovery.

Phase two of Jacob's chemotherapy protocol is called "Consolidation". We were hoping that after phase one, the treatment intervals might slow down, but actually the opposite is true. The treatment is still scheduled on a weekly basis, but it will involve multiple days of treatment each week. For now we will enjoy the peace and quiet for the next few days and take on the next phase on Friday.

It's been three months since he woke up feeling sick and this is the first time he has been at a friend's house socially. My plan was to drop him off and then pick him up when he called. He does not trust himself behind the wheel since he has been on steroids.

Five

PHASE II
CONSOLIDATION

DAY 40, FRIDAY, MARCH 11, 2011

Today is the first treatment for the clinical study that Jacob is participating in. So far, all he has done for this study is to have a bone marrow biopsy. Now he will actually have a drug called Nelarabine. We don't know much about what this drug can do to help. Dr. Gordon said that it might help kill cancer faster in some patients. The only thing that he would really tell us is that there should not be any negative effects for Jacob. This treatment consists of one outpatient treatment per day for five straight days. The treatment can only be given at the Med Center in Omaha. It's not available in Grand Island, which would be much closer to home. Not knowing how Jacob will react to this drug, we decided it would be best to stay in Omaha every night instead of spending four hours on the road every day driving back and forth to Aurora. The American Cancer Society has a program where they will find lodging for a family for just these situations and since it is free to us we felt this was the safest path to take. You have to notify them at least a week in advance to reserve the room, so we could not afford to wait and find out how Jacob reacts to treatment.

Shari and I decided to split our time on this treatment. She would take Jacob to Omaha today and then I would trade off with her on Sunday. That way neither one of us will get too burned out and Jacob will have a little change of pace with someone different to talk to. I also took advantage of this time to actually go to work at my office for the first time since January 28.

Jerod and Dalton have been very helpful so far during this process. They understand that Jacob's treatment is the main priority in our lives right now, so I wanted to reward them this afternoon by taking them out to a friend's farm to shoot some guns. Jacob has no interest in guns, but Jerod and Dalton love anything to do with firearms. This past Christmas they both asked for Scheel's gift certificates, so we all pooled together and bought a pistol that we have not had a chance to shoot yet. Dalton also got a restored World War II Russian rifle that he has not shot yet. We all needed to blow off some steam and this was a great way to do it. We took out Dalton's new rifle, our new pistol, my 30/30, and the .22 rifle. We shot every bullet we owned and the boys had a blast. It was nice to see some joy back in their lives and it was a great distraction for me.

Shari and Jacob were staying at the Coco Keys Hotel and Indoor Water Park. At 10:52pm I got a call from Jacob that someone had pulled the fire alarm and they were forced to evacuate the building. They were staying on the fifth floor and had to walk down all of those stairs and then stand outside in the cold. I told Shari to require a room change as soon as they were allowed back inside. Luckily they were able to move to a room on the ground floor. Jacob complained about the alarms going off on his IV tower during his first inpatient admission to the hospital. He called them sleep detectors and felt that their only job was to keep him from sleeping. Now he has a fire alarm doing the same thing at a hotel. The rest of the night was peaceful though.

Day 44, Tuesday, March 15, 2011

Today was the last of the five Nelarabine treatments for this round. Jacob will have two more rounds of this treatment later on during this phase of treatment. The treatments don't take that long so we spend the vast majority of our time just lying in bed at the hotel. When I traded off with Shari on Sunday, I brought Jacob's TV and his PS3 with me to help him pass the time. Until then, they were stuck watching whatever was on TV at the hotel. Now Jacob has access to his games as well as Netflix.

I brought Jerod and Dalton with me on Sunday and since Jacob was not having any side effects we all went out to eat as a family. I took him out to eat on Monday night, and except for treatment every day this was really the only time that we left the room. We are all very nervous about being out in public and exposing him to an outside infection. We are probably being too overprotective, but he is participating in a clinical study and we have no idea what the side effects might be or when they will arise.

Day 47 Friday, March 18, 2011

After two quiet days at home we are on our way back to Omaha. We left at 5:45am for an appointment to start receiving IV fluids. Today's treatment will require a minimum amount of fluid prior to receiving chemo and a minimum amount of fluid after. At 10:00am we had an appointment with Dr. Gordon. He said that according to Jacob's labs, all is going well and Jacob is responding to treatment extremely well. After the appointment they had to check the protein level in Jacob's urine. This will determine if he has had enough fluid to begin chemo. The first test came back too concentrated so he continued on fluids for another hour. The second test also came back too concentrated so he continued on fluids for another hour. Finally, the tests were acceptable and he began receiving chemo at 1:00pm. At 3:30pm the chemo was complete, but now he has to have a minimum of four hours of IV fluids before we can go home. Thank goodness he brought along his homework and his computer to pass the time. At 7:50pm the alarm goes off on his pump and we are free to leave. Even though we had spent almost all day sitting in chairs doing absolutely nothing, we were all exhausted when we got home at 10:00pm.

Tonight there is a party at Corey and Tracy Ohlson's house because tomorrow is the Alumni Basketball Tournament in Aurora. My life used to revolve around this weekend. I looked forward to it all year. Even though I have never been a good basketball player, I enjoy the weekend because of all the alumni that return each year. The tournament was started in 1990 and my graduating class has had a team in it every year. I was on crutches that first year and could not play. Since then I have only missed two tournaments, both because of weddings. When I had my shop/office on the south edge of town, I would invite my returning classmates to supper every year. After the local bars closed for the night, EVERYONE would go directly to my shop for the "after hours" party. This was a tradition for several years until I sold that building. Now the tradition is that everyone goes to the Ohlson's house for the entire evening. I have had a lot of people ask if Shari and I will be in attendance tonight and I have told them that since Jacob was having chemo today we would probably not go out. I was too tired to go back out after we got home anyway, but in no way did I ever even consider going out tonight. I have no desire to pretend like everything is fine and to be surrounded by people that are trying to have a good time. Another reason is that my presence would just lead to more discussions about my family's situation and I don't want to be a downer for everyone else tonight. Let them have fun. I will stay home with the most important people in my life. Besides that, Jacob has to be at the Cancer Treatment Center in Grand Island tomorrow morning at 8:00am for the start of another treatment.

Day 48, Saturday, March 19, 2011

Today Jacob starts the first of three straight days of outpatient treatments in Grand Island with a drug called ARA-C. This is the drug that will really have a negative effect on his immune system. Until now, his immune system has handled the treatments well. His counts have dropped, but have always stayed within acceptable levels. This drug is supposed to wipe them out.

The Treatment Center in Grand Island is only a thirty-minute drive from our house. It is really nice to be able to have these treatments so close to home, unlike the Nelarabine treatments. I could tell when we left this morning that Jacob's stress level was down because he knew he would be at home instead of another hotel. The actual treatment only takes about 30-45 minutes, so we were home by mid-morning and he got to go back to his futon downstairs.

Day 54, Friday, March 25, 2011

In stark contrast to last week's treatment, today's treatment went pretty quickly. We arrived at 9:00am for labs followed by an appointment with Dr. Gordon. After a short visit in the clinic, we went to the Post Anesthesia Care Unit (PACU) for Spinal Tap #4 followed by a short chemo treatment and we were on the road by early afternoon.

After we left the Med Center, Jacob was craving Buffalo Wild Wings. He decided that today was the day to try the Blazin' Challenge. The challenge consists of eating twelve of their hottest buffalo wings in less than six minutes. Since Jacob has been on steroids, he has lost some of his taste buds. Food tastes very bland unless it is extremely salty or spicy. I have been making his lunches while he is at home and almost every meal has to have jalapenos or jalapeno juice mixed in and EVERY meal must have a two-chili-pepper garnish. If I don't include the garnish, he will sit at the bar in the kitchen and stare at me without saying a word. I haven't done my job correctly until I provide the garnish. He has always liked spicy foods, but the steroids require a much higher level of heat before he gets the flavor. He finished the challenge in 5 minutes and 31 seconds and picked every bone clean. The prize for this accomplishment is a black T-shirt and severe indigestion.

Tomorrow we start three more days of ARA-C treatment in Grand Island.

DAY 57, MONDAY, MARCH 28, 2011

Today was the last day of the ARA-C treatments at the Cancer Treatment Center in Grand Island. Jacob has not been feeling well at all. Shari and I both knew that he was feeling worse than usual because he did not attend the basketball team's potluck supper on Sunday night. It's not in Jacob's character to miss a team function, especially when he does not have many opportunities to see his friends. He has also lost his appetite completely. I think all of this chemotherapy is finally catching up with him. The biggest side effects that he faces are headaches and nausea. He says that he always has a headache. Sometimes it's just a lot worse than others. He has not had a problem vomiting from the nausea because he does a good job of catching it early and taking his Zofran. However, Zofran causes headaches so it is definitely a vicious circle.

Day 60, Thursday, March 31, 2011

As usual, Jacob is feeling a lot better on Thursday. Tonight he went up to the track and walked a ½ mile and then jogged a ½ mile. I'm sure that his doctors would not have recommended this course of action, but I think he knows his body the best and if this helps him mentally, I'm all for it. Plus, he knows that after tomorrow's treatment, he won't feel like working out for at least another week.

Day 61, Friday, April 1, 2011

Jacob received his first blood transfusion today. His counts are down as expected, but for the first time his red blood cell counts are low enough to require a transfusion. He was a little freaked out when they listed HIV as a possible risk factor from getting blood products, but Dr. Gordon did a good job of easing his mind. Other than that, today was a typical Friday: labs, clinic, spinal tap #5, followed by chemo and then the blood transfusion.

Today was also the first day of the University of Nebraska Football Coaches' Clinic. I have been attending this as a guest of our varsity coaching staff for the past few years. Basically it's two days of listening to successful coaches talk about their systems and programs. I have learned a lot from attending these clinics and I have been fortunate enough to listen to coaches like Sonny Lubick, Barry Alvarez and Bobby Bowden. This year the featured speaker is Bob Stoops from Oklahoma. Missing this event crossed my mind a couple times during the day, but it was never a distraction and I never even considered letting Shari take Jacob to treatment without me. Jacob asked me about it a couple of times and I think he felt bad that I was missing it, but there will be more coaches' clinics in the future. We only get one chance to get this treatment right.

Day 67, Thursday, April 7, 2011

Jacob missed about half of his sophomore basketball season and will miss the entire track and field season and he has accepted that, but today he sadly stated, "They started option drill today". Option drill is when the high school quarterbacks and running backs get together a couple of days a week before school and practice running the option in the gym. Jacob has been participating in these drills since he was in 8th grade. His goal was always to be the varsity quarterback his junior year. This was the first chance that he would have this year to earn that position and it was passing him by. My heart ached for him as I know that it was tearing him apart inside. We have talked about the probability that he would not be able to play this year, but it has always been just that—talk. Now it was real. HIS team was moving on without him and he was helpless.

Football is a young man's game. Even if someone is fortunate enough to play professionally, by the time they reach their mid-30's they are considered "old". When you consider most of the other sports played competitively, football is one of the few that is not played recreationally later in life. I have personally played in a recreational basketball and softball league and I know of several men who still play well into their 40's. In fact, there is an adult baseball team in our small town that has several players my age competing. Of course, anyone can golf as long as they can walk and swing a club. Although far fewer, I still know people my age and older who continue to compete in running events like a 5k, 10k, or even triathlons. Football is a young man's sport and you only get one chance to compete in high school. Every practice that goes by, every game that is played is one less opportunity in a finite amount of opportunities. No one is more aware of this point than Jacob. He is one of the rare individuals who enjoys practice almost as much as the game. He loves every minute of the preparation and competition for position that practice provides.

Before he began his sophomore season, I sat down with him and gave him one piece of advice: Don't waste one second. I told him that he was about to enter one of most exciting and memorable times in his life. For those who have never played it might be hard to understand, but high school football is truly an experience that most people will never forget. Some people spend the rest of their lives reflecting back on those days as the best of their life. I asked Jacob to not waste one second of that opportunity. Give everything that you have on every play and every drill. I told him that the worst thing that he could do is look back and say, "I wish I would have worked harder". Leave no doubt in your mind that you gave every effort to improve yourself and your team. By doing this he would always be able to look back and know that he and his team achieved everything possible. If there is a chance at regret, then there can always be the thought that "we could have done better". This is a lesson that we all have learned as we get older. Jacob is one of those rare individuals who learns from others' mistakes, and I believe that he could honestly look back at his sophomore season and say, "I did my best".

Day 68, Friday, April 8, 2011

Consolidation consists of (2) five week protocols. Today is the fifth and final treatment in the first protocol. As usual we start out with labs, followed by an appointment in the clinic with Dr. Gordon. Even though Jacob developed a rash overnight, Dr. Gordon says everything looks good. Jacob's counts are rebounding nicely and he seems to be feeling better. The only drug that he will receive today is a Vincristine push into his IV line which only takes a few minutes and we are once again on our way home by mid-afternoon.

When Dalton got off of the bus from school today, he had a wonderful surprise for us. Two of Jacob's classmates had ordered wristbands in honor of Jacob. We were totally caught off guard. We had no idea that anyone was doing something like this. Beth Morris was Jacob's first "girlfriend" when they were in sixth grade and Bryce Hewen has been one of Jacob's best friends since kindergarten. These two kids took it upon themselves to order and pay for 400 bracelets to show support for Jacob. The bracelets are half red and half white with the letters JP3 and a superman symbol molded into the wristband. Jacob was very touched by their thoughtfulness and both Shari and I cried when we realized what a wonderful gesture this was.

Day 69, Saturday, April 9, 2011

Since Jacob did not have another spinal tap yesterday, he is not battling a headache today, and we are learning how to control his nausea. So today he got to attend some of the Aurora Invitational Track Meet. We did not spend a lot of time at the meet, but we did get to watch some of his friends compete and we stayed just long enough to watch the finals of the 400m. He is not supposed to stay out in the sun too long, so we went home before the meet was over. He has to wear his mask out in public and he does not like being seen as the cancer patient, so he didn't really argue when I told him we needed to go home.

Day 75, Friday, April 15, 2011

Week 6 of Consolidation is a week off from treatment. Tonight Jacob got to go to his friend Rick's house for poker night. He has been looking forward to this all week. He finally has an opportunity to hang out with the guys and feel "normal". It's been three months since he woke up feeling sick and this is the first time he has been at a friend's house socially. My plan was to drop him off and then pick him up when he called. (He does not trust himself behind the wheel since he has been on steroids.) I actually ended up staying upstairs with Rick's mom and stepdad along with some other adults who stopped over. This is really the first time that I have had a chance to unwind and relax with some of our friends. It was nice to have some fun with people that we have known and shared a lot of good times with. Like usual, Jacob lost all of the money that he brought, but we both had a great time.

Day 82, Friday, April 22, 2011

Today was the first day of the second five-week protocol in the Consolidation phase. This will also be the start of the second five-day outpatient Nelarabine treatment. Just like the last time, Shari took Jacob to Omaha this morning and I will trade places with her on Sunday. This time the American Cancer Society has arranged for us to stay at the Hilton Downtown Omaha. The Hilton is a brand new hotel right across the street from the Qwest Convention Center and TD Ameritrade Park. It is definitely a step up from Coco Keys Water Resort. There was a home baseball game tonight and Shari and Jacob got to enjoy an awesome fireworks display from their room after the game.

Day 84, Sunday, April 24, 2011

Today is Easter. I dropped off Jerod and Dalton at my parent's house so that they could spend the day with their grandparents and then I went to Omaha to trade places with Shari.

In the afternoon, Jacob and I got a visit from Jim, Melinda, Reid, and Ryan Allen. They were on their way back home after spending Easter weekend with Melinda's family. Jim has been a friend of mine for over 25 years and was my college roommate for a while. Melinda and Shari were roommates at the end of our time in college and we have all been close friends ever since. Reid is a year younger than Jacob and Ryan is the same age as Dalton. About a week ago Jim forwarded a story that Ryan wrote in school. I have included it below.

Being Sick isn't always Bad

I dropped back and saw the blitz coming. I had to do something quick. Carson Johnson, our best wide receiver, in the end zone with his hand sticking up in the air, signaling that he was open. This throw would win the game! My eyes glance up at the glowing red scoreboard with 30 seconds left in the 4th quarter. I throw the ball as hard as i could... which ended in being too hard. The ball sailed at least 20 yards past him. One more chance to win.

I remember being a kid and throwing the ball back and forth with Carson. The hot, sticky days in the deep summer of Nebraska. That's all we would do from dusk to dawn. Although Carson has never really been the best at throwing, he could catch the best on the block. He would perfectly follow any route I commanded. We never lost a pickup game in the neighborhood. My best friend was football, I almost literally lived, breathed, and ate football. I loved the sight of the ball floating through the air, the smell of cut grass, and the birds flying over my head. Nothing were better than those days.

*   *   *

"C'mon dude," Carson spoke.

"I don't know what happen," I explained. "I never miss that," saying while I recall the scoreboard, which states that there are 26 seconds left. I quickly call the play. It's another pass.

My mind wasn't prepared, but I didn't have time to get ready. I slowly walked to the center, opened my mouth and start the cadence for the last time in high school, "Down, Set," I yelled with my mouth guard about as clear as mud. "Hike." All the players on wide-outs went on a fly pattern as I faked the handoff. Nobody (obviously) fell for the fake. My next thought was then interrupted by a smack! Somewhere in my mind told me that I couldn't go down, not after getting this far. In my luck the linebacker had tried to arm-tackle me, which, always fails on me. I then broke the tackle and bolted up the field. It was easy at first, shedding the bad mistakes people were having, up to the 20-yard line. Which only meant one thing, 20 yards to go. Their top defensive backer, Michael Doty started to run after me. There was no chance of me surviving a blow from him, so I had to take a different course. With ten yard to go I thought I lost him for sure but, yet again I was wrong. I had one and only one option and that was to lower my shoulder and take the hit. That's what had to happen. At the 4 yard line is where it all happened, something horrific and uncalled for. Michael hit me with all his force +10, knocking the mouth guard out of my mouth, and more importantly, knocking me out.

It's only when I woke up was I happy. Right then and there I saw the referee, standing, blowing his whistle signaling that I had scored. My most powerful feeling was relief that I'm still alive. Although, I did have a painful sensation in my chest.

*   *   *

Here I sit in the hospital lobby waiting for the doctor to come back with the results on the x-ray of my chest. Remembering that night, last night, was almost all a blur. We'd won the semifinals and we were going to state. Playing in the great Memorial Stadium. This has been the longest 5 minutes of my life. Hoping, praying that nothing had happen to me. As if on cue, the doctor came walking out of the double doors. "I have good and bad news," the doctor exclaimed. "Good news first please, dad replied. "There were no results on any broken bones," the doctor articulated. "But, there was a sign of a small tumor developing in your son's chest," the doctor placed. No one said a word. All I felt were warm tears rolling up in my eyes, and the rock in my throat. "We must take you to a room now," the doctor says emotionally. I couldn't talk at all. Especially knowing that my cousin had died at the age of 6, 2 years ago. With the same disease. I lost all hope and, my body lost all energy.

For about the next two days my tumor got worse. It was definitely a learning experience. I gained some hope back but just not enough yet. My parents have been keeping me strict on chemotherapy and medicine. People have written stories on me, but I don't get why I'm so special.

*   *   *

Today had been the state championship and we'd won by 2. My backup had an amazing game, or at least better than I would've played. Our school has been sending cards from the students that I really didn't need.

Months passed this time, getting a tiny bit better every day, slowly but surely is what my doctor had said. In fact, I'm only a week away from being done with chemo. Over these days I've received 6 assuring scholarships from 6 schools including Nebraska, Florida State, Syracuse, Iowa, Minnesota, and Virginia Tech. Today is also one of my rare days out of the hospital, where I would be accepting one of the scholarships. I wanted Nebraska more than anything, but that was the only college that I wasn't guaranteed to start on the football team. My parents told me to choose whatever one I wanted. All of the kids at school suggest I go to Nebraska so, I took that into consideration and, that's why I went to Nebraska.

*   *   *

Almost a year later, I sit in the room awaiting America's decision to vote for me to win the heisman. I'd already been waiting for hours with interviews and pictures. My dream had come true and I started for their football team for the whole season. The votes were in and counted, and it was time! just seconds away of anouncing the winner... and... I got second! I was joyed and a mix of emotions at the same time. LaMichael James got first in front of me by 235 votes. I called my dad up and told him to figure out that he already knew about it . He is always positive and told me that I still had another 3 years to win it. I'm looking very forward to next year!

*   *   *

My heart was filled with joy as I drove home to visit my family for spring break. I entered the door with my dad greeting me to the couch. For the rest of the day, for the rest of the week, we told stories of our long and much longed for, lives.

"You don't have to get sick to get better."

- Jacob Peters

I have known Ryan Allen his entire life and have never heard him say more than two words to me. I cried like a baby as I read this story and when Jacob read it, he was speechless—and that never happens.

DAY 85, MONDAY, APRIL 25, 2011

After treatment today, Jacob and I decided to go to the Henry Doorly Zoo to pass some time. Even though we are staying at a really nice hotel it still feels like a prison sometimes. I was surprised that he wanted to go to the zoo, but I knew that he just wanted to get out for a little while and it didn't matter where. (He does like the penguins at the aquarium, though. They make him giggle like a little boy.)

The weather is overcast and a little chilly, so we only went through the enclosed exhibits. The Henry Doorly Zoo has several world class enclosed exhibits: the Lied Jungle, an aquarium, a desert dome and under the desert dome is a swamp. We walked through all four of those areas and Jacob really seemed to enjoy himself, even though he is still very self-conscious about wearing his mask in public.

After we got back to the hotel, Jacob complained about a slight pain in his abdomen similar to a pulled muscle. I think maybe we overdid it today at the Zoo, so we will spend the rest of the day lounging in our room. Tomorrow is the last day of this Nelarabine treatment and I don't want to mess this up and extend his stay.

Tomorrow is also the Central Nebraska Track Championships in Grand Island. In order to participate in this event you have to qualify by having one of the best marks in your event in the area. Jacob qualified in the 400m last year as a freshman. The athletes with the top 16 times are invited to compete and Jacob had the 15th fastest time, but he finished the race in the top 10. Jacob has always been the kind of person that produces his best results when the pressure is on and when he feels that he has something to prove. He was really looking forward to improving on his performance this year and he loved the idea of competing against the best athletes in the area.

DAY 89, FRIDAY, APRIL 29, 2011

The pain that Jacob started feeling in his abdomen moved into his chest and then his arms. I stayed home to work today so Shari took Jacob to Omaha for treatment and they found out he has Rhabdomyolysis. Basically, his muscles are deteriorating due to the Nelarabine that he was given. According to what Shari and Jacob were told, he is only the second person ever to develop this condition from this drug, and the other case just happened not too long ago. We don't have much more information as this is all part of a clinical study and they can't give us too many specifics about someone else's condition. We were also told that this situation may mean the end of the clinical study on Nelarabine.

There will be no treatment today. Jacob was sent home and will have to be on IV fluids overnight at home for the next six days. He will also have to drink 136 ounces of water during the day. 136 ounces is a lot of water when you are just lying around all day. Jacob is extremely angry about getting off schedule and losing time. I talked with him on the phone while they were driving home and tried to calm him down and keep him focused. He didn't want to hear it, so I backed off and just let him be angry for a while. He has every reason to be angry. He has bought into the protocols and has done everything he could to stay on track. The worst part about knowing the schedule that lies before us is when you deviate from that schedule unexpectedly. Once again, Jacob sees things in black and white. There is a treatment scheduled today and falling a week behind will only mean finishing a week later and cutting into the time he has to rebuild his body for competition. When we first got started, Dr. Gordon was somewhat vague about timeframes and schedules. Now I understand why. Dr. Beck had warned us at the start of Consolidation that there would be setbacks, but Jacob did not think that warning pertained to him—he is Superman. Setbacks and delays are for other people.

After Jacob went to bed tonight he called me into his room. I knew that he would want to talk tonight, so I was prepared to try to calm him down. I was completely caught off-guard when he said, "I found out today that I am not Superman". Up until this point he was certain that he would push through this treatment like no one ever has. He would be the amazing young man that stayed on schedule and took all of the chemo in stride and came out the other side a better and stronger person. To hear him make that statement broke my heart. His external strength comes from his internal strength and now that internal strength was in question. After I regrouped and gathered my thoughts, I tried to convince him that even Superman had a weakness. Superman's weakness was kryptonite and Jacob's weakness was Nelarabine. I also explained that he had done an outstanding job up to this point in staying on schedule and this setback should not deter his will to fight. He was frustrated that we had signed up for this clinical study to try and help other people in the future and now we find out that we wasted two weeks, endured ten days of outpatient treatment and prolonged his completion date only to find out that Nelarabine does not work. I do remember Dr. Gordon saying once that a negative answer is better than no answer at all. We had gotten a negative answer about Nelarabine which may end the study, but it was a definite answer and that will lead the research into a new direction. I think Jacob understands the overall meaning behind this theory, but it doesn't make it any easier for him to accept. In his mind he is now three weeks behind schedule in starting his comeback.

Jacob will have to go to the hospital in Aurora once a day for the next few days to have labs drawn to monitor his kidneys and liver to make sure that there are no lingering effects or permanent damage from the Rhabdomyolysis.

Day 93, Tuesday, May 3, 2011

Today the local Relay for Life Coordinator called to ask if Jacob would be interested in doing an interview with the local newspaper. She wanted to do an article on cancer survivors in the weekly edition prior to the annual Relay for Life event next month. Jacob immediately declined stating, "I don't want to be known for this." He does not like the attention that he gets because of his cancer. He would rather be recognized for his achievements in competition or academics. Jacob is also very superstitious. He does not consider himself a "cancer survivor" because he has not beaten this disease yet and he does not want to jinx himself by calling himself a survivor too soon. He also despises the use of the terms "brave" or "courageous" being applied to him and his fight. Jacob told me that he was not "brave" or "courageous" because he did not choose this fight, it chose him. When you choose to stand up and fight for something, like the men and women of our Armed Forces, or when you defend someone else, then you can be considered "brave" or "courageous". In Jacob's opinion he has no choice but to fight. What is the alternative? When you don't have a choice then you do whatever you must to find the will to fight—every day.

Day 96, Friday, May 6, 2011

Lab work done yesterday in Aurora shows improvement so we are back on the road to Omaha again today. Treatments resume after a one week delay and

Jacob's mood is improved. He was uneasy about having to delay treatment for another week if labs were not acceptable. It sounds weird, but he was glad to start getting chemo again. We will go to the Treatment Center in Grand Island for the next three days to receive the ARA-C treatments just like he has in the past.

DAY 97, SATURDAY, MAY 7, 2011

The Central Conference Track Meet is being held in Aurora today. After we returned from treatment in Grand Island, I took Jacob up to the school so that he could watch the meet. As we were walking around we ran into Coach Buck from Holdrege. Jacob had never met him before, so he took this opportunity to thank Coach in person for all of his support. Coach Buck has sent a couple of hand-written notes of encouragement to Jacob over the past few weeks and he appreciates every one. If Jacob is learning nothing else through this ordeal, he is learning to show gratitude. The support he is receiving is uncommon and he needs to realize how thoughtful his supporters have been and show them that he is appreciative. Of course we stayed at the track meet until the 400m was complete around 3:00pm. In order to keep the sun off of his skin he has to wear sweat pants, a long sleeve T-shirt and a floppy hat and of course his mask. The only part of his body that was uncovered was his cheeks and he managed to come away with a slight sunburn. Getting a sunburn while on chemo is a bad idea. Hopefully this will not lead to another setback, being at the track meet today was important to him. He is also becoming less self-conscious about being seen wearing his mask. His friends are all getting used to it and he just stopped caring what other people think. It might not be mandatory for him to wear it outdoors, but we have all agreed that it's not worth taking any chances.

DAY 101, WEDNESDAY, MAY 11, 2011

We have some outstanding friends here in Aurora. A few weeks ago we were approached by Jeff Ashby, his son Cole is one of Jacob's oldest friends, and he asked if we would be OK with a group of families organizing a benefit golf tournament for Jacob. We have been asked by several people if we would be organizing a benefit and I have always said that we are not planning anything. This was different. These people were asking permission to organize and host a benefit for my family. I conceded and thanked him for his thoughtfulness. The reason that I mention this now is because in this week's newspaper there was an article advertising the golf benefit right next to the article about the track team winning the Conference Championship. I found this hard to look at since Jacob does not want to be known for having cancer and he would have been a contributor this year on the track team. Instead of being proud of his team's accomplishment, he is being singled out for having cancer. Sometimes life seems more than cruel.

On a brighter note, the Team Jacob T-shirts arrived today at the school. After Jacob was diagnosed, Coach Gordon Wilson came up with the great idea of getting T-shirts made to show Jacob support from his schoolmates. The design of the shirt is awesome. On the front there is an Under Armour logo and a Husky logo with the phrase "Protect this House" in the middle. "Team Jacob" is centered just above the logo. Coach Wilson cornered Jacob one day in the halls of the school and asked for a quote that they could place on the back of the shirt. It didn't take long for Jacob to say, "You don't have to get sick to get better". The quote is in all caps on the back of the shirt and it sends a great message that is truly Jacob.

DAY 102, THURSDAY, MAY 12, 2011

Since March, I have been working on a logo to represent Jacob. I have tried to find a graphic artist that can help, but I have not been able to find someone with any creative abilities. I finally gave up and took my sketches to the local newspaper to have them clean them up and make them look professional. Today the logo is complete and I am happy that it is a broad representation of Jacob's life. It incorporates all of his interests along with some subtle notations of when he was diagnosed. We plan on using this logo on stationery and T-shirts that Jacob can use as a fundraiser. As I finished talking with the designer, one of the local reporters asked me if Jacob would be interested in granting an interview for an upcoming edition. I told her that Jacob would probably decline, but that I would ask. I did ask, and again Jacob declined.

Today the track team won the District Championship and will be one of the favorites to win the Class B Championship at next week's State Meet in Omaha.

Day 103, Friday, May 13, 2011

Jacob has a huge muscle butt and he is proud of it. He has stretch marks on his butt and his thighs and he considers them badges of honor earned from hours of hard work in the weight room. I have heard him talk about his stretch marks multiple times and they were never a cause for concern. Today, however, we are concerned that they have gotten very dark and pronounced. We asked Dr. Beck to examine them just to be on the safe side. She feels that they have darkened due to the chemotherapy and not a sign of something new. During this conversation, Jacob asked her how long the port would have to remain in his chest. Dr. Beck responded that usually the port stays in through the end of the Maintenance phase. What we have been told so far is that the first four phases of treatment—Induction, Consolidation, Interim Maintenance and Delayed Maintenance—would take six to eight months to complete. Hypothetically, Jacob should be done with these phases around the first of October. The final phase, known as Maintenance, lasts for two years. Two years of monthly visits to the Clinic and oral medication. Needless to say, hearing that the port would stay in the entire time was not what Jacob wanted to hear. His plans are to complete the first four phases, have the port removed and begin his comeback for his senior seasons. Jacob simply stated upon hearing Dr. Beck's response, "That's not gonna happen." He told her that it doesn't matter if they have to poke him every day for labs, the port will come out when the Maintenance phase begins.

After his discussion in the clinic, we went back down to the PACU for another spinal tap, then back to the Treatment Center for chemo before heading home. Once again, Jacob will go to Grand Island for chemo the next three days.

Day 108, Wednesday, May 18, 2011

Today Jacob completed the work for his core classes on time. He will only need to take one class this summer in order to stay on track academically. His GPA for this semester is 4.0. Today was also the meeting for all boys who want to play football next season. Another reminder that time is slipping away.

With the loss of Shari's job we will also be losing the insurance benefits for her and the boys. They will be covered in the interim by the Cobra plan. We met with a Social Worker with the Department of Health and Human Services a while back to discuss our future insurance options. She informed us that since Jacob is the patient and has no income, he would qualify for the Medicaid Waiver program as his secondary insurance. He also qualified for a program through the State of Nebraska that would pay the premiums for the policy that he was on. In turn, Shari, Jerod and Dalton's premium would also be paid since they were all on the same plan. To make a long story short, the State of Nebraska would pay for the Cobra premiums as long Jacob required "Nursing Level" care. The Social Worker will review his status every few months to determine whether or not he fit the parameters of the program. This was a huge burden off of our shoulders. The Cobra premium is approximately $987 per month. Without this program, this would have been a huge problem for us financially in a very short period of time. Knowing that this program is short term, we set up a meeting today with a local insurance agent to try and figure out a way for us to obtain private health insurance. This is a major point of stress for both Shari and I right now. How are we going to get private health insurance for a cancer patient? How will Jacob obtain health insurance later in life? Securing health insurance will be the dominant factor in his future career plans. I believe that he will have to find a job with a major corporation or a government entity in order to be able to be insured. I don't see how he will ever be able to obtain private insurance on his own. He can stay on our family policy until he is 26, but after that he is on his own. This thought keeps me up at night.

After our meeting with the local insurance agent, I felt no better about the situation. We will fill out the application for private health insurance and will probably be declined. At that point we can move to the next step in the process and deal with more paperwork and red tape. I have no confidence in this process at all.

DAY 109, THURSDAY, MAY 19, 2011

Every year the 7th grade students do a class project titled "People of the Past". Each student chooses a person in history and coordinates a comprehensive overview of that person's life. It is quite an involved project and it takes a lot of time and effort. The project culminates with an evening presentation held in the Commons Area and Varsity Gym at the Middle School. Each student is dressed as their chosen subject and stands motionless in front of a story board that outlines highlights of their subject's life. Each student places a can on the floor in front of their position for people to drop donations into. When someone donates money, the student comes to life and recites a speech about their subject's accomplishments. It's quite a production and believe it or not I think the students actually enjoy performing.

Another purpose for this project is to raise money for charity. Each year the 7th grade class votes on one international charity, one national charity and one local charity. This year the local charity is to benefit Jacob Peters and his family. Jerod is in 7th grade and he was very proud when he came home to tell us that three local charities were nominated, but his class overwhelmingly chose to support Jacob. Jerod and Dalton have not been heavily involved in Jacob's treatment. We have tried to keep their lives moving as normally as possible these past few months. I think Jerod is excited to feel like he is doing something to help his family.

Today was the Middle School Honors Convocation and we were presented with the donation in the school theatre in front of the entire Middle School student body. I was asked to say a few words so I thanked the students for their generosity. I also spoke with them about "getting better" every day. Most, if not all, of these kids have seen the "Team Jacob" T-shirts by now. I wanted to explain the meaning behind the quote on the back of the shirt, "You don't have to get sick to get better." I spoke about Jacob taking advantage of every opportunity to become a better athlete and better student while he was healthy, but now that he was sick he was changing his focus to getting better medically. You can choose to get better at something every day, it's your choice. Don't waste the opportunity.

DAY 110, FRIDAY, MAY 20, 2011

After the standard port access and lab draw, we had our standard clinical appointment. Jacob has been asking about the timeframe for his return to lifting almost every week. Finally, he got permission from Dr. Beck to begin the summer workout program, in moderation, on May 31. Jacob immediately grabbed his phone and posted the good news on Facebook before heading downstairs for spinal tap #7 then back upstairs for more chemo.

Today is the first day of the State Track and Field Championships. Blake Williams, one of Jacob's best friends, qualified in the 300m hurdles for the first time. We have been hoping all week that treatment would go as planned and we would be able to make it in time to support Blake. We actually got out of the Treatment Center earlier than anticipated so we went to Scheel's to buy Jacob some new white sweatpants and long sleeve shirts for the coming summer months. As we left the store, Jacob broke out in a terribly itchy rash. Apparently he was having an allergic reaction to trying on the shirts at Scheel's. His skin is so sensitive that any fabric that touches his skin must have been washed at home. Not only was he now battling a rash, he appears to be catching a cold and it's raining heavily. After a short time his rash went away, thankfully, and we stopped at a restaurant to regroup and decide if we still wanted to try to attend the track meet. Ultimately, with the rash, the cold, the rain, the spinal tap and the chemo, Jacob elected to just go home. Just add this to the list of activities that he has been forced to miss. He really wanted to be there to support Blake.

Shari dropped Jacob and I off at home and then went to the grocery store. After she checked out, the young man that was helping her with the bags turned to her and said, "I heard that Jacob gets to start lifting again". Word travels fast in a small Nebraska town.

Day 113, Monday, May 23, 2011

Twice every year the football team holds what they call "The Iditarod". Team Captains are chosen and then they take turns drafting players onto their Iditarod teams. Each player completes a series of physical tests and the individual scores are tallied into a team score to determine a team champion. The physical tests consist of running the length of the football field continuously for two minutes, a one minute agility drill, standing broad jump, how many times you can flip a tractor tire in two minutes and how many reps you can complete on the bench press. Jacob had the highest score of all the returning athletes and he was confident that he would have the highest overall individual score this year. Just outside the entrance to the weight room there is a list of the top 10 individual scores of all time and he was confident that he would make that list his junior year. However, instead of participating this year he spent the evening holding a clip board, writing down scores and encouraging his teammates. He was not even sure that he wanted to attend this event earlier in the day. He thought it would be too painful to watch his teammates competing while he was helpless to compete. In the end he decided that it would have been more painful to sit at home knowing what was going on at the school without him. He loves his team and his teammates and I'm glad that he realized where he needed to be before it was too late.

Since there is some question as to when the port will be removed from his chest and he is determined to be a part of the team this year, Jacob started working with Coach Peterson on place kicking after the Iditarod. If he has a port in his chest he will not be able to have any contact. I remembered watching an NFL kicker when I was young that had to run off the field after kickoffs to avoid contact due to a previous traumatic head injury. He was good enough at kicking the ball deep that the team kept him on the roster. Our plan is for Jacob to learn how to kick and spend the summer getting good enough to kick-off and then run to the sideline. Nebraska High School Rules state that once the ball goes into the end zone it is a dead ball and will be placed at the 20-yard line. I told Jacob that if he could kick it into the end zone on a regular basis, the Coaches would probably let him kickoff. If nothing else, this will serve as a distraction to him and give him another goal to reach for this summer.

DAY 117, FRIDAY, MAY 27, 2011

Consolidation ends on Shari's birthday. Jacob has had 24 doses of chemo in the past 77 days. We knew that Consolidation would be more involved than Induction and Jacob has weathered the storm remarkably well. He has lost his hair, but his weight has remained basically the same and he has a minimal amount of side effects. I am proud of the way that he has followed the protocol to the letter and kept his mind on the ultimate goal—being cancer free.

The next phase is called Interim Maintenance and we have been told that the treatment schedule will now go from 7 day intervals to 10 day intervals. We are looking forward to a few more days in between treatments. Hopefully Jacob will have a few more days of feeling good in between rounds of chemo.

When we got home tonight we registered Jacob for the Elite Quarterback Academy at the University of Nebraska. He will not get to attend any other football camps this summer because he can't be out in the sun for that long. This camp has a lot less outdoor time. The players spend a substantial amount of time in the film room and classrooms. There will still be quite a bit of out-door activity, but Jacob will just have to take part in moderation. He loves attending football camps and since the rest are out of the question, we felt it was important for his mental health to sign him up for this one. He and I will stay in a hotel in Lincoln instead of letting him stay in the dorms. This will allow us to come and go as necessary to keep him out of the sun and out of trouble with the Oncologists.

Day 121, Tuesday, May 31, 2011

Exactly four months after the X-ray that revealed the tumor in his chest, Jacob is starting summer workouts at the high school. I went up to the school with him this morning to capture the moment on video. Bald, out of shape and of course wearing his mask, he still had a spring in his step and an attitude that we have not seen since the diagnosis. He is back where he belongs and he loves it. As the athletes were milling around on the gym floor I started crying when I heard Coach Jones yell, "Peters… get'em going". Without skipping a beat Jacob barked out a command and the entire group started their warm-up as directed by Jacob. Fighting back the tears, I followed the group to the weight room. Everyone made their way over to an open station and I followed Jacob over to his. He was told to lift in moderation and to start slowly to ease his way back into shape. I was alarmed but not surprised when I saw that the lift he had chosen to start out on was the jammer press. This is a whole body lift that looks extremely violent. This is one of Jacob's favorite lifts because it improves the explosiveness of the entire body. I wanted to capture the moment of his first lift on video as well. He got into position and paused for a moment. Four months of torture and excruciating anticipation had brought him to this point and he savored the moment for a few seconds before exploding into his first set of reps. He was home. This was also Dalton's first day ever in the weight room. Not wanting to interfere with the boys any more than I already had, I went home and left them alone.

This is not supposed to happen. This type of lymphoma is very treatable and the vast majority of patients are cured with no relapse. Jacob's case is made even more unique because he relapsed while undergoing chemotherapy, not after.

Six

—

RELAPSE

DAY 123, THURSDAY, JUNE 2, 2011

In preparation for the Interim Maintenance phase, Jacob was scheduled for a CT scan and chest X-ray in Omaha this morning. We received a phone call this afternoon telling us that the results showed something new on the left side of Jacob's neck. He has a swollen lymph node about half way between his jaw and his clavicle. Dr. Gordon is not sure what it is. It could be something old that was overlooked earlier and is now shrinking. It could be something new and growing, or it could be unrelated and of no significance. Treatment tomorrow has been postponed until we learn more about what we are dealing with. Jacob will be scheduled for surgery on Monday to remove the lymph node and have it biopsied.

We have had the rug pulled from under us again. We are hanging on to the fact that we do not know what we are dealing with. Dr. Gordon told us not to spend the weekend worrying because "9 out of 10 Jacobs that have this cancer don't develop new cancer". One of the hardest things to deal with is when you are waiting for information. I try not to let my mind run wild because I do not have all of the facts and I must rely on whatever information Dr. Gordon has given us. Until now, everything has gone pretty much as planned with only one major setback due to the Rhabdomyolysis. I guess we have taken for granted that the therapy was working as planned. We have had no indications to the contrary. Just like with his original diagnosis, Jacob is showing no symptoms of any new problems. How could this have happened? Today feels a lot like day one. I find myself re-living a lot of the same emotions and chasing the memories of that day out of my head. The bottom line is that we do not have any answers and we have to stay positive and move forward. Spending the weekend in tears will do no one any good. Especially if this turns out to be nothing or unrelated to his condition.

Day 124, Friday, June 3, 2011

Today was supposed to be the first day of Interim Maintenance, the third phase in Jacob's treatment. We will not be going to Omaha today due to the newly discovered swollen lymph node. Jacob is frustrated with another delay in treatment. He knows the plan and wants to stay on schedule. It is against his nature to do it any other way.

Tonight was the local Relay for Life event. Jacob was very apprehensive about attending because he thought he might get special attention since he was so recently diagnosed. Thankfully, there was no special attention and he stayed at the event for quite a while before wanting to go home. He would not wear his purple "cancer survivor" t-shirt and he refused to walk in the survivor's walk that is part of the ceremony. Simply put, he does not feel that he can be considered a survivor because he has not beaten this disease—yet. On top of that is his superstition about jinxing himself now by calling himself a survivor before he is cured. It's pointless to argue with him and most of all, if we make him participate and things go badly with the upcoming surgery and biopsy, he will look to this moment as the point where everything went wrong. At this point it is best to just let him have his way if that's what makes him happy.

Team Jacob has swelled in numbers. A bunch of people got together to decorate the luminaria bags a while back and they are all on display tonight. They did a fantastic job decorating a large number of bags. It seems like every other bag is in honor of Jacob and it is humbling to see this support. It is also heartbreaking when the candles in the bags are lit after dark and the grim reminder of the toll that cancer has taken on this community is illuminated on the town square. It was a night full of emotions, but mostly filled with hope for a brighter future. We know that we have this new development hanging over our heads, but we refuse to let it smother our hope for a cure.

I stayed as long as I could before getting tired. I went home to check on the kids and then learned about a storm that was about to blow through town.

One thing about summers in Nebraska is that storms can literally spring up in minutes and they can be severe. The organizers of the event were notified of the impending weather and they elected to move everyone to a building at the county fairgrounds to continue the evening. I scrambled back to the square as quickly as possible and Team Jacob had already disassembled the tent and were packed up and ready to leave. Tammy Spellman, a new friend of ours whose daughter is battling leukemia, had picked up all of Jacob's luminaria bags so that they would not get damaged in the storm. I can't imagine how I would have felt if they had all been blown away never to be seen again. It was an exhausting night of emotions, both good and bad, but we will never forget it.

Day 125, Saturday, June 4, 2011

Tonight is the annual Shrine Bowl All-Star football game at Memorial Stadium in Lincoln. Two of Aurora's coaching staff have been selected to participate for the South Team, Head Coach Randy Huebert and Offensive Coordinator Kyle Peterson. Along with those two coaches, quarterback Tyson Broekemeier and linebacker Kyle McCarthy will be playing in the game. The three remaining coaches on Aurora's staff will be assisting from the press box. It was truly a special night for Aurora Football. The South Team won the game 41-20 and Tyson Broekemeier was chosen as MVP. He broke almost every major offensive record in the books. This was a showcase for the Aurora Football Program. Jacob was thrilled and could not have been more proud of the accomplishments tonight. Listed below are some of the records broken by Tyson.

Most completions = 30 (the old record was 15, he had 18 at halftime)
Most passing yards = 371 (the old record was 206, he had 233 at halftime)
Most touchdowns = 5
Most all purpose yards = 407

He did all of this wearing jersey #3, but he did not do this as a tribute to Jacob. Uniform rules state that the South Team wears odd numbers and the North Team wears even numbers. I still thought it was pretty cool that he broke all of those records wearing Jacob's number.

I took Jacob and Jerod to the game tonight, but Jerod was the only one sitting with me. There were quite a few high school kids from Aurora in attendance, so Jacob got to go sit with them. I spent almost as much time watching him interact with his friends as I did watching the game. It was comforting to see him being goofy with his friends and blending into the group, even with his mask and floppy hat. He has been separated from them a lot and hopefully it was a nice distraction for him.

DAY 126, SUNDAY, JUNE 5, 2011

Last night we drove to Lincoln for the Shrine Bowl. Today I went back to drop Jerod and Dalton off at Husker Youth Football Camp. We have a tradition of getting to Lincoln early and eating at Sonic Drive-In. Jacob started this tradition several years ago when he first started attending the Husker Youth Camp. His brothers are adamant that we continue it now.

The Varsity left for camp at Hastings College this morning and Jacob did not get to go along. The camp lasts through Tuesday and the entire team stays in the dorms at the college. There is no way that we are letting him stay in a dorm with 60 of his teammates right now. I did agree to take him to Hastings for the 7:00pm practice though. This is a full contact camp that scrimmages against other teams. This is the first true test for the upcoming season and it can decide positioning on the first depth charts. His first real opportunity to earn the starting job and lead this team was to be at this camp. This opportunity was now here and passing him by. He again had reservations about attending this camp without being able to participate fearing that it would be too painful to watch everyone else doing what he loves most of all. In the end he agreed that it would be even more painful to sit at home knowing that he could be with HIS team right now. I stood across the street and took some video of him interacting at practice, but mostly I just wanted to stay out of the way. Normally parents are not in attendance at camp, so I did not want to interfere with his experience. We have spoken many times about finding new ways to lead his teammates since he cannot be on the field right now. Tonight is a great challenge for him to explore and find those ways.

Tomorrow morning he is scheduled for surgery and I think that fact weighed heavily on him as he said his goodbyes tonight before we left for home. He is feeling more anger now than worry. I can't imagine how hard it was for him to first of all attend camp not being able to participate and secondly to leave camp early knowing that he might not be back. There is a very good chance that he will not be able to return to camp this year if the surgeon does not allow it. Our busy weekend is over. Now we take on a new challenge in the morning.

Day 127, Monday, June 6, 2011

We left at 7:00am this morning in order arrive and be prepped for surgery at 10:15am. We had never noticed the bump in Jacob's neck until the Resident came in to mark the spot for the Surgeon. The bump was about the size of a large grape and it was right in the most muscular part of Jacob's neck.

Dr. Raynor spoke with us briefly about the procedure and how he did not foresee any complications. However, he did say that Jacob might be more sore than usual because of the size of the muscles in his neck. He said that might make it more difficult to excise the lymph node and they might have to move things around a little more than normal. That actually made Jacob smile.

Dr. Raynor returned about 11:45am to let us know that the procedure had gone very well. We were called back to the recovery room shortly before 1:00pm and Jacob was already sitting upright in a chair. He still had his gown and floppy surgical hat on when he asked, "Can I go to practice tonight?" The surgeon told us to just keep the area clean and dry and had no problem with him watching practice, but he was to have NO ACTIVITY. We left the recovery room around 1:30pm and were back on the practice field in Hastings by 7:00pm. He looked the same as he did yesterday only now he had a giant bandage on his throat. It didn't take long for him to grab a football just to carry around. Soon he was tossing the ball to a friend underhanded, and soon after that he was throwing and catching passes with the guys. So much for NO ACTIVITY. Once again we stayed the entire two hours, which mostly consisted of scrimmaging against other teams. It was easier for him to say goodbye tonight because he was already planning on returning tomorrow for the last day of camp.

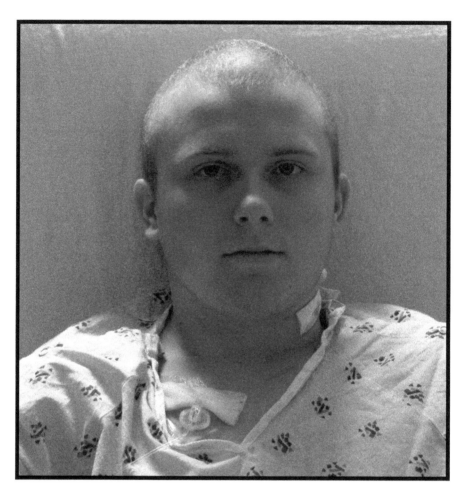

DAY 128, TUESDAY, JUNE 7, 2011

Since everything went so well at football camp yesterday we decided it would be OK for Jacob to return today for the last day of camp. I stayed in Aurora to work, so Shari took him to Hastings in time for the first practice at 8:30am. The morning was nice and cool and the practice lasted until 11:30am. When the teams broke for lunch, Shari and Jacob went to my construction manager Jessie's house for lunch. No one was home, but we called him and his wife Brandie last night to make arrangements and they were kind enough to let Shari and Jacob crash for about an hour and a half. Afternoon temperatures these last three days have been in the mid to upper 90's and the humidity has also been pretty high. The last practice started at 1:00pm and lasted until 3:00pm. He has been covered from head to toe and has avoided getting a sun burn somehow. He started out being apprehensive about attending camp but ended up attending a portion of camp all three days. His attitude has improved, even after having endured another setback and surgery, because he now has a feeling of being a part of that team. I know it was pretty risky letting him attend camp considering his treatments, compounded by the fact that he also had surgery, but seeing how much better he feels now made it worth the risk.

Day 129, Wednesday, June 8, 2011

Now that the team is back from camp, lifting has resumed up at the school. We told Jacob that he is not allowed to lift weights until he has the stitches removed, but he could ride the stationary bike to get a workout. We did not clarify how long he could ride the bike. In the morning session he rode 10 miles. He came home and spent the rest of the morning and afternoon lying on the futon downstairs and then returned to the gym for the afternoon session. He rode 10 more miles in the afternoon.

At 5:00pm, while Jacob was at the gym and I was at the office, Shari received a phone call from Dr. Gordon. The lymph node biopsy was positive for more lymphoma and we were scheduled to be back in Omaha on Friday for another chest X-ray and consultation with Dr. Gordon. She called me and told me to come home immediately and I knew it wasn't good news. Shari stood in the doorway between the dining room and living room and was visibly shaking from head to toe as she told me the content of the phone call. I did not cry at all this time because I think that deep inside, I expected this result. I think it would have been too big of a coincidence for this to be unrelated and it would be illogical to believe that it was unseen originally and shrinking at a slower rate than the rest of the cancer. I am also numb and extremely scared. Jacob got home from the weight room shortly after 6:00pm and we sat him down in the living room to break the bad news to him AGAIN. He was extremely angry and he feels like he just can't catch a break. I called Dr. Gordon back to discuss the details with him personally. After he explained everything to me I stepped outside to ask Dr. Gordon a question that I did not want anyone else to hear. "What does this do to his chance of survival?" Dr. Gordon's response, "It's not good". He would not elaborate any more than that and tried to redirect my thoughts to what path we will follow from here. He then tried to persuade me not to over-think the situation and wait until we had more treatment information. I went back inside and did the best that I could to convince my family not to panic.

Jerod and Dalton both went back to their rooms just like they did on day one. The rest of the night felt eerily similar to that very first night over four months ago. We even decided to rent another movie since we were all basically speechless. Again, I think we all needed time to process what had just happened. We tried not to worry about this result all weekend, but we all knew it was a possibility. Now we were faced with a much more serious challenge. We have been told by several people that Jacob was at a very low risk of relapse, but that is precisely where we find ourselves now. We all understood that the original diagnosis was a very dangerous situation, now it just got much more serious. I think we have been lulled into a false sense of security by the weekly treatment routine and the way that Jacob has powered through the side effects.

Day 130, Thursday, June 9, 2011

I stayed home from work today, knowing that I would be absolutely no good to anyone. I was supposed to go to Waverly with Jessie, but we were waiting for the nurse to call with the arrangements for Friday and I wanted to be there when the phone call came. I have missed a couple of treatments and was not at home when the call came when the lump was found or when the biopsy results came in. I feel guilty for not being with Shari when she got those calls.

Early on in this process someone asked Jacob what he does to deal with stress. He stated that before he was diagnosed he did not have that much stress, but if he did, he dealt with it in the weight room. Today Jacob went back to the weight room and did another 10 miles on the stationary bike. Afterwards he went to McDonald's with a good friend and classmate Ehren Schwarz. Ehren then spent the rest of the morning and most of the afternoon downstairs with Jacob. I was worried about how he would handle this latest setback, but was comforted to know that he was spending time with a friend. I know that he is tired of being at home alone or stuck with his Mom and Dad either at home or in the hospital in Omaha, so being with Ehren is good for his mental health.

Later in the evening Jacob rode along with Coach Huebert and a couple teammates to the football team's 7on7 scrimmage in Grand Island. His involvement with the team this week has really helped his spirits and distracted him from this setback. After they returned from Grand Island, Jacob joined several of his friends at Ben McQuiston's house for the evening to play poker. He called home at midnight to let us know that he was winning and asked if he had to be home at any certain time. We said that he could come home whenever he wanted to. Curfews and rules have been suspended until further notice. He got home at 2:50am down $10.00, but he enjoyed himself. He had a great day despite yesterday's bombshell.

DAY 131, FRIDAY, JUNE 10, 2011

We arrived in Omaha for the chest X-ray at 10:30am and then we met with Dr. Gordon at around 11:30am to discuss what exactly was happening. We were anxious to hear what the treatment protocol would be at this point. He told us that he had sent Jacob's information out to several doctors and had been waiting for a return call with an expert colleague and ironically the call came in the middle of our consultation. Dr. Gordon stepped out of the room to speak with his colleague for what felt like an eternity. The end result is that Jacob will start a new chemotherapy regimen and abandon the old protocol. We could tell that Dr. Gordon was somewhat flustered and not entirely confident in what he was planning on doing from this point forward. He was stuttering and stammering and had a hard time finding the right words. He finally came right out and stated that he and his staff are good at curing lymphoma, but admitted to not being as confident with relapsed lymphoma. This is not supposed to happen. This type of lymphoma is very treatable and the vast majority of patients are cured with no relapse. Jacob's case is made even more unique because he relapsed while undergoing chemotherapy, not after.

My mind has been working overtime these past few nights trying to rationalize how this happened. One theory that I asked Dr. Gordon about was the Nelarabine treatments. Remember, we agreed to take part in the clinical study for this drug and by doing this it was stretching out the Consolidation phase by three weeks. I was concerned that by lengthening the intervals of regular treatment we diluted the effects of the standard protocol. Jacob went through two rounds of Nelarabine treatments and then had a one week delay due to the Rhabdomyolysis which was caused by the Nelarabine. Did these delays lead to the relapse? Dr. Gordon did not believe that it did. He told us that Nelarabine has been undergoing tests for quite a while and they had no evidence to suggest that could be a problem. I will never be convinced that it was not a contributing factor.

Hoping that we would be able to start treatment immediately, Jacob did not have anything to eat or drink after midnight. It's called being NPO and it is a pre-requisite to having any surgical procedure. Our experience allowed us to plan ahead for a possible spinal tap and bone marrow biopsy and avoid another delay. Somehow Jacob's outpatient case manager, Jeannine, was able to schedule a spinal tap and bone marrow biopsy for 1:00pm with a PET scan to follow at 3:00pm. This was amazing because none of these procedures were scheduled to be done today and things just don't happen that fast at a hospital as large as UNMC. By 5:00pm we were already checked in to our room at the Nebraska House in the Lied Center and Jacob was on his way to his patient room. We will be in Omaha at least until Tuesday.

I also called the Husker Football Office to let them know that Jacob would not be attending the Elite Quarterback Academy Sunday thru Tuesday. He has really been looking forward to this camp because there is a lot of classroom time as well as outdoor practice. Coach Baldus has also made arrangements to work on placekicking individually with Jacob after camp ends on Tuesday. Jacob is planning on calling Coach Baldus on Monday to explain his absence. Add another item to the growing list of things that he will miss this year.

Day 132, Saturday, June 11, 2011

Jacob's new chemotherapy regimen is called ICE. That stands for Ifosfamide, Carboplatin and Etoposide. This new protocol calls for inpatient treatment to be given over 3-4 days every three weeks until he is back in remission. Once he is back in remission he will be scheduled for a stem cell transplant. The transplant will require him to be hospitalized for at least a month and mostly confined to his room. There are some major complications that can arise after a stem cell transplant not the least of which is an infection because his immune system will basically be destroyed for a while. After the transplant is complete he will be on anti-rejection medication for a year. The transplant is not guaranteed to work, but at this point they believe it's his best chance to be cured.

Today Shari told me that last night Jacob told her he believes he has played his last football game and his athletic career was probably over. He also stated that he now has no goals to work toward. This is very concerning for me. To hear my son, who is so driven to succeed, admit that he now has no goals is frightening. He has always been a fighter and has been incredibly strong throughout this process. I fear that if he feels that he now has no goals and no future that his mental and physical strength will fade along with his recovery. Somehow, I must convince him to put those other goals on a shelf and develop new goals pertaining to beating cancer, but for now we need to develop more short term attainable goals.

Shari's brother, Pat, stopped by for a couple of hours and ended up playing poker with Jacob. Shari and I went to Blockbuster and rented four of Jacob's favorite movies. We watched one and then went to bed. Goal setting will have to wait until another day.

Day 133, Sunday, June 12, 2011

Jacob asked Shari and I to both stay at the Nebraska House last night. Until now I have been sleeping in the room with him. I think he just wants to be alone for a while. When we are at home he spends most of his time alone in the basement with limited interruptions by the family. I believe that this is standard operating procedure for a 16-year-old boy.

Therapy went as planned today and Grandpa Beran brought Jerod and Dalton to Omaha along with some supplies for our stay. We had a nice afternoon just hanging out in the room and even played another game of poker. After the boys left we watched another movie and then game six of the NBA Finals. Before the basketball game started I told Jacob that I would bet everything I owned that Dallas would beat Miami tonight, and they did. If Dallas had lost tonight then game seven would have been on Tuesday night. We watched the final game of the NFL season, the Super Bowl, in his hospital room and we will not be in the hospital on Tuesday night, so that guaranteed a Dallas victory tonight. We are hopeful that we will not be in the hospital during the deciding game of the World Series in October, but if we are, that would complete the World Championship trifecta.

Day 139, Saturday, June 18, 2011

Today was the Golf Benefit for Jacob. The day started at 10:30am when the high school kids teed off to unofficially start the four man scramble. It was a perfect day for golf, the sky was clear the temperature was in the low to mid 80's with a slight breeze out of the south. A storm actually rolled through the area overnight and several people said that they woke up at 3:00am wondering if we were going to be able to hold the tournament today. It could not have been more ideal conditions. People started showing up around 1:00pm to check-in for the tournament and by 2:00pm there were 19 teams on the nine hole Poco Creek Golf Course ready to start. Shari and I stayed at the first tee box and took pictures of all the teams as they arrived. I didn't want to golf today. Instead I chose to thank everyone as they came by for coming today to support my family.

After the golf tournament concluded, more people began to arrive for the social hour and steak supper. The number of people was overwhelming. Rob Marlatt and Chad Johnson cooked the most amazing steaks. Usually when you have a steak feed the meat is a little tough and the flavor is just OK, but my Dad even enjoyed the steak and he is the most difficult person to cook for in the world. Matt Thomas donated all of the steaks, the Aurora Youth Football Families provided the potatoes and the Aurora United Methodist Church organized the donation of all the salads and desserts. It was a great meal even though I could not finish my meal because my stomach was tied up in knots. I have a hard time with charity.

The auction started on time at 7:00pm. The organizers of this event were hoping for 30-40 items to be donated for the auction. They ended up with close to 60 items. Once again I was blown away with the quality and quantity of the items that were donated. After the dust settled, the auction alone brought in over $15,000.00. Rob Marlatt came over to me after the auction and gave me a big hug and we both lost it. Rob has been one of my closest friends since grade school. He and his twin brother Randy are both large individuals with blonde hair just like me. In college, people thought we were triplets and some of their own extended family gets me confused with the twins. As we bear-hugged each other, Rob whispered in my ear, "I never thought it would be this big", referring to the size and scope of the auction and the entire day. We both stood there locked in a powerful embrace and cried.

It was an emotional roller coaster all day. We were overjoyed with just the thought of people taking the time to organize and attend such an event, and then to see it grow beyond the organizers' expectations was the most humbling experience of my life. I laughed and cried with old friends and Shari and I both rode the waves of emotion all day long. It all started even before the high school kids teed off. Jeff Ashby pulled me aside and said that he had something special for Jacob. We went to his car and he pulled out a personal letter and autographed picture from NBA Hall of Fame Legend Larry Bird. Jeff's son Cole had written a letter to Larry explaining Jacob's situation. Larry actually read the letter and took the time to personally respond. I don't think any of us truly understand how cool this actually is. The generosity of our friends is beyond description. Many items that were auctioned were sold for at least 4-5 times their actual value. Dean Garfinkel, whom we have known for less than a year, bought an autographed Husker Football for $400 and then gave it to Jacob. My construction manager Jessie McCoy paid $1,000 for two tickets to the Nebraska v. Northwestern football game this fall. My father-in-law paid $400 each for two custom-made knives that Jerod and Dalton wanted badly.

At the end of the night, I made it a point to go thank each of the four families that organized the event. Mike and Linda McQuiston, Jeff and Heidi Ashby, Kelly and Karen Grossnicklaus and Jody Griffith are all parents of Jacob's closest friends. As I spoke with Jeff Ashby he stated that in all his years of coaching and teaching, he has never seen a class of boys as close as Jacob's friends. Ben McQuiston, Alex Hunt, Cole Ashby, Rick Schmidt, Ben Grossnicklaus, Tanner Griffith, Blake Williams, Troy McDonald and Brock Henderson were all on the flag football team that Jacob loves so much. They became teammates in 2nd grade and have played together on almost every team since that time. They are like brothers to Jacob. I feel the same way about the guys that I graduated with. Jacob is lucky to have such friends. After the golf tournament was over these boys went to work. They helped set up the food tables, they got beverages for people, waited tables and then bussed the tables when people were finished. They really worked hard all evening and were a great representation of the quality of the kids in our community.

As I was thanking Linda McQuiston she explained to me how easy it was to get people to help and how the whole event snowballed into something much bigger than they had planned. She told me how eager the Youth Football Families were to help out and I broke down for the second time. I have stated earlier that support for my family makes me cry and this event was support overload.

I had choked up several times during the day including when I spoke with Ryan Allen's aunts and uncles about the short story he wrote in school, but I always kept it together. This time my emotions boiled over. None of us will ever forget this day.

Day 143, Wednesday, June 22, 2011

We returned to Omaha this morning for more labs and another consultation with Dr. Gordon. Jerod and Dalton went along with us for the first time. We were all being tested as possible donors for Jacob's stem cell transplant. Dr. Gordon spent about 45 minutes explaining what the next steps would be and all of the possible ways of completing the stem cell transplant. Basically, it comes down to using Jacob's own stem cells and taking the chance that the sample that they extracted from Jacob still had some cancer cells, or take stem cells from a donor that was cancer free. If one of the family is a match, then of course that would be the best bet, but if no one matches then they will have to go to the national donor registry. The stem cell transplant is basically a way of giving an extremely high dose of chemotherapy. The side effects are basically the same as they have been, but may be a bit more extreme. Jacob has not suffered much from the side effects of the chemo. He has continued lifting and working out Monday through Friday most weeks and has a fairly active social life right now. I even asked Dr. Gordon if there was a way to increase his dosage now because the current dosage doesn't seem to affect him that much. The side effect that is the most concerning to all of us is Graft vs. Host disease. Any time there is a transplant the host body usually tries to reject the donated tissue. This is expected and can be treated with medication. However, with the stem cell transplant the donor cells can actually try to reject the host which is much more serious and could even be fatal. But it is a chance we have to take if Jacob is going to beat this disease.

Jacob received a package today from Brandon Cool, the Head Football Coach at Kearney High and an Aurora High School Alumnus. Inside was a 2011 Kearney High football T-shirt with the Senior Class motto on the back and very nice handwritten card with some excellent words of encouragement from Brandon.

Seven

A CANCER PATIENT'S SUMMER

Day 145, Friday, June 24, 2011

Jacob had more labs today. The results showed that his counts have hit an all time low, which was expected. He also has a rash around his port and his upper body. This afternoon he went to the Cancer Treatment Center in Grand Island to see Dr. Ramaekers about the rash and to have his second transfusion. We decided from now on that we will wait for the results of the labs before he is allowed to workout that day. This morning he went to the gym as usual, but we did not know that his counts were this low. Hopefully he won't pay a price for this mistake. His plans for the weekend have now been changed. He will now sit in the basement alone instead of playing poker or hanging out at his girlfriend's house.

Day 146, Saturday, June 25, 2011

Tonight was my 25th high school class reunion. I have been torn for quite some time about whether or not to attend. The decision is being made even more difficult since Jacob will be confined to the basement all weekend. In the end I decided to participate with great reservations. Jacob's disease has brought a different perspective to our everyday lives. I have looked forward to this date as a fantastic weekend to cut loose and have a great time with some old friends. Now I look at it as possibly the last opportunity to see some of the people that I grew up with. I have always been the first to arrive and the last to leave a party. If things were normal this year, I'm sure that this would be the expectation for the weekend. Now I just want to spend some time talking with people that I haven't seen in years and appreciating this time that we have together. Most of my classmates were aware of our situation, but I tried not to dwell on it as a topic of conversation. Once again, these people were looking forward to a good time this weekend and I don't want to bring the mood down. We had a nice time together at the house of one of our classmates, then the crowd started to break up and move on to other parties. This was my cue to leave. Like I said, normally I would have gone with my friends to the next party and tried to make the night last as long as possible. I am now completely content to come home early accomplishing all that I had set out to do.

Day 148, Monday, June 27, 2011

My cousin Bruce from Colorado and his daughter Christine have been visiting relatives in Nebraska all weekend. They stopped over this afternoon for a visit. Bruce is a few years older than me and we had lost touch over time until he called a couple of years ago trying to re-establish contact. I really appreciated his efforts because since our grandparents died, the family has drifted apart. Now we are at the age where some of our aunts and uncles are passing away and the family will split even further apart. He brings an interesting perspective because he grew up in Colorado and was only back in Nebraska for special occasions. He has a different point of view than those of us that grew up in Nebraska and since he is a few years older, his memory is more vivid.

Bruce is now a Catholic and so he brought along a few things from his Church. He brought a small bottle of Healing Oils and a kerchief blessed by the Tears of Christ. Bruce placed the Healing Oils on Jacob and then presented him with the Tears of Christ and they read a prayer aloud together. Bruce asked our permission first not knowing whether we would approve of this blessing since we were not Catholic. Our response was that we were not in a position to judge someone else's religious beliefs and if the Catholic Church believes that this could help Jacob then we were all for it. Jacob does have some serious reservations about religion and where he should place his faith. I'm not sure if he believed in what Bruce was telling him, but he was willing to listen and participate. Our church has been basically absent this entire period which is also not helping his faith at all. We have been talking for some time about asking an influential person from my youth, Paul Nauman, to meet with Jacob to answer some of his questions. We need to take action on this if we want Jacob to believe in God.

Day 154, Sunday, July 3, 2011

Some friends of ours are building a house on a lake north of Aurora. They are hosting an all day party complete with fireworks this evening. Shari took Jerod and Dalton up to the party early in the day, so that they could enjoy swimming, fishing, and boating all day. Jacob wanted to bring his girlfriend along and he also wanted to drive to the party, so I sat in the backseat and chaperoned. We showed up just in time for the fireworks. He is still a little scared to be around a lot of people so he used that as an excuse to sit behind and away from everyone else during the fireworks display. I know it was really so that he could have a little alone time holding hands with his girlfriend. Apparently he's not worried about her germs.

Day 155, Monday, July 4, 2011

Jacob has never been deeply interested in 4th of July celebrations. He has had the typical boyhood fascination with blowing things up, but he mostly likes just being around his friends. Last year we celebrated the 4th in Hastings at Jessie and Brandie's house. Jacob helped me light off all the fireworks for the first time instead of sitting on the lawn and watching. I think he liked the thrill of lighting the fuse and running from the explosion. This year I tried to get him to sit on the driveway in the afternoon and light some firecrackers and some smaller fireworks, but his interest faded quickly. In the evening we did get him to come down the street to our neighbor's house to watch the neighborhood display. He arrived with his friend Bryce just in time to watch the display and then went home soon after. He just doesn't have any energy to do anything that is only marginally entertaining. He saves all of his energy for working out and socializing with his friends. I guess I can't blame him for that.

Day 156, Tuesday, July 5, 2011

Lab results today showed that all counts have improved enough for treatment except for his Absolute Neutrophil Count (ANC). His ANC has to be at least

1000 before they will begin treatment and today he was at 875. He will not be admitted for treatment tomorrow and will be re-tested on Thursday.

Day 159, Friday, July 8, 2011

Lab results on Thursday showed his ANC was now 1600 so we went back to Omaha today to be admitted for another round of ICE therapy. During his visit to the clinic Jacob asked Dr. Gordon this question: "You can clone a goat, but you can't fix this any faster?" Now that is funny.

We should be in Omaha until Monday.

Day 162, Monday, July 11, 2011

I went home yesterday so that I could do some things in Aurora this morning for work. Jessie was on vacation last week and today was his first day back so we spent an hour catching up on jobsite progress. Jacob got a visit from Tammy and Madi Spellman this morning. Madi was back for her monthly post-stem cell transplant check-up and wanted to stop and see Jacob. She is actually a great role model for Jacob. Here is this sweet, tiny little girl who has handled her leukemia treatments like a champ. She understands what he is going through like no one else can and she has been very supportive. It's amazing to see a nine-year-old girl being a strong example for a 16-year-old young man.

I got back to Omaha today shortly after 11:00am and they had just cleared Jacob to be released. He was sitting on the edge of his bed and was packed up and ready to go. His stomach is upset and like usual he slept the whole way home. He hasn't really eaten anything since Saturday night because he gets nauseous whenever he eats or drinks. He is bloated from the IV fluids and has been peeing every 30 minutes or so, which is annoying to say the least. He also says that the smell of the hospital food makes him sick. I'm sure that this is a psychological byproduct of having to stay in the hospital. During the first admission he ate like a horse. Now he insists that the food is terrible and just the smell of it makes him nauseous. Steroids have also changed his taste buds, so the food probably doesn't have the same flavor either. His weight has remained fairly stable so we are not pushing him too hard to eat right now.

DAY 163, TUESDAY, JULY 12, 2011

Mr. Frazier came over this morning to work with Jacob on his Sports Nutrition summer class for about an hour and a half. Jacob was pretty wiped and out and didn't feel very good when they finished. He had more labs today at 11:00am. The chemo is taking more and more of a toll on his stamina. He has to realize that he just got home from four days of treatment and needs some time to rest, but that is not in his nature. He enjoys this class and wants to do well so that he can maintain his 4.0 GPA from last semester. He not only wants to conquer cancer, but he wants to do it with a perfect GPA.

DAY 164, WEDNESDAY, JULY 13, 2011

Representatives from Make-A-Wish came over tonight to get the initial paper-work started for Jacob. He has never seriously considered what his wish might be. We were all stunned when they brought up Make-A-Wish at the hospital because we all assumed it was for someone with a terminal illness and we have never looked at this as terminal. It is a little unsettling. In the beginning, Jacob did not feel that he deserved to be granted a wish and felt strongly about letting someone else have a wish granted. Now he is thinking that he might want to host a concert in Aurora to celebrate beating cancer. We have had a pretty good time discussing what performers he would like to have at this party. It started out fairly small and grew into Zach Galifiniakis as the emcee with the band Shinedown opening for Metallica. In the end he said that the girls would probably not attend that concert, but he thought they would if Blink 182 performed and he could live with that. I love the fact that he dreams big.

DAY 165, THURSDAY, JULY 14, 2011

For the first time all summer he got to go to a baseball game. Tonight we went to watch the American Legion Juniors beat Wayne in the first round of District baseball. This team is mostly made up of Jacob's classmates and the class below. Even though Jacob has not played baseball for two years now, he still loves to support those guys. His last summer of baseball was 2009 when his team won the 14-and-under League Championship completing a perfect season at 15-0. Jacob played centerfield all season and thoroughly enjoyed the entire summer because he knew it would be his last playing baseball. In the summers to come he was planning on attending more and more football camps that would force him to miss quite a few games. Like everything else that he does, if he can't completely commit he will not participate.

Day 169, Monday, July 18, 2011

For the past few weeks my mind has wandered to places that I do not want it to go. I have been visualizing Jacob dying either in his bed or on the futon in the basement as I sit next to him. I find myself thinking about his funeral while I drive down the road. Mostly this is brought on by listening to certain songs on the radio as I drive or in the moment right before I fall asleep. I catch myself and try to redirect my thoughts to something else only to find that I have wandered back to those same thoughts. I hate it and I get extremely angry when I do it. It's easier to redirect when I am driving down the road. I can change the station on the radio or pick up my phone and call someone, but when I'm trying to sleep that is a different matter. Quite often I will find that I have fallen asleep for 20-30 minutes only to wake up picturing one of those thoughts. Now I am wide awake and pissed off. The longer I lay in bed and try to find enough peace and calm to relax the more frustrated I become. At this point I just get out of bed and go to the living room to watch TV for a couple of hours. I have no doubt in my mind that Jacob will beat this disease and live a great life, but this all started when he relapsed back in June. Maybe subconsciously I feel differently. Either way, I cannot and will not show any sign of weakness in my belief and support of Jacob. He will never know what I have been imagining. My strength must be bulletproof.

Day 173, Friday, July 22, 2011

Labs this morning revealed his lowest counts to date. His ANC has been 0 all week and now his red blood cells and platelets are too low. The Med Center called and told us that Jacob would need to go to Grand Island and receive two units of blood and one unit of platelets today. This is the most he has had at one time. The whole ordeal took seven hours.

Day 175, Sunday, July 24, 2011

Jacob noticed a small spot on his ankle that looks like a bug bite, but it was not there yesterday. We called in to find out what we should do and were told to email a couple of pictures to Dr. Beck at the Med Center. She reviewed the pictures and prescribed an oral antibiotic that our good friend and pharmacist Jim Morris brought over at 10:30pm. The pharmacy is not open that late. He went in on his own time to fill the prescription. It's great to live in a small town and have great friends.

Day 176, Monday July 25, 2011

The spot on his ankle has grown from 5mm last night to 8mm this morning. Once again we called in to report the change and were told to stay and give the antibiotics some time to work, but monitor any new activity. We have an appointment in Grand Island tomorrow to have someone look at it regardless of whether or not it changes today.

Varsity Football Camp started tonight, so Jacob was gone from 5:00pm to 9:00pm. While he was gone, the spot grew from 8mm to 13mm. It had stayed the same size all day long, but it grew substantially while he was at football camp. We immediately called the Med Center and Dr. Coulter recommended that we go to the Emergency Room at St. Francis Medical Center in Grand Island to have a Doctor look at it right away. The initial thought was cellulitis and Jacob was given a new antibiotic prescription and we were told to double the Bactrim and Cephalexin that he was already taking. We got home around 1:00am.

Day 177, Tuesday, July 26, 2011

Jacob had labs this morning and also went to see the Physician's Assistant at the Cancer Center to look at this spot. The spot has grown to from 13mm to 19mm overnight and he was prescribed a different antibiotic because Dr. Coulter now believes that Jacob has MRSA, which is a particularly nasty staph infection. We were told that if it is either the same or smaller tomorrow morning we will continue with this drug. If it gets worse then we will have to go to Omaha for treatment. Undeterred, Jacob went to football camp again tonight.

Day 178, Wednesday, July 27, 2011

It appears that the spot got bigger overnight so Shari called the Med Center and they told her to bring him in for a consultation and probably admission for treatment. I had to work today so Shari and Jacob went without me and got to Omaha around 2:00pm. Jacob was admitted again only this time he is in the pediatric unit on the 6th floor. Until now he has always been in the Oncology, Hematology Special Care Unit (OHSCU) on the 7th floor, but since he is not being admitted for chemo he will be on a different floor. We have not been on the Pediatric floor before and the rooms are not set up for teenage boys. The border around the top of the wall consists of black and white cows wearing scuba gear or surfing and some have mermaid tails. Everything is set up for children much smaller than Jacob, but as long as he has his phone and his computer he couldn't care less what is on the walls.

At this point his stay will be determined by his reaction to treatment. He will receive IV antibiotics and shots to help boost his white blood cell count. Remember, his ANC has been at 0, so he basically does not have an immune system right now.

We are not sure how he got this infection. It could have come from contact with something in the weight room or it's just as likely that he contacted something while he was getting his transfusions last Friday night in Grand Island.

The first message he sent was to the football coach to let him know that he would not be attending camp tonight.

Day 179, Thursday, July 28, 2011

The spot has gotten better fairly quickly. Today he was told that he would be released tomorrow morning. While he was admitted, the Oncology team took advantage of the time and did a bunch of tests that will precede his stem cell transplant. At least these tests will be out of the way and maybe this will eliminate another trip back to Omaha in the future.

Cheryl Beran's mother passed away recently and her service is this afternoon. Cheryl is married to Shari's brother Dave and they live in Huntington Beach, CA. Cheryl's mother requested that she be buried wearing her JP3 wristband. She had never met Jacob. What a wonderful, thoughtful, selfless woman.

Day 180, Friday, July 29, 2011

Jacob was released from the Med Center today as planned. Upon his return he got to attend the final night of the high school football camp. Missing the last night would have been very hard for him to accept.

Day 181, Saturday, July 30, 2011

I went out to the garden shed this morning to mix some weed killer to spray on the lawn. The first thing that I noticed was that our dog, Sammy, had not eaten her food from yesterday and that it was spilled all over the floor. Then I noticed that she wasn't moving and there was a small pool of blood under her chin. She had died sometime after Dalton had fed her on Friday. We got Sammy on the last day of school when Jacob was in 1st grade because our last dog, a Jack Russell Terrier named Archie, had died on the last day of kindergarten, one year earlier. He was having a hard time with the one year anniversary of Archie's death and a good friend of ours was moving into a new home and didn't have a place for Sammy. Shari and I agreed to adopt Sammy and would surprise the boys on the last day of school. I sat down at the end of the driveway with Sammy as Jacob got off the school bus that last day of school. He was so excited when I explained that she was now his dog. I can vividly remember Jacob and Sammy running up the driveway together like two long lost friends. She was two years old when we got her and we had her for nine years.

Today was the Aurora 7-on-7 tournament. Teams playing were Aurora Varsity, Seward, Giltner, Crete, and the Aurora JV's. Last year Jacob was the JV quarterback and lead them to a 3rd place finish with eight teams in the tournament. As a freshman Jacob took a bunch of his classmates and a couple sophomores to 4th place out of eight varsity teams. This year the JV did not win a game.

Day 182, Sunday, July 31, 2011

Jacob's girlfriend broke up with him today. I never quite understood why a girl would want to start a relationship with a boy battling cancer, but she made Jacob happy, so we didn't ask too many questions. Of course he was upset, but I think he understands that there are more pressing issues in his life right now.

July for Jacob has been like a bad Country and Western song. He got a staph infection, his dog died, and his girlfriend left him. Hopefully August will be better.

Day 183, Monday, August 1, 2011

Labs this morning revealed that his counts were great and we are scheduled to be in Omaha on Friday at 8:30am. Tonight we met Chad Johnson at the high school track at 8:45pm to work on Jacob's running mechanics. Chad was a decathlete in college and has a wealth of knowledge. He showed Jacob quite a few exercises that would sharpen his running mechanics. Jacob has been going to the track and running a ½ mile, recovering, run ¼ mile, recover, run ¼ mile, recover then walk ¼ mile. Chad is working with him on running very short distances and doing certain techniques perfectly. Although Jacob is not able to officially start his comeback, he wants to correct any imperfections in his technique now, so that when the time comes he is ready to go. He really struggles with his cardio-vascular conditioning and wheezes quite a bit while he runs. I think these shorter distance exercises will be much better for him right now. Today is also the deadline that he gave Dr. Beck several months back. He was originally told that he would have 4-6 months of chemo and then start maintenance. He told Dr. Beck in no uncertain terms one day that they (the doctors) had until August 1 to cure him so that he could return for this year's football season. Today is six months and we have no idea what the schedule is now.

Day 184, Tuesday, August 2, 2011

Tonight was the sign-up and first practice for our Youth Football team. Jacob did not help this year and he always has in the past. He usually throws passes to the kids as we teach them to run pass routes and works with the kids when we teach quarterback techniques. But this year he declined and I did not press the issue.

At the end of each practice we have one specific player that we always allow to ask the last question. This tradition was started a couple of years ago with a young man named Austin Allen. I found that this was a good way to punctuate the otherwise endless amount of questions posed by 9, 10 and 11-year-olds. This year the young man's name is Ian Boerkircher and tonight he asked if the team could dedicate their season to Jacob. I replied, "If that's what the team wants, then I am fine with it." Ian asked the team and they responded with a thunderous "yes". It was all that I could do to fight back the tears as the team huddled to break, signaling the end of practice. The thoughtfulness of others is always amazing to me, especially kids.

Day 185, Wednesday, August 3, 2011

Today was the end of summer Iditarod conditioning test. We all agreed that Jacob needed to be there to support his teammates and continue to find a new way to be a part of the team and lead in a different fashion. Jacob returned home at 9:15pm with the biggest smile we have seen in a long time. His shirt was dirty and you could tell he had been sweating. He then proceeded to tell us that he had competed in the pro agility, broad jump, bench press and tire flipping tests. Shari and I were speechless. We would never have given him permission to test in the bench press OR tire flipping because of the port in his chest. We probably would have allowed him to compete in the other tests because there was no danger of damaging his port. Once he got around his teammates, his competitive nature took over and he actually did quite well. He did 14 reps with 135lbs on the bench press (only 6 less than his best performance one year ago), and he flipped a large tractor tire 22 times in one minute. The only thing that he did not compete in was running the length of the football field and back repetitively for two minutes. Ironically that is the one event that we would have definitely permitted him to do. He was full of adrenaline and was really excited about his performance. He had an exuberance that we have not seen in months. He was not only excited about his performance, but he was thrilled by the thought that he had inspired his teammates with his efforts. This is the first competitive activity that he has attempted in six months. That is the longest span of time without some sort of competition since he was six years old. I'm sure that it is one of the rare times that he felt "normal" again.

Day 186, Thursday, August 4, 2011

Tonight was the football team's Fun Run. The entire team meets at the high school and then runs to the Country Club and back which covers a distance of over two miles. Jacob won this event last year as a sophomore and was looking forward to defending his title. This year, however, he will ride his bike and encourage others to compete. Even though we have allowed him to go up to the track and jog a few laps, we are not allowing him to participate in the Fun Run. Once again, knowing Jacob, he would push himself to compete which would probably lead to more problems. During track practices in Middle School he would push himself until he vomited almost every day. If he didn't push himself that hard, he didn't feel like he was giving his best effort. When he got to High School, the "rule" was that the underclassmen were not allowed to pass the upperclassmen during workouts. This unwritten rule was one of the reasons that he stayed after practice for additional work. The upperclassmen were dogging it during practice and he was not getting better by just following them around the track. How many kids have that kind of internal drive and discipline?

Eight

ANOTHER RELAPSE
AND MORE SETBACKS

Day 187, Friday, August 5, 2011

The second protocol did not work. At our clinic appointment Dr. Gordon informed us that today's CT scan revealed that both affected areas have gotten slightly larger since June 2. Normally, we check in at the Clinic early and we usually get in for our appointment early. Today we were at least twenty minutes late going back to the room and I began to think that this was a bad sign. To me this meant that the CT scan showed a problem and that Dr. Gordon was probably asking a lot of questions prior to meeting with us. This turned out to be exactly what was happening. We have not had any good news since week five and this is now week twenty-six. The best way to describe how I felt when we heard this news is "hollow". We were so optimistic that this latest protocol was working because his counts had gotten so low and his hair was completely gone. The chemo was killing cells and we were encouraged by this. It just wasn't killing cancer cells. There's not much to say at this point that will alleviate Jacob's anger and frustration, so we just let him process those emotions on the two-hour ride home. Nothing that we can say or do will change how he feels and he has every right to feel those emotions and more.

Dr. Gordon sent us home for the weekend so that he could talk to some colleagues about the best plan of action at this point. We are scheduled to go back to Omaha on Monday for spinal tap #8 and bone marrow biopsy #4. Jacob will then possibly be admitted for approximately four days of yet another new chemotherapy.

Day 190, Monday, August 8, 2011

Shari and Jacob left at 7:30 this morning for labs, consult, spinal tap #8, bone marrow biopsy #4 and admission. I stayed home to work for a few days. To make matters worse for Jacob, today is the first day of two-a-day practices for the football team, the official start of the season. Instead of being done with chemo and moving on to maintenance, he is enduring yet another setback and once again being removed from his team.

This weekend was full of frustration, anger, sadness and a little depression for all of us. My mind continues to wander to places that I don't want to go. I had a hard time sleeping again last night. Quite often I will fall asleep for about thirty minutes only to awake to thoughts about a not-so-bright future for Jacob. Then I struggle to fall asleep again. I can't imagine what is actually going through Jacob's mind right now. I know that his mind usually goes into overdrive at bedtime and I can't imagine the emotions that he must be feeling.

The newest chemotherapy will start tomorrow.

Day 191, Tuesday, August 9, 2011

Jacob's new chemotherapy is a 24-hour infusion of Methotrexate through his IV. Up until now he has been receiving small amounts of Methotrexate with each spinal tap. This time it will be given in a much higher dose. After the 24-hour infusion is complete, Jacob will be on regular IV fluids and an anti-dote drug until the Methotrexate levels in his system dilute down to a reading of .10. The antidote is given to help protect the non-cancerous cells that we are trying to save. This could take the rest of the week. No one is certain.

Day 193, Thursday, August 11, 2011

Today is Dalton's birthday. Jacob slept all morning. Jerod, Dalton, and I stayed until noon then left for home. Before we left, Dr. Gordon stopped in and I asked him why Jacob has not been back on Prednisone. Prednisone is one of the steroids that Jacob was taking during the Induction phase. This was the first phase in his treatment and we saw dramatic results. The tumors shrank quickly and every test was negative for cancer cells. Phase two of the treatment, Consolidation, did not include any steroids which coincidentally is the same time period that Jacob relapsed. We haven't had any good news since he stopped taking Prednisone after the first 28 days and I believe that there is a direct correlation. The steroids seem to have the most impact on the cancer cells. Dr. Gordon said that he would get back with me and let me know.

Jacob figured out the problem he's been having with the Netflix connection at the hospital, so he now has access to all of his TV shows and movies. I have no idea what the problem was and he just got tired of waiting for someone from the hospital's IT Department to figure it out, so he fixed it himself. He is always the one to fix any computer problem that we have at home and he likes to give Shari and I a hard time about being technologically illiterate. Fixing this problem will make the time go much faster during his admission. This hospital can do some amazing things and has some of the best medical technology in the world, but the TV system is at least thirty years old. Jacob is known as being the kid who brings his own TV to the hospital and I have gotten some strange looks as I carry it through the halls. But having his own TV, PlayStation3, and Netflix makes him more comfortable and definitely helps us all pass the time more quickly.

Later in the evening he and Shari went for a three-hour walk and found the Teen Room on the Pediatric floor. Shari said that this helped his state of mind quite a bit. They were all over the hospital tonight. If a door was unlocked they tried it. If there was an unexplored hallway they explored it. They even found themselves in the "tunnels" below the hospital that interconnect the buildings below ground. Anything was better than just sitting in that room with the "Dairy Cow Mermaids" and "Scuba Diving Cow" wallpaper border.

DAY 194, FRIDAY, AUGUST 12, 2011

Jacob was supposed to come home today, but he still has too much Methotrexate in his system. He has been on an antidote drug since Wednesday along with IV fluids to dilute the Methotrexate levels down to .10 before being released. They will test him again Saturday morning.

He missed every practice during two-a-days this week.

DAY 195, SATURDAY, AUGUST 13, 2011

Jacob's Methotrexate count this morning was .15. He was told he couldn't go home until he was at .10. Tests later in the morning resulted in a count of .22, which is confusing to everyone. They have never seen a count like this go up. He has had no new Methotrexate introduced into his system, therefore the counts should not have gone up. A 5:00pm test showed the count at .19. He will spend another night in the hospital and be tested again Sunday morning at 6:00am.

DAY 196, SUNDAY, AUGUST 14, 2011

I awoke this morning to a text from Shari stating that the Med Center did not have any more testing material necessary for Jacob. There was none in Omaha and they were waiting to hear from the Resident. More frustration and disappointment, but Jacob was asleep while this was transpiring. Shari told me that they were calling Lincoln hospitals to try and find any more testing materials, but the nurse felt that the previous tests were inaccurately showing Jacob's levels rising instead of falling. Shari was hoping that they would release Jacob anyway along with a prescription for the antidote drug and let us keep an eye on him at home since he was showing no side effects from the treatment. While Jacob was angry that he might have just spent two more days in the hospital for no reason, he was thrilled at the prospect of getting to go home now.

Jacob called at noon to let me know that they were on the road home after seven days and six nights for only one day of treatment.

Day 197, Monday, August 15, 2011

Today started for Shari and I with a meeting at 8:30am with High School Principal Doug Kittle to review Jacob's school schedule. He is planning on taking a full schedule of classes and is excited to return to the regular schedule of a typical school day. Jacob's day started a little earlier though. He went to football practice at 6:00am and then met up with us at the meeting with Mr. Kittle.

The day ended with Rev. Paul Nauman and Gregg Kremer coming over to the house at 9:00pm to help answer some of Jacob's questions about religion. He is confused and skeptical. He sees most Christians as hypocrites that use their religion either as a crutch or a weapon. Jacob asked some very good questions and we all talked for about an hour and a half. Some of his questions were:

> What was God's purpose before Creation?
>
> Does God have a plan for our life from birth until death?
>
> If he does, then we cannot be held responsible for our actions or decisions, and prayers can only be for gratefulness. A prayer for change could not be answered.
>
> If someone has never heard the Word of God will they go to hell when they die?
>
> How do you explain the genetics behind Adam and Eve being the only original source of reproduction? Wouldn't the eventual in-breeding lead to birth defects and other health problems?
>
> Where did the water recede to if the entire Earth was flooded?

Paul and Gregg offered to come back another time to continue this discussion and Jacob was very receptive to that idea. Paul commented that he saw Jacob as a "Seeker" and he was glad that Jacob was asking these questions. Gregg thought it was encouraging that Jacob would ask questions like this at the age of 16 because when Jacob is satisfied that he has all of the information necessary to make a decision on where he places his faith that Jacob will "own" that decision. It will not be something that he has been force-fed by his parents. It will be his decision, he will take ownership in that decision and his faith will be unwavering.

Jacob loves to argue about religion with his friends. He always takes the side of the skeptic, not necessarily because that is what he truly believes, but because that view will spark the best argument. Ultimately, what he is doing is checking the validity of your faith. Do you have the answers and the knowledge to back up your faith or are you just regurgitating what someone else has told you to be true? Most young people have not spent the time to develop a deep knowledge of their own faith. They may have attended Church and gone to mandatory classes, but they are just memorizing information given to them by an authority figure. Jacob does not simply accept something as fact just because someone stated it as fact. He wants to tear it down to its basis and evaluate its validity from the ground up. This is the point where he struggles with his religious faith because religion is not based solely on facts, it is a leap of faith and acceptance. This concept will be a great struggle for Jacob to accept. That is why I have turned to Paul and Gregg for help. They will tell him the truth as they believe it to be and answer his questions directly. They will not lie to Jacob and that is of the utmost importance. If Jacob feels that you are not telling him the truth as you know it to be then he will turn away from your message immediately. He has an excellent "BS" detector. If he feels you have no basis or are being elusive he will turn up the heat and try to get you to break mentally or emotionally. He is strong in his convictions and expects that same strength from others.

DAY 198 – TUESDAY, AUGUST 16, 2011

We found out at 4:00pm that Jacob now has cancer in his bone marrow. Dr. Gordon said it was a very small amount and that the scheduled treatments will not change. He also stated that he would be prescribing a steroid as part of the ongoing treatments. At this point I think he is as lost as we are. I asked him five days ago why we had not gone back to using the steroids since they seem to be the only thing that works and even though Jacob hates the steroids he knows that they might be his best hope.

We waited to tell Jacob until he got home from the team barbeque. He sat on the couch and I told him the news. He was obviously disappointed, but not as crushed as he was with the first relapse back in June. We talked about it for a moment and then he decided that he needed to start selling the fundraising cards for the football team. He picked up the phone and called most of my subcontractors and some family friends and ended up selling 75 cards at $20 apiece in about an hour and a half. He was running around the house and yelling with excitement every time someone bought multiple cards. It was hard to believe that this was the same kid that was just told the cancer had now spread into his bone marrow. Maybe it was denial. Still, it was good to see him that happy and excited again.

Day 199, Wednesday, August 17, 2011

Today was Jacob's first day of school. His only restrictions are that he has to wear a mask and he must use his hand sanitizer—a lot. He took his brothers with him to lifting this morning. As a junior he is supposed to be taking lifting as a class this year, but since he will be gone for his transplant, he can't make up work in a lifting class, so he will lift with the younger kids before school.

Tonight is the last night of sales for the fundraiser. After practice the kids break into groups and "blitz" the town door-to-door. In the end, Jacob led the entire team in sales with 102 cards total and he had only been selling them for two days.

Day 200, Thursday, August 18, 2011

It's amazing how something as simple and normal as going to school for a full day can seem so monumental. Jacob actually looks forward to going to school in the morning. He hasn't had a normal day at school since January.

After the high school practice Jacob came over to the youth practice for a while. He helped with some of the quarterbacks and running backs a little but mostly just observed. After practice I thought it would be appropriate for him to speak to the team since they have dedicated their season to him. He did a nice job talking about "getting better". He referenced the TEAM JACOB shirts and what the phrase on the back of the shirt meant. His message was simple. "If you're not getting better you're getting worse."

DAY 201, FRIDAY, AUGUST 19, 2011

Tonight was the annual Sports Drink Scrimmage. Everyone who brings some kind of sports drink to the game is admitted for free. This was a test for all of us. I was not sure how I would react seeing all of Jacob's teammates participating in the scrimmage without him. It wasn't easy, but seeing his interaction with his teammates and seeing his obviously positive attitude on the sideline made it bearable. His job at this point is to help signal in the plays using color-coded boards and hand signals. You could see the determination in his stride and he was heavily involved with his teammates congratulating them on doing well and encouraging individuals that needed some help. After the scrimmage, he and a bunch of kids from Aurora went to Grand Island to Buffalo Wild Wings for the evening. He ultimately stayed out until about 2:00am and neither Shari nor I had a problem with that. He should be doing this. It is "normal".

DAY 202, SATURDAY, AUGUST 20, 2011

Shari made the observation that the PS3 hasn't even been reconnected in the basement since Jacob came home last Sunday. Seven straight days with no video games or Netflix. He has been so busy with two-a-days, school, and hanging out with friends that he hasn't spent much time on the futon in the basement. This has been a really good week for him.

DAY 203, SUNDAY, AUGUST 21, 2011

I didn't say anything to anyone today, but I think that I can see noticeable swelling on the left side of Jacob's neck right below where the most recent biopsy was done in June. It scares me to think that it has grown to the size that is noticeable. I try not to let myself think about it and I am self-conscious about staring at it and concerning Jacob and Shari. We will be going back to the Med Center soon and I will mention it to Dr. Gordon then. I do not want Jacob to stress about it unnecessarily. He has been doing so well lately. Something has to work soon.

DAY 205, TUESDAY, AUGUST 23, 2011

The Med Center called today to let us know that Jacob would not be home in time to go to the Seward game Friday night if treatment went ahead as planned. The plan right now was to be admitted tomorrow (Wednesday) for four days of treatment and then released on Saturday. Dr. Gordon did offer to see Jacob on Saturday morning instead of tomorrow, so that Jacob could attend the opening game of the season. I went to the school to ask Jacob his opinion and of course he wanted to move treatment to Saturday. We have never delayed treatment during this entire process, but he has been looking forward to this date for a long time. Even though he can't be on the field, he wants the season to get started and he has been feeling fantastic.

We thought that when we moved treatment to Saturday that the following weeks treatment would also be moved to Saturday. However, Dr. Gordon is off next weekend and he wants to see Jacob before treatment begins, so we had to tell Jacob that he was going to miss the McCook game completely. I was not home when Shari told him, but he was extremely angry. McCook and Aurora are perennial powers and it is usually the game of the week in Class B. We have talked to the school about setting up an internet stream of the game so that Jacob can watch it on his computer, but that system has not been tested. When I got home from youth football practice I went downstairs to talk to Jacob and he was sitting in his room staring at the wall. He said he was "cooling down". He has known for quite some time that he was going to miss some games this season, but now it has hit home and reality sucks.

Day 206, Wednesday, August 24, 2011

Jacob went to lifting this morning, attended a full day of classes and football practice. When he got home from practice he looked really tired. He came to the conclusion that he is not eating or sleeping because of his anger. He does not feel like eating when he is angry and bedtime has always been hard for him, especially now. His mind has always run wild when he goes to bed. Even when he was little he would talk about the deepest subjects when I would tuck him in. He would ask me if he was an over-achiever or say "my life isn't very good", "I don't ever have any fun". I always thought it was just a stall tactic so that he wouldn't have to go to sleep, but now I realize that his mind was in overdrive.

He doesn't eat when he is in the hospital because he is usually bloated from all of the IV fluids. He also hates the smell of the hospital food and the smell brings back the memories of our first stay back in February. I think that the memories linked to that smell is the real reason that he doesn't want to eat. I can't really blame him.

I am having a harder time falling asleep also. I still wake up after about thirty minutes and my mind starts racing about all of the things going on in our lives right now. In the mornings I am so tired that I can hardly drag myself out of bed, but I don't want him to see me as anything but strong right now.

Day 208, Friday, August 26, 2011

Tonight was the season opener for football. This is a day that we have always had in our mind as a benchmark of sorts. Originally Jacob was to be finished with chemotherapy 4-6 months after diagnosis. Six months expired back on August 4. Then we learned that chemotherapy would last until approximately September 30, his birthday. Jacob then thought he would learn to kick-off, so that he could still suit up for tonight's game. Things unraveled from there to where we are now.

Jacob did a nice job of encouraging and "coaching" his teammates. He was involved in some passing drills during warm-ups and flashed the color-coded cards as part of the offensive play calling. Needless to say, he was disappointed that he could not be on the field, but I think he handled it about as well as could be expected. Aurora won in a close game. He would have definitely helped his team if he was on the field.

Day 209, Saturday, August 27, 2011

We left for Omaha at around 6:45am. Jacob had blood drawn and we had a consult with Dr. Gordon and were expecting to be admitted for four days of ARA-C treatment along with a steroid. Then the nurse came in and said that Jacob would now be having another chest X-ray and an ultrasound to check his liver function. This was totally unexpected and we immediately knew that this was not good. The treatment room felt a lot like the patient room that we were in on day one. The same feelings of denial overshadowed by impending doom darkened the room. This was a smaller room than normal and it seemed darker than normal and more ominous. It also felt a lot like the day I took Jerod to the doctor in Hastings which led to his cancer scare. The nurse scurried in and out of the room and never gave us any real information. I have learned one thing about reading people through this process. When they scurry into the room repeatedly to ask only one question, then scurry back out only to return with another question means something unexpected has happened and it's not good. Dr. Gordon finally came in to explain that labs showed there was something irritating Jacob's liver and that it could be the remnants of the Methotrexate from August 9 or it could be more swollen lymph nodes blocking the bile duct. I then mentioned that I thought that there was now a visible lump on the left side of Jacob's neck where the second biopsy had been done, but Dr. Gordon felt the area and did not think that it was dramatically different than the last time he had examined Jacob. He did say that sometimes a tumor will swell as it is being destroyed, so we should not be too concerned about it right now.

Ultimately Dr. Gordon told us that the chest X-ray looked pretty much the same as the last one and that the ultrasound on Jacob's liver was "unremarkable". However, he felt it was in Jacob's best interest to go home for a couple of days before starting the next treatment. Since nothing showed up on the X-ray or ultrasound, hopefully whatever is irritating his liver will pass on its own. We went home feeling somewhat relieved that we did not get more bad news that day even though we were returning home without having treatment. We are scheduled to come back for treatment on Monday.

Day 210, Sunday, August 28, 2011

Shari, Jerod, Dalton and I went to Grand Island and Hastings for a while and Shari's mom came over to get some respite care hours in for the month of August. It was a pretty quiet day until Jacob went to bed. He called me down at around 10:15pm and told me that he had a bad feeling about tomorrow. He said that he had felt some "difficulty" breathing at certain times during the day. Shari took him in for labs in Aurora at 9:00am and he said that he coughed quite a bit on the way to the hospital. This was not a total surprise to me considering the visible swelling on the side of his neck, but the coughing was nowhere near as bad as it was in January. We talked for almost two hours. I told him that we need to focus on the positive and enjoy the good days and good news as much as possible. We will get more bad news as we continue this journey, so don't waste time projecting that bad news on good days. As we were talking I mentioned that I understood if he felt like he was "helpless" to affect the outcome of the football season, and that touched a nerve. He broke down and started crying as he told me that his greatest fears were not being in control and feeling helpless. He has always been the strong-willed child that can will his way to victory or persevere through adversity until he achieves the desired outcome. In this situation he feels helpless, as we all do. I explained to him again that being in control is an illusion. People think that they are in complete control of their lives until something like this arises and reminds everyone that we are not in control.

That led us to another discussion of religion and believing in God. I asked him if he would rather believe that everything happens randomly or that God oversees everything and allows things to happen for a reason. I told him that after the nurse came in on Saturday to tell us that he needed a chest X-ray and an ultrasound of his liver, I said a prayer asking that he give us some good news, so that Jacob could see some hope and compassion that might strengthen his faith. I told him that when we found out that the results were "unremarkable" I felt that maybe God did answer that prayer. Lately all that we been hearing has been bad news, and while this was not great news, it wasn't bad either. Jacob then informed me that lately every time he has prayed he has gotten bad news the next day. I then told him that he might need to offer himself to God instead of just asking to be healed. Maybe God wants he and/or I to break down and beg on our knees for forgiveness and healing and offer our lives in exchange for a cure. Jacob immediately reeled at the idea that God would punish us that way for not believing when non-believers are cured of cancer all the time. I didn't quite know what to say to that and I told him that we would need to speak with Paul Nauman about that in more detail.

We ended the lengthy discussion with the idea that it couldn't hurt to believe in God and ask for forgiveness. There is no downside to living a Christian life. He will still receive medical help for his cancer and the spiritual help could not have a negative effect. He agreed with that, but I can tell he is still hesitant to commit fully. I asked him to look at the positive influence that Christian men have had on his life and consider their faith and the reasons for their faith. We talked about his head football coach Randy Huebert, Jeff Sutter, Gordon Wilson and Tom Osborne as examples of how to live as a Christian man without being hypocritical. Hypocrisy is still a major issue that Jacob has with Christians.

It's been seven months to the day since we first heard "lymphoma".

...the steroid is really messing with his mind right now. It causes paranoia and increased anxiety, so he did not signal plays in from the sideline tonight. I think this was a wise decision on his part. The pressure of signaling the plays in quickly and correctly would cause way too much stress on a kid who is already fighting paranoia and anxiety attacks.

Nine

———

RE-INDUCTION
BACK TO SQUARE ONE

DAY 211, MONDAY, AUGUST 29, 2011

Another early morning departure for Omaha. We arrived at the Med Center around 9:00am for more labs. The results showed no improvement in his liver function. Dr. Gordon wants to get a CT scan of Jacob's head, neck and pelvic region just to see if anything new has popped up. He also stated that we would be getting a visit from the Radiation Oncologist to discuss starting a radiation treatment for the lump in his neck. We were taken to the Pediatric Ward and shortly after our arrival Dr. Gordon showed up to tell us that the cancer has now spread to Jacob's blood. The first thing I thought was, "How did Jacob know last night that we would be getting bad news today?" Technically this means Jacob now has leukemia and lymphoma. Dr. Gordon stated that we were again going to change therapies and return to something similar to the Induction phase that Jacob started with. I have been thinking for the past month that this is what we should be doing, but I am a contractor not a doctor. Dr. Gordon feels that we need to try something like this because the cancer is progressing at a faster rate than he had anticipated. The blood tests that were done two days ago either did not show cancer or the cancer cells were missed. Either way, we hope that we are catching this early enough that Re-Induction will have similar effects that it did in February.

Jacob fell asleep shortly after Dr. Gordon left the room. He did say that he was tired of being right when he felt something bad was going to happen. He has called himself "the unluckiest kid in the world". He just hasn't been able to catch a break lately. I'll bet anything that he said another prayer last night after I

125

left his bedroom which was followed up today by more bad news. This is going to make it even more difficult to get him to believe in God. He is not only in a fight for his life, but also for his soul.

Day 212, Tuesday, August 30, 2011

I have been planning on leaving the hospital after lunch and go back to Aurora for a couple of days. I have youth football practice and we don't want Jerod and Dalton to feel abandoned. I also have work that needs to be done at the office. Right before I left, Jacob reminded me that he needed to borrow my computer to write a letter to his teammates since he has been told that he would not be attending the football game this Friday night. His words:

> Coach, please read this to the team in the locker room before the game, whenever works best for you.

> To my teammates and brothers,

> There is only one place in the world I want to be tonight, and that is right there with you guys, but I can't. If I was there, I would prepare as hard as I can, but I can't. If I was there I would warm-up as hard as I can, but I can't. If I was there I would play every single down as hard as I can, but I can't. I would do every single thing as hard as I can, but I can't. You all have an opportunity tonight that I would do anything to have. Take full advantage of every single second. You should never be able to look back and say "maybe I could have gone harder, then we would have won." Don't allow that to even be a possibility. Give every ounce of energy you have, every play. Leave that field with no regrets. Know that you did everything you possibly could have to help the team. Play every single play like it's your last, because you never know when it will be. You may only have one chance at McCook, don't allow yourself to be beaten. We've worked too hard for too long to lose. Don't do this for me, do it for your teammates, the coaches, and yourself. No regrets. Kick some ass. We are Aurora, now go play like it!

> Jacob Peters

He has been depressed the last few days knowing that he is not improving and that he would be taken out of school and away from his team this week. He is starting to show signs of breathing difficulties and the lump on his neck cannot be overlooked anymore. The stress of this situation has got to be taking a toll on him, but he refuses to show it outwardly. I told him that I thought it was a well-thought-out letter and well written. This is his way of trying to overcome the feelings of helplessness as his team prepares to play 300 miles away without him.

About an hour after I had left the hospital I got a call from Jacob saying that Dr. Coulter had just left the room and he stated that he was not worried about the lump in his neck. He actually thought that the tumor had started to dissolve according to test results. Dr. Coulter also stated that the CT scan only showed growth in his neck, everything else seemed stable and the best news was that they saw no new infected areas. Jacob was cautiously optimistic that this treatment might be working. His voice was full of strength and hope as it seems like he might actually be catching a break this time—finally. Approximately an hour after that first call he called back to let me know that he and Shari would be meeting with a Radiation Oncologist tomorrow morning to discuss radiation treatment to try and eradicate the lump on his neck. He has not had any radiation treatments thus far and the fear of an unknown treatment is looming in the background of this good news.

Day 213, Wednesday, August 31, 2011

It's been seven months to the day since we first heard "lymphoma".

Jacob called me this morning and excitedly asked, "Are you ready to drive 115mph to get me to McCook on Friday?" Dr. Coulter had just told him that they would stop IV fluids on Thursday night, monitor him overnight and release him sometime on Friday. He was so excited about the opportunity to go to the game he overlooked the fact that the treatment must be working. We later found out that the Radiation Oncologist said that Jacob would not need the radiation treatment right now. This would have been a much bigger deal than we had thought. Apparently Jacob would have received five outpatient treatments every week for three straight weeks. That is much more involved than we ever would have thought, but we would have made it work. We have become very adaptable. She also stated that she was surprised when she saw Jacob. When she had looked at his scans she expected to find a child who was near death and not breathing very well. Jacob jokingly stated that "my insides don't match my outsides". They prepared him with a mask and some information about the radiation process, just in case it will be administered at a later date, but right now he is doing better.

Jacob also told me that he can already tell that he is breathing better. He never really came out and said that his breathing was getting worse. I think he was in denial. Now he admits that he can breathe more easily without any raspiness and he sounds much better on the phone. I am so glad that we might be on the right path because as we have progressed through this week we are learning that the situation was much more serious on Monday than we had thought. We knew he was getting worse, we just did not understand how fast the cancer was progressing and how bad he really was. But the words from the Radiation Oncologist have stuck with me even though I was not in the room. She expected to find a child near death when she saw Jacob's scans. That is a sobering statement. A scan this morning seemed to reveal even more reduction, so we remain cautiously optimistic.

Day 214, Thursday, September 1, 2011

Shari called this morning to let me know that recent labs did not reveal any cancer in Jacob's blood. He will get a platelet transfusion tonight and they are taking him off of IV fluids this afternoon and monitoring him in anticipation of releasing him tomorrow morning. He will need to be on IV fluids at home overnight until Tuesday when we will return to Omaha for treatment. This has been the longest string of good news we have had in three months and we are all relieved that it appears that Re-Induction is working. Hopefully we are finally getting on top of this thing.

Day 215, Friday, September 2, 2011

Today was a marathon. I left for Omaha at 7:00am to bring Shari and Jacob home. I got there shortly after 9:00am and he was released at approximately 10:15am. When I got to his room he was sitting on the edge of his bed tapping his foot impatiently on the floor. Everything was packed up and ready to leave at a moment's notice. He has traveled from the depths of despair earlier this week to the happiest I have seen him in a long time. He will be with his team tonight.

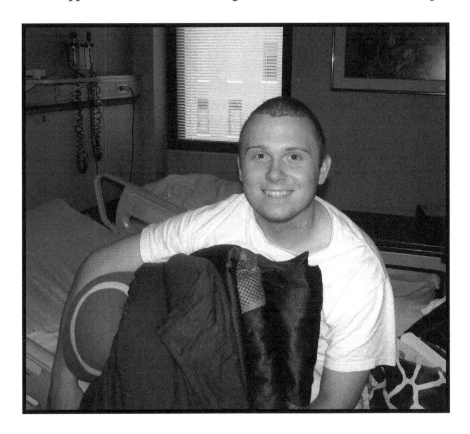

Just before we left Jacob's room, Gregg Kremer called to tell me that Alyssa Sandmeier passed away last night. Alyssa was a 10-year-old in Aurora who had been fighting leukemia for six years. We had just run into her parents at the Med Center on August 11 and they told us that she was back at the hospital due to headaches and some numbness in her face. After that we only heard that they received bad news on August 12, but no details. She only made it three more weeks after that conversation. Our excitement is tempered by this loss.

When we got to Aurora we ate a quick lunch, picked up his new prescriptions at the pharmacy, filled the tank with gas, picked up Jerod from school early and then we hit the road for McCook. For most of the week Jacob was told that he would not be able to attend this week's football game, but as the week progressed so did his outlook. We stopped at the school to pick up some things from his locker and he stopped in the coaches' office and told them that they could throw away the letter he had written because he would be at the game tonight. He said everyone's jaw dropped when he walked in the room. We have learned that things can change very quickly, so we have not told anyone that Jacob would be attending the game tonight, plus I wanted him to have the pleasure of looking his coaches in the eye when he surprised them with this news.

We got to McCook early enough to stop and eat some supper. Thursday night Jacob ate two hotdogs, but before that he had only eaten saltine crackers and drank a little Sprite, so it was good to see him tear into a double cheeseburger. We arrived at the field as the players were being taped up, so we took this opportunity to tape Jacob. He has to take in 1000ml of IV fluids over 6½ hours every day until Tuesday, so his port has to remain accessed until then. Before we left Aurora I stopped at the hardware store and bought a shallow plastic electrical box to place over his port during the game. It took two tries before we got everything positioned right, but we did finally get the box placed over his accessed port and taped securely in place. He stood on the sidelines the entire game and helped signal in the plays just like he did last week. Unfortunately, the Huskies lost the game in double overtime after basically controlling the entire game and failing to capitalize on key plays several times. Jacob was understandably frustrated after the game as I helped him take off his jersey and cut off his tape. As we removed the electrical box I noticed that at some point during the evening he had bumped the box and it had partially pulled the needle out of his chest. I ran over to some people from McCook and asked them how to get to the local hospital. We went to the Emergency Room and Shari called the Med Center just to make sure they were aware of the situation. The nurse removed the needle and thoroughly sanitized the port area and after the doctor looked at it we went back to the field. The local booster club had made some food for the team so the boys were just finishing up and getting ready to load the bus. Jacob sat on a short concrete wall with some of his friends for a brief time and then we started our journey home. McCook is approximately three hours away from home, so as the day progressed I drove two hours to Omaha and two hours home with Shari and Jacob. Then we drove three hours to McCook, attended the game, went to the Emergency Room, back to the field and finally drove three hours home (approx. 450 miles round-trip).We got home at 1:30am. I would do it all again tomorrow to see him that happy.

DAY 219, TUESDAY, SEPTEMBER 6, 2011

Today is Alyssa Sandmeier's funeral. We are in Omaha for treatment, so we are unable to attend. Truthfully, I don't know if I have the courage to attend her funeral after what we have endured in the past few months. This hits way too close to home. I have been battling the thoughts of Jacob dying ever since he relapsed in June. I just don't think I could handle a child's funeral right now. I need to stay positive and control my thoughts and emotions.

As soon as we arrived at the Med Center, Jacob was started on IV fluids. His urine has to be diluted down to a certain level before treatment can begin. We have been told at least four hours of fluids prior to treatment. As usual, we had our clinic visit with Dr. Gordon and he was pleasantly surprised at the reduction in the size of the mass in Jacob's neck based on his physical examination. He stated that there were no cancer cells in his blood and that his labs looked very good. Jacob will get another round of chemotherapy this afternoon and then we will be on our way home. However, treatment lasts for at least two hours and then he will need IV fluids for an additional 3-4 hours before being sent home.

DAY 222, FRIDAY, SEPTEMBER 9, 2011

Jacob's glucose level was high today, so they are considering giving him insulin. He drank four Cokes yesterday and that is what Shari and I believe is the problem. He will be checked again tomorrow. Jacob did not attend school at all today and I met with his principal to discuss his schedule. We are going back to just meeting with teachers during their prep periods and hopefully reduce some of the "busy" work. Ever since school started this fall he has been trying to attend regular classes, but it's just becoming too much for him to accomplish. He did feel good enough to attend the Huskies 28-27 win against Adams Central. However, the steroid is really messing with his mind right now. It causes paranoia and increased anxiety, so he did not signal plays in from the sideline tonight. I think this was a wise decision on his part. The pressure of signaling the plays in quickly and correctly would cause way too much stress on a kid who is already fighting paranoia and anxiety attacks. When the game was over he asked to go straight home which I found odd until he told me that he wasn't sure that he could control his feelings and didn't want to say something to offend someone in his mind's altered state. Is this a higher level of maturity on his part or more paranoia?

DAY 224, SUNDAY, SEPTEMBER 11, 2011

Today was our first youth football game of the season. Jacob was up in the press box acting as my "eye in the sky". He did a nice job and was very helpful for the first half. He started feeling bad at halftime and told me he was going to go home.

Jacob had drawn up a play for me to use this year and we installed it during practice this past week. All day the kids had been asking to run this play as the first play of the 3rd quarter. I asked Jacob to stick around for the beginning of the 3rd quarter so that he could see his play executed. He stood next to me on the sidelines and watched with the kids as they executed his play perfectly for 18 yards and a first down. He was smiling from ear to ear and the kids were jumping around and cheering as they were excited and proud of what they had done and who they had done it for. The play is very simply called "JP3". It was a nice moment.

DAY 225, MONDAY, SEPTEMBER 12, 2011

Jacob called me at work today to frantically tell me that he now weighs only 148lbs. He started this journey weighing 174lbs. I was shocked to hear this. I did not think that he looked that much smaller so we are going to check his weight records and see when he started losing weight. If my memory is correct, he checked in to the hospital on August 29 weighing 168lbs. When he left the hospital three days later he weighed 158lbs because all he would eat was saltine crackers during the week he was admitted. He has been eating a lot better since he got home from the hospital, but somehow he is still losing a significant amount of weight. This is the first time that he has had any substantial weight loss throughout this entire process. He is still taking two liters of fluid overnight every night for twelve hours. His sodium is still low and we are careful with his sugar intake. Today is the last day of the steroid so maybe things will even out once that gets out of his system.

Jacob called me again at 4:00pm to tell me that he got a letter from Stanford today requesting film from his junior year. Is this good or bad? He is excited to get the letter, but crushed that he will not have any film to send. Sometimes life sucks and then sometimes life is cruel. This is the letter that he worked for his entire life. It's almost like an insult or a slap in the face. He has worked so hard for an opportunity, then the opportunity presents itself, but he has cancer and may never get to fulfill the dream that is now literally in his hands.

Day 227, Wednesday, September 14, 2011

We went to Omaha today with an uneasy feeling. Jacob is dehydrated and his sodium is still low. We were told yesterday that if things did not look better today that he might be admitted to the hospital. Jacob admits that he is battling depression and he knows that all of his problems right now are being amplified by the steroid. Knowing this does not make it any easier to deal with. It just gives him a different perspective. We are learning a lot about seeing things with a different perspective.

After his spinal tap today he admitted that when he was at his lowest point a couple days ago, he entertained the thought of getting drunk to escape the misery. Our liquor cabinet is unlocked and readily accessible to him in the basement very near his beloved futon. He knew that he would never act upon this urge, but it was the first time that he truly had the urge to "escape". These are tough words for a parent to hear, but I'm glad that he felt he could share that with me.

Thankfully, Dr. Gordon was very happy with the results of Jacob's labs today. Everything appears to be within normal ranges except his sodium. He will have to stay on IV fluids for ten hours a day, but hopefully now that he is off the steroid, his body will start to balance itself.

For the first time in a long time we went out for supper after treatment. Jacob was craving Applebee's. This time he ate a ton of food and did not upset his stomach. That was really good to see for a kid who has not been eating well and losing a lot of weight.

Day 229, Friday, September 16, 2011

After lunch today we got a call from the Med Center. Jacob's sodium is still below normal and now his glucose has spiked to over 500. His glucose has been up and down for the last week, but we have been able to correct it with diet adjustments. It was just over 100 on Wednesday when we were back for treatment. The low sodium level and high glucose level combined with the fact that he has lost even more weight mean that we have to bring him back to Omaha today to be admitted. He is now down to 145lbs. Three weeks ago when he was admitted for treatment he was 169lbs. We can't understand why he continues to lose weight. He is now eating well. After treatment on Wednesday he ate two complete entrees and ate part of my meal as well.

Once we arrived and the paperwork was complete they started him on another normal saline IV with potassium added. His blood sugar came down to 300 before they had even given him an insulin shot and the Resident was hinting that Jacob may not have needed to be admitted today after all.

The most disappointing part of the whole day was the fact that Jacob will now miss tonight's football game in Beatrice. We are rated in the Top 5 in both polls and Beatrice is rated in the top 10. We got the news that we would be going to Omaha about three hours before we were scheduled to leave for the game. Jacob called Coach Huebert immediately to tell him that he would not be making the trip to Beatrice. As Jacob was talking his voice started shaking and he was trying hard not to cry. Not only has the cancer taken away his ability to play, it is now separating him from his teammates and coaches. I thought that Jacob would be inconsolable and extremely angry as we prepared to leave, but he was amazingly calm and mature about the whole situation. Unfortunately, he has been forced to learn how to deal with crushing disappointment frequently. I can't imagine how hard it must be for him to see his peers living normal lives as he trudges his way through a life filled with roadblocks and setbacks. Luckily, we found a local Beatrice AM radio station that was streaming the game online. We had to listen to the biased hometown announcers for three hours, but at least we got to listen to the game.

Aurora committed three turnovers and dropped a sure touchdown pass in the first half and trailed 16-0 at halftime. Neither Jacob nor I were too concerned at halftime because our coaches do a great job making adjustments at halftime. Aurora came out in the second half and scored on our first two possessions. However, we also allowed Beatrice to score twice as well. With seven minutes left in the game we were behind 29-15. After forcing Beatrice to punt, Aurora took over at the Beatrice 31 yard line and threw a TD pass to cut the lead to seven, 29-22. Beatrice tried to run out the clock, but picked up only one first down on their final drive. They were forced to punt and we took possession of the ball at our own 13 yard line. 87 yards away from the endzone with 1:17 left. A few plays in to the final drive we found ourselves 4th and 15 to go. Our quarterback completed a pass to one of Jacobs' best friends for 18 yards to keep the drive alive. The team stayed focused and kept fighting and found themselves on the eight yard line as time was running out. Our quarterback took the snap, rolled to the right, and found a receiver in the endzone with no time left on the clock. We are still behind 29-28. The big question is do we kick the extra point for the tie or do we go for two and the win. I asked that question to Jacob and he replied, "We're Aurora, we go for the win". That is exactly what we did. At this time the nurse came in to check Jacob's IV and see if he needed anything. It was a surreal scene as Jacob is lying in his hospital bed hooked up to an IV and being checked by a nurse as all of this drama is unfolding through the speakers on my laptop. As the running back crossed the goalline and the radio announcers sluggishly informed us that the two point conversion was good our room briefly erupted into a mixture of cheers and SSHHH's. Somehow, some way, those young men found the strength and confidence to complete one of the greatest comebacks in school history. 23 points in the 4th quarter against a highly rated team, on their home field, and as we found out later—it was their Homecoming. It's probably a good thing that we were not in attendance because Jacob would have been on the sideline amidst the entire team as they stormed the field in celebration. We ended up in the emergency room in McCook after a loss. I don't want to imagine what could have happened on the field after this win.

Shari and I stayed in Jacob's room for about another hour and then decided to go to our room for the night. As we were leaving his phone was beginning to flood with text messages from his teammates. We left him alone to try and connect with his friends and become a part of their celebration. I was wide awake and he would not be getting any sleep for quite a while either.

Day 231, Sunday, September 18, 2011

Jacob had a rough night last night after we left. We are having a hard time stabilizing his blood sugar. He has been on slow-acting insulin and fast-acting insulin and his blood sugar has dropped dangerously low twice overnight. He called me this morning thinking that he would not be coming home today as planned. Luckily, as the day progressed it appeared that things were leveling out. He is basically enduring the same process as someone with diabetes because ultimately he now has diabetic symptoms as a side effect of the chemo. He has to check his blood sugar every couple of hours, count his carbs and give himself insulin shots based on his food intake, blood sugar count and several other variables. Dr. Gordon also has him on an IV 24-hours a day. This is all being brought on as a side effect of the chemotherapy and although Jacob does not like it, he understands and accepts that it is a small price to pay if the cancer is going away. Shari will have to wake him up at home at midnight and 3:00am to monitor his blood sugar until this passes, but at least we get to go home today.

Day 232, Monday, September 19, 2011

Jacob called me at the office this morning to tell me that he weighed 152lbs. He was excited to have gained seven pounds over the weekend. Of course, he is now talking about lifting and riding the stationary bike and his energy level is the highest it has been in a month. The rollercoaster ride continues.

Day 234, Wednesday, September 21, 2011

Today we are back in Omaha for the last regular treatment in the Re-Induction Therapy. Dr. Gordon was pleased with Jacob's lab results and it appears that his hyperglycemia is passing. His blood sugar has not spiked like it did last week and they took him off of insulin yesterday. The only thing that concerned Dr. Gordon was some "blasts" that appeared in Jacob's blood test. Blasts are immature cells that could be either more cancer or just bone marrow cells regenerating. All of the other test results were good news, so we will wait until September 26, when Jacob will have another spinal tap and bone marrow biopsy, to find out if the cancer is coming back or not.

Day 235, Thursday, September 22, 2011

Jacob was having a good day at home until he spiked a fever late this afternoon. Shortly before 7:00pm his temperature hit 100.5 degrees which automatically means a call to Omaha, so Shari called the Med Center and was told to take him to the Emergency Room just to be safe. I stayed home with Jerod and Dalton while she and Jacob went to St. Francis Medical Center in Grand Island. We stayed in touch by phone over the next couple of hours and then at around 10:00pm she called to tell me that Jacob would be transported by ambulance to the Med Center in Omaha due to the fever and extremely low blood sugar. Shari stayed with Jacob until the ambulance left the hospital, then hurried home. We quickly packed a few things and left for Omaha at 11:00pm. Jerod and Dalton are staying home by themselves.

Day 236, Friday, September 23, 2011

Jacob is feeling pretty good all day and everyone is hopeful that he will be released in time to make it to Waverly for the football game. At 9:15am Dr. Lowas came in to check on Jacob and was hopeful that he would get to go home today if he met the following criteria by 3:30pm:

1. No more fever
2. He feels better
3. The blood cultures taken last night in Grand Island are negative for infection

They checked him frequently all day and unfortunately at 3:15pm he spiked a temperature of 101.3 and that means at least another 24 hours in the hospital. Jacob's doctor, nurses and techs were all disappointed that he didn't get released in time for the game. They all know how much it means to him. Once again we were lucky enough to find a local radio station that broadcasts the games on the internet so we listened to the game online again. This time we lost and lost pretty badly. It was an even more depressing night than usual in the pediatric ward.

Day 237, Saturday, September 24, 2011

No temperature at 4:00pm means that it was 24 hours since his last fever and he was released in time to watch the Husker game at home tonight. He sat upstairs with Shari and I for the entire game. Usually he is down on the futon the second that we get home. It was nice to watch a game with him at home where we belong.

Jacob sobbed as he stated, "I just want to be normal..." and he covered his eyes with his hands as the tears began to flow. Normal has never been good enough for Jacob and now normal is what he yearns for. He will never be "normal" again. He knows that, and it eats at him constantly.

Ten

—

NORMAL?

DAY 239, MONDAY, SEPTEMBER 26, 2011

Today we went back to Omaha for a scheduled bone marrow biopsy and spinal tap. Dr. Gordon stated that some blasts had shown up in Jacob's labs last Wednesday, then were gone on Friday and then re-emerged on Saturday. Everything else looked good though, so he thought that they might just be immature cells being regenerated by his bone marrow. After an appointment with the Endocrinologist at Children's Hospital we were on the road home early in the afternoon and were just settling in at home when Dr. Gordon called with more bad news.

I was up at the school, around 5:30pm, watching the Junior Varsity football game from the parking lot while I was waiting for Jerod and Dalton to come out of the locker room after their practice. I was going to call Shari to tell her that I might stay at the school and watch some more of the game when Jacob called to tell me, "Dr. Gordon is on the phone talking to Mom... and it's not good." At this time, Jerod and Dalton had just left the locker room, so we jumped in the truck and sped home.

We found out that there was a substantial amount of cancer in Jacob's bone marrow. Dr. Gordon told Shari that Jacob needed to come back to Omaha tomorrow to try yet another new treatment. This was a setback of monumental proportions. He then stated that he believed Jacob could still be fixed, but questioned how far we were willing to go. What were we willing to put Jacob through to try and fix him? This was the first time that anyone has suggested that we are near the end of our rope. At what point does a parent say that it is time to stop treatment and let their child die? We know that we are not at that point yet, but with all that he has been through and we keep falling further and further behind, at some point you have to say enough is enough. Jacob's case manager Jeannine had told Dr. Gordon that he needed to stop looking at this situation through rose-colored glasses and he did just that.

Jacob had a similar reaction to this news as he has had in the past. He sat on the floor in the living room staring blankly at the wall. We talked about what had worked for him in the past and what had not and that we would just have to find the right "cocktail" to fix this now. We discussed the fact that he would be going back on the steroid and that he is strong enough mentally to deal with the depression and anxiety that go along with the steroid. He stated, "I can take anything… but why do I always have to." He is right. He has battled through everything that has been thrown at him only to find a new battle waiting for him. This time he will be admitted for 7-8 days of treatment and the stem cell transplant is being postponed.

Shari started to do laundry and prepare Jerod and Dalton's schedule for our absence. I went downstairs, sat with Jacob and watched some TV. At first he seemed fine. He was watching Family Guy and laughing like he usually does. Then he got up to go to the bathroom and when he sat back down he told me that he knew what Dr. Gordon meant by "how far were we willing to go". He looked me square in the eyes and said, "I'm not scared of that". This is the first time that he has alluded to death in front of me. He told me that when he is lying downstairs alone for hours on end and the steroid is messing with his mind, "death is not unwanted". I told him that I was glad that he was strong enough to talk about that outcome because dying from this disease has been a possibility since day one, but we have not dwelt on it. In fact we have only talked about death when referring to that first night when he could have suffocated at home or on the operating table when they placed his port and how close he was when he was admitted on August 29 with the lump in his neck. I guess after you have faced death multiple times and have had this many setbacks and complications, coupled with the side effects of the drugs, he has accepted death as a possible, but not impending, outcome.

Since the June relapse, Jacob's death has continually been in my thoughts. I try to block those thoughts out of my mind only to find them recurring quickly. I am terrified of losing my son, but yet how long can he go on when all of his goals and dreams are shattered? We still talk about his possible return to football, but every day that goes by he gets farther and farther away from that reality. He hasn't been able to even go to school to meet with his teachers and now he will be in the hospital for another week and a half and fall even further behind. He asked me if this latest setback meant the end of school for this semester and I told him that I was not even the least bit concerned about school right now. We are only concerned about getting him into remission and getting the transplant. He hasn't even really wanted to workout that much lately, either, which is understandable. He has restarted a workout routine so many times, only to have it derailed by setbacks, that I think he doesn't see the point in it anymore. I have told him many times that there is way more to look forward to in life than just playing sports and he understands that. He finally broke down during our conversation when I mentioned the word "normal". Jacob sobbed as he stated, "I just want to be normal, so f…king bad" and he covered his eyes with his hands as the tears began to flow. Normal has never been good enough for Jacob and now normal is what he yearns for. He will never be "normal" again. He knows that, and it eats at him constantly.

Day 240, Tuesday, September 27, 2011

We got to the hospital around 11:00am and waited until around 3:00pm for Dr. Gordon to come see us. Jacob felt anxious, as if we were just wasting time. He kept saying, "I feel like I should be doing something right now." I was very apprehensive about meeting with Dr. Gordon. I feared what he might have to say. Information has changed so quickly lately that I was worried that he would come in and tell us that there was nothing more that they could do and we should go home, prepare ourselves for the worst possible outcome. I had prepared a timeline of Jacob's victories and setbacks and how they related to the drugs he was on during those times. I thought that if we eliminated some of the drugs that apparently didn't work and concentrated on a mixture of things that apparently did, that we could possibly get him into remission long enough to stay on schedule for the transplant. Dr. Gordon explained to us that the transplant process cannot be used in that way. Jacob will have to be in a solid remission for 2-3 weeks before they will proceed with the transplant.

Dr. Gordon sat with us and outlined the plan at this point and I asked him if he was still conferring with the same doctors that he had been earlier. He alluded to the fact that those people had given up on Jacob after hearing about this last setback. The last time that he had contact with them, they told him that the best we could do was to try to make him comfortable, but there was nothing more medically that could be done. I felt the weight of the world land on my chest when I heard this news—it was a crushing blow. Then Dr. Gordon stated that he did not feel the same way and he was not ready to give up if we were not ready to give up. Thank God that Dr. Gordon does not feel the same way as the others. He still wants to try some different drugs and hopes to find the right combination to get Jacob into remission. I told him that I understand that there could come a time that Jacob is too weak to continue this fight, but we are not there yet. He agreed that Jacob still looks like he can fight and sees no point in stopping now unless those were our wishes. Jacob spoke up and told Dr. Gordon, "If there is a chance that it will work, regardless of the side effects, I am willing to try it. I can take it."

DAY 241, WEDNESDAY, SEPTEMBER 28, 2011

Dr. Beck was making rounds today and stopped by with Mandy and a pharmacy student. She said that Jacob's labs showed 40% cancer in his blood up from 4% just a few days ago. This has been a very aggressive cancer from the beginning, but it has also dissolved very quickly when attacked with the right drugs. However, with every treatment the cancer could become more and more resistant to the steroids, and if they stop working, then I believe that nothing will work. We have reached the last possible chance for Jacob to get well. If this treatment does not work he will not get the stem cell transplant. Everyone believes that the transplant is Jacob's best chance to be cured, but if he doesn't get that transplant and the cancer is resistant to chemotherapy, then there is no other alternative.

When he was first diagnosed I feared for his life, but after we had talked to the doctors we were confident that Jacob would recover and live a "normal" life again. I felt that way until his relapse in June. We were even talking to people about when we could have his port removed so that he could get back to sports while he was in the Maintenance phase. After the June relapse, Jacob's death from cancer has been a mountain hanging over my head. It infiltrates almost all of my thoughts. From then until now I have had re-occurring thoughts about the process of watching Jacob die, preparing for and attending his funeral and how to live afterwards. If this process leads to Jacob's death, at least he will not have to endure anymore of the mental and physical decline. I will be relieved that he will no longer have to fight a battle that he did not choose, but I will miss him more than my mind can imagine. He is my best friend as well as my firstborn. He and I can talk about anything and we both have the same opinions about almost everything. He is everything that I am not. He is glorious and magnificent, intelligent, motivated, hard working, dedicated, athletic and funny. I can't stand the thought of living every day of the rest of my life without him. THIS TREATMENT MUST WORK.

Jacob fell asleep around 3:30pm and slept until 4:30pm. Before he fell asleep he was feeling pretty good, but after he woke up things had changed. Dr. Beck and Mandy stopped in to check on him and buy a fundraiser card for the football team and he was disoriented and slurring his speech while they were talking to him. His eyes were blinking very slowly almost as if he had been sedated. They will monitor this situation closely.

Shari and I got him up for a walk around the 6th floor and ended up in the Teen Room shooting baskets on a pop-a-shot game. His sluggish symptoms seemed to have improved and he did pretty well for a guy whose fingertips are numb, and can't really feel his feet. Several times during the walk, though, he acted as if he was drunk or one of his legs gave out. I likened it to stepping onto a ship for the first time. He looked like he hadn't gotten his sea legs yet. I told his nurse about the problem and she informed the Resident. The Resident came in and did a quick Neurological exam and could find nothing wrong with him. There is a very good possibility that the combination of the new chemo, high blood sugar, lack of sleep and high stress level are contributing to this problem.

Just before Shari and I were ready to leave his room for the evening, Jacob asked Shari to step out of the room so that he could talk with me. He doesn't like to see his Mom cry and he knew this conversation would be a rough one. First of all he asked me if I thought his story would make a good movie. My initial reaction was yes, but I told him that it would only make a good movie if he survives. I haven't told him this before, but I do believe that his story would make an excellent movie. As a father I am biased, but his story is compelling and he has done things during this process that are truly remarkable.

- Attending Camp in Hastings on the same day as the tissue biopsy
- Competing in the Iditarod
- Travelling 300 miles to McCook for the football game the same day he was released and then ending up in the Emergency Room before going home
- Getting a 4.0 spring semester 2011
- Elected to Student Council
- Elected Class Treasurer
- Elected to the football team's Unity Council
- Watching his dreams pass by without his participation, but still finding ways to display leadership

I told him that no one wants to watch a movie where the main character dies after persevering the way that Jacob has. Maybe I was just trying to motivate him to keep fighting. Maybe no one really cares if the main character actually lives or not. That led me to talk to Jacob about what a difference he could make in other people's lives by telling his story. He could motivate people of all ages to fight through adversity and never give up. This could become a career for him, but only if the movie ends with him throwing a touchdown pass. He immediately burst into tears and I thought that he wanted to talk about dying when he said, "You aren't going to want to hear this, but I think that I am done playing football."

I was relieved. I told him that I didn't care if he ever played football again. To hell with the movie, just live to tell your story. He said that all that he has done in his life has been to prepare him to play football with his team, with his friends, for Aurora.

He loves his teammates and especially his classmates. He is proud of how they have stepped up this year and played key roles in their first varsity action. I responded to his proclamation by saying that I do not believe that he is done playing. I told him that we can't waste time right now worrying about playing football next year. All of our efforts need to be channeled into getting him through today and then tomorrow—one day at a time, one hour at a time one minute at a time. He really wants to go outside and throw a football, but he can't because of the needle in his chest. The site has become irritated because it has been accessed for about a month now. This past week has been the lowest that I have seen him. He has been segregated from his friends and his team by his recurring trips to the hospital and that is taking a large toll on his mental health.

He also said that he feels like he is in a fight with God. He said that he prayed every day in September and at the end of the month things were worse than the beginning.

"Why is God punishing me?"

"What good is prayer?"

"Every time I feel closer to God he pushes me away."

These are some of the statements that he was making. I don't have the answers for him. I really want him to find peace in his heart, but I don't know if that will happen. He feels that he is being abandoned by God. I have no idea how to persuade him otherwise. Sometimes I feel like we are being abandoned or punished.

Jacob told me that there were three words that always break him emotionally. This was ironic because I had also picked up on three words that I swore that I would not use around him anymore. His three words were normal, helpless, and football. My three words were normal, helpless, and control. Using any of these words around Jacob will bring an instant emotional reaction. At the end of our discussion I told him that he needs to let his emotions out more often. Everything that he is going through emotionally is compounded by the steroid and he will now being receiving an insanely high dosage. I told him that he needs to scream and yell and cry whenever the need arises. Holding it in will only lead to larger meltdowns and more stress. The hardest time for him has always been right before bed. I have a feeling that trend will continue and undoubtedly be magnified.

He also told me that he was afraid that this would be his last birthday. How do I respond to that?

I think more than anything the stress of his circumstances along with the onset of the steroid side effects brought on tonight's meltdown. He let Shari come back into the room around 10:45pm and said that he wanted us to stay until he went to bed at 11:30pm. We were watching "the Office" on Netflix and the current episode ended around 11:15pm. I asked him if he wanted us to leave or if he wanted to watch one more episode and he said he wanted us to stay. I then asked him if he wanted one of us to stay overnight in his room and he said yes. He was not even watching the TV, he was on his computer the whole time trying to trade players in his fantasy football league. He just didn't want to be alone. He almost always wants to be left alone at night so I knew that his emotional turmoil was not over. Shari left for our room around midnight and I transformed one of the chairs in Jacob's room into a bed and settled in. Jacob had different plans. First he decided that he needed to do lunges and squats beside his bed (remember its midnight) then he needed to write a note to his teammates and send it to them on Facebook. He said that there were some new security settings that would only allow his teammates to read his note. The team is playing Gering High School on Friday night and once again, Jacob will not be in attendance, so he wants to do whatever he can to help and this note is his way. It took a long time for him to type the note because he can't feel his fingers. Once he got it done he gave it to me to proofread. By this time he was extremely tired and having a hard time with his fine motor skills. He was getting mad at his computer and frustrated with Facebook when the problem was actually his clumsy mind and clumsy fingers. After we got the text of the note correct he then started tagging the players that he was going to allow to read it. He went through his friends by memory and then asked me for help in remembering everyone else. I told him that the easiest way to do that was to start with jersey #1 and go through all of the numbers, so we did. #1 AJ Farrand, #2 Troy McDonald, all the way through #88, Josh Lawton, until we had identified every player on the roster. We had to start completely over multiple times due to him pressing the wrong key or accidentally bumping the touchpad or the computer freezing. He finally completed this process at around 2:30am. By this time he was barely coherent and his speech was garbled at best. As he rolled over onto his left side he asked me if today was Sunday and before I could answer he was asleep. The most important thing in the world that night was to reach out and inspire his teammates. I hope he succeeded.

Day 242, Thursday, September 29, 2011

Jacob is still groggy and not quite up to speed again this morning. He probably will get worse as the steroid dosage increases. Dr. Beck and Mandy came in around 9:00am and told us that labs today showed the cancer in his blood had gone from 40% to 20% which was what we were expecting to hear. The problem is not getting it lowered, the problem is keeping it away for 2-3 weeks.

We also asked them what other options we might have somewhere else if this treatment does not work. Dr. Beck cautioned us about travelling too far from home, but said that there were leukemia specialists in Minnesota, Denver, and Kansas City if we were interested. She offered to have Dr. Gordon send Jacob's information to other hospitals to see if anyone else had another treatment option that showed any signs of success. We told them that we are not looking for a magic pill, but if this is the last chance we are given with Dr. Gordon then we would like to know if someone else "outside the box" has any suggestions. They both agreed that it was a good idea to get that process started now, being proactive instead of reactive. We are at the end of the line and no suggestion can be dismissed without consideration.

Mandy came into the room early this afternoon to see if we needed anything or had any questions. It does seem that we are getting more attention now than we have had during previous stays. She asked Jacob if he would like a Psychologist to visit and he said yes for the first time. I am glad to see him give this another try. I think talking with a professional could possibly help him in more ways than just opening up to me or his Mom. Jacob also asked Mandy what will happen to him if this therapy does not work and the transplant is cancelled. She stated that the leukemia cells would eventually take over his blood vessels and constrict the flow of blood to his extremities and then his organs. She explained that it is very painful and at that time they would start him on pain management to keep him as comfortable as possible. I wanted to get up and run out of the room while she was describing his possible demise. I started trembling and I could feel my heart pounding in my chest. I did the best that I could to hide my reaction and quickly told Jacob that we are not crossing that bridge right now. We will deal with that if and when it needs to be.

Later Jacob asked me what my beliefs were about the afterlife. Again, I did not have a good answer for my son. I told him that most of the stories that I have heard about the moment before dying are very peaceful. I told him that he would find out the answers to his questions about God immediately. I reminded him that he told me the other night that he was not scared of death. He then tearfully told me that he is scared of Hell. He does not believe that this treatment will work and he believes that he will die soon. My response was that he has this chance to find peace with God and ask for the forgiveness of his sins. A lot of people are not given the opportunity to assess their beliefs prior to dying. He has been given a chance to make a decision now and prepare himself for what lies ahead. In my opinion he will still need some additional input from other people before he truly believes in a God that he feels he is fighting sometimes.

My continued advice is to live today, one goal at a time. He is having a blood and platelet transfusion now, so let's get through that. Then let's get to the start of the College Football game on TV tonight. Then let's try to get a good night's rest tonight before taking on tomorrow. Let's not plan for his death while we are still fighting for his survival. He did say that if there was another treatment option later that was considered experimental or a long shot that he would elect to try it rather than give up and prepare to die. The warrior is still alive inside, but sometimes he just needs to be revived.

Day 243, Friday September 30, 2011

Today is Jacob's 17th Birthday. We have heard through the grapevine that today is JP3 day in Aurora. A friend of ours has asked everyone to wear either their Team Jacob or JP3 STRONGER T-shirts today and send pictures to us. The football team always wears their game jerseys on Fridays, but they decided that today they will all wear their T-shirts in support of Jacob. There was also an announcement made at school that students attending the game tonight should wear either shirt to support Jacob.

All four of Jacob's grandparents are coming to Omaha late this morning to celebrate his birthday. Jacob told me during a long walk through the hospital last night that he is afraid of what he might do today in front of his grandparents. He is afraid that he will break down in front of my parents and make them cry also. He does not like making anyone cry, especially my dad. I told him that we would probably all be crying at some point, so let it out, no one will blame him for being emotional.

Everyone arrived shortly before 11:00am. We all sat in Jacob's room for a while and he dosed off and on as we visited. Shari ordered Applebee's to go and we all went down to a conference room on the 3rd floor. We have not told the grandparents the severity of the situation and probably won't until we know the results of this round of chemo. My mom and dad are not in good health and don't need any additional stress right now. After lunch we went back to Jacob's room and he quickly fell asleep. Everyone said goodbye and they were all headed home by 2:00pm. Jacob handled everything very well. He did not break down in front of his grandparents like he thought he might. We will see how he does tonight at bedtime.

Around 3:00pm Jacob got a visit from two Hooters Girls. Some friends of ours back home arranged the whole thing. The girls brought him a T-shirt, 50 wings, a birthday cake, and a Husker football autographed by 2001 Heisman Trophy Winner Eric Crouch. Jacob was asleep when they arrived and was not really happy to be awakened for unscheduled visitors. Once he saw the girls his attitude changed pretty quickly. Shari shot some video as they walked in the room and got plenty of pictures for Jacob to share with his friends.

Coach Huebert informed Jacob via text message that he would read Jacob's latest note aloud to the team tonight before the game against Gering.

During the game the radio announcers mentioned that today was Jacob's birthday and that he was having some health problems, but I was in the restroom and missed the whole thing. Aurora played hard but sloppy and just couldn't put Gering away. Gering came back and scored a touchdown with less than two minutes left in the game to pull within one point, 36-35. Gering then went for the two point conversion and failed. Aurora ran out the clock and won. Three out of the last four games have come down to a two point conversion late in the game and another game was decided in double overtime. He can't help but think that he would be making a difference in all of these close games.

Jacob got a call during the game telling him to watch the Channel 5 sports broadcast tonight. We streamed the entire broadcast to make sure that we would not miss whatever it was we were watching for. Then at the end of the regular broadcast and just before the "Sports Extra" portion started the online streaming stopped. Sports Extra shows the highlights from local games and had the footage of whatever happened in Aurora tonight. We will just have to wait until the segments are posted online.

Jacob has been receiving text messages and Facebook messages all night. Now that the game is over his teammates are filling him in on all of the details of the game. Apparently a couple of his classmates were in tears again tonight after the game. Those boys are struggling to process all of this too and I hope people understand and appreciate that they need to process their emotions as well.

Jacob's closest friends have been basically the same since 1st grade. As all friends do, they have had good and bad times, but through it all they have remained like brothers. These are the boys who volunteered to help with Jacob's golf benefit and the ones that he leans on for support. In the notes that he has written to the team he refers to them all as teammates and brothers. These bonds are very strong and will last for the rest of their lives. We heard that there were plans made tonight for a bunch of guys to come tomorrow for a visit.

It's a cruel coincidence that 17 years ago on a Friday night we were in the hospital in Lincoln celebrating the birth of our first son. Here we are 17 years later on a Friday night fighting to save his life.

DAY 244, SATURDAY, OCTOBER 1, 2011

Ten of Jacob's friends showed up shortly before noon today. Jacob's hospital room is smaller than the average motel room so fitting ten high school boys was tight.

Brock Henderson, Rick Schmidt, Ben McQuiston, Tanner Griffith, Troy McDonald, Blake Williams, Trevor Thorell, Bryce Hewen, Alex Brechbill and

Ehren Schwarz. About an hour and a half into their visit, Chris, Tina, Alex and Bradley Hunt showed up for a visit as well. We took all of the boys downstairs to an empty waiting room so that we would have more room. Bryce just had knee surgery so I got him a wheelchair to make it easier for him to get around. I then mentioned that there were a large amount of wheelchairs just around the corner by the front entry. Immediately the boys raced down the hallway to obtain their own. Of course races and crashes ensued, followed by everyone trying to balance on the back wheels only, and culminated in a wheelchair joust between Bryce and Ehren. They wedged one of Bryce's crutches between their leg and the side of the chair and tried to ram each other. It was great to have that kind of energy around us again. Jacob really needed to see these guys today and we will be forever grateful to them for giving their entire Saturday to Jacob.

At one point Jacob's IV fluids ran out, so I took him upstairs to get the bag changed. The boys followed us upstairs and Jacob wanted to lie back down in his room. I left them all alone and returned to the waiting room on the 1st floor with Shari, Chris, and Tina. We had a nice visit. A short time later the boys came down from the room and walked past us as they were leaving. I thanked them for coming all this way to see Jacob. They are all good boys. The four of us then went up to Jacob's room for a while until the Hunts left shortly after 4:00pm.

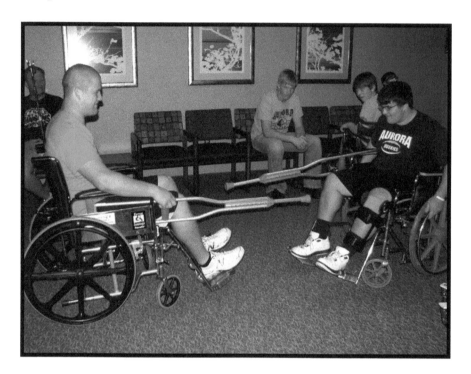

DAY 245, SUNDAY, OCTOBER 2, 2011

Today was another busy day with visitors, which is great because we have not had many visitors during our previous stays in Omaha. Shari's mom and dad brought Jerod and Dalton to Omaha today. They arrived around 11:30am. We visited for a while and then we met Shari's brother and his family for lunch at the Olive Garden. Shari and I haven't left Jacob alone during the day this whole week. He was heavily engaged in his fantasy football league between his Blackberry, Netbook, and the TV, so we thought he would be fine alone for a little while. It was good to eat something besides hospital food and to see some different scenery.

My youth football team secured the Division Championship today by beating York 20-0. This is the first game in eight years that I have missed and I am glad that my absence did not have an adverse affect on the team. The assistant coaches are good men and we have been preparing for this scenario all year. I am really just an organizer and manager at this point and everyone stepped up and completed my responsibilities perfectly. I am very proud of our program and this is a testament to the entire team, players, coaches and parents. Last year another team had to play one game without their head coach due to the death of the coach's father. The team lost that week and the coach told me that the kids were just not ready to play and his absence really affected their play. I preach every week at practice about being mentally tough and prepared for the game. It is their job to come to the game ready to play regardless of the circumstances. This is their team and they are the ones that have to execute what we have taught them. The coaches can't make them do the right thing. The other component that could have led to a letdown this week was the fact that at least half of our starters were at hunter safety education last week and missed both Tuesday and Thursday practice. This group has a great opportunity to do something very special.

Day 246, Monday, October 3, 2011

Today is our 19th wedding anniversary. I want to spend my 20th anniversary at home with all three of my kids and my wife.

Day 249, Thursday, October 6, 2011

Yesterday we got to go home, but this morning Jacob woke up with a headache and upset stomach. He ate some breakfast then went downstairs to lie down again. I left to run some errands in Grand Island and was planning on going on to Kearney after that. At 11:45am Shari called to tell me that Jacob had a fever and they were preparing to leave for the Emergency Room in Grand Island. I told her that I would meet her there. I arrived at the ER shortly after 12:00pm and checked with the front desk to see if I could do anything to speed up his admission and inform them of his condition. I sat in the waiting room for a couple of minutes and then received a phone call from the Police Dispatcher telling me that an ambulance had been dispatched to my home and Jacob was unresponsive. As I left Grand Island all that I could think of was that Jacob would be dead by the time I saw him again. I was certain that he would be transported to Omaha immediately and if he wasn't dead already he would be dead by the time I got to him. Thankfully, Paul Graham, a Lieutenant with the Aurora Police Department, called to update me on the situation. He told me that Jacob was in the bathroom with Shari and the EMT's were there ready to take him to the Emergency Room in Aurora so that he could be stabilized. I was relieved to hear that I wasn't too late.

When I got to the hospital, Jacob was groggy and only wanted to go to sleep. His blood pressure had dropped to 71/30 and his heart was racing at 120 beats per minute. Shari then told me that while Jacob was downstairs he started having heavy diarrhea. When he came upstairs to let her know, he got light-headed and nauseated. He went out through the patio door and onto the deck where he vomited. Shari went outside with him and when he got up she had to catch him to keep him from falling over. She then called 911 and while she was on with the phone Jacob's eyes were rolling back in his head and he kept telling her how tired he was. Somehow she got him to the bathroom before he had another bout of diarrhea. This time there was also blood in his stool. Paul Graham was the first on the scene and stayed just outside the door until the EMT's arrived and he was taken to the Emergency Room in Aurora.

Around 1:00pm Dr. Widhalm asked us which way we preferred to have Jacob transported to Omaha, by ground or air. We told him to do whatever they felt was best. They decided to go by air ambulance. At 2:10pm we heard that the helicopter was in the air and should be here soon. At 2:30pm we heard that they had to stop for fuel and would be there around 3:30pm. At 3:15pm we heard that they had stopped for fuel in York and would be there around 4:00pm. Meanwhile Jacob had been on two 1000ml normal saline IVs pumping at full speed known as a bolus. This brought his blood pressure up and his pulse down. After the fluids ran out they put him on one 1000ml IV at half speed. Almost immediately his blood pressure dropped and his pulse was racing again. Shari and I were getting very frustrated with the absence of the helicopter and we could tell that Dr. Widhalm and the nurses were getting concerned about Jacob crashing again. The helicopter showed up shortly after 4:00pm. The nurses evaluated Jacob's condition for about twenty minutes and then he was loaded up and taken away. Shari and I went home, packed our bags again and left for Omaha around 5:00pm. Mandy, Jacob's in-patient case manager, called us twice during the trip to update us on what was happening. Jacob was stable and several doctors were on site consulting on a treatment plan.

Jacob was admitted to the Pediatric ICU so that he could be more closely monitored until they diagnosed his condition. The rest of the evening was spent with Doctors, Residents, Attending Physicians, Nurses and Techs constantly flowing in and out of his room. I spent the night in his room because he was too weak to stand alone and pee. My once powerful son who was best known for his strength and tenacity now could not stand up on his own. Dr. Coulter also asked us at one point if we were aware of what a DNR (do not resuscitate) was. I told him we were aware of it, but were not ready to go down that road yet. It literally sent chills through my body to be discussing a DNR about Jacob. Somewhere down the road if this treatment does not work, we will have to discuss a DNR as a possibility. I don't want to ever quit trying, but if all doors are closed I would rather have him go quickly and peacefully than the slow painful death that Mandy had described to us last week. My nightmares all pertain to watching Jacob die slowly at home in our basement. How could we possibly live in our house after that?

We stayed in the PICU all day Friday and were transferred to the regular Pediatric Unit Saturday morning. He has responded well to all of the antibiotics and steroids. He has a bacterial infection from bacteria that we all have in our bowels. Because of the chemo, the lining of his bowels has weakened and some of that bacteria got into his blood. Luckily, the bacteria responded quickly to the treatment and there was no infection in his port. For a while they were concerned about bacteria in his port and there was a possibility that the port would have to be removed and a new one implanted on the other side of his chest.

While all of this was going on, my company was literally falling apart by the minute. A few years ago I built an apartment project in Gillette, Wyoming. We had massive cost overruns and the project seemed to be doomed to fail from day one. For the past three years I have been trying to catch up from those financial losses. I thought that if I just kept working harder I would catch up. I was wrong. Since I have been gone so much, some of the people I owe money to started calling around and asking questions. My banker told the developer that I needed some money to cover a couple loan payments and that started the domino effect. I have been behind for three years and have basically just been juggling money to the people who were the farthest behind or were screaming the loudest. My construction manager even called the developer to ask him if he could pay some people for me so that they would show up for their scheduled work. He did this with the best intentions, but again this just added fuel to the fire. While we were in the Emergency Room in Aurora my lumber salesman called because the Developer wanted to know what my account balances were at the Lumberyard. I told him to give him whatever information that he wanted. I had reached the end of my rope. I would rush out of the emergency room and answer calls in the parking lot trying to answer questions from my business associates and then rush back into the emergency room to check on Jacob. At one point the nurse told us that they were having a hard time reaching one of the doctors in Omaha and they were starting to get a little frantic. Then they reached the doctor in Omaha only to find that they didn't know where the doctor in Aurora had gone. People over-use terms like surreal or chaotic, but this was the definition of both. All of this was whirling around us like a storm while Jacob laid on the hospital bed drifting in and out of consciousness. The doctors and nurses were scurrying in and out of the room and we were being updated on the status of the helicopter which ended up taking over three hours to arrive in Aurora.

On Friday I made a phone call to Matt (the Developer) and we had a long talk about the situation. My house of cards has fallen and there is an enormous mess that will need to be cleaned up. I'm not sure how this will unfold. There is some money available to pay some of the vendors, but not nearly enough to take care of the problem. In a way, I am relieved that I can stop living with this burden hanging over my head. I had two projects that finished late and two projects that started late this summer. Had those projects been completed on time and started on time, I probably could have moved money around to keep people happy for a while longer. That would have only prolonged the inevitable. My company was doomed when I signed the contract to build those apartments in Gillette five years ago.

The next few days were a blur. We were getting information on Jacob's infections and treatment and I was fielding phone calls and emails trying to summarize the financial losses of the business. I would sit in Jacob's room and pound away on my computer and Blackberry trying to answer questions and formulate a plan to fix the business. Once again, I would step out of his room and walk down the hallway to have my phone conversations and try to re-enter his room showing no signs of what was happening. At this time no one in my family knew what was happening. I was trying to shield them from any additional stress and worry. After a few days, I did end up telling them what was going on and Jacob had already told Shari that I had been acting weird. I tried to appear strong for them and tried to shield them from the wreckage all while it was tearing me apart inside. I remember a strong pain/pressure in my chest along with dizziness that would not go away. It was like the feeling that you get right before you black out or when you stand up too quickly and get a severe head rush. Sometimes I have difficulty breathing. I will feel the emotions building inside me and then I will feel my breath becoming more short and shallow and I will then force myself to re-direct my thoughts and take a long deep breath and exhale slowly. I have never had a panic attack, or anxiety attack like Jacob had when he was on steroids, but this feeling is what I envision to be the beginning of an attack similar to that. When Jacob was having his blood pressure checked I would always tell him to control his breathing and any time he had pain, or felt a panic attack coming, I would remind him to focus on his breathing techniques and it would always calm him down. There were times that Jacob was indefinitely connected to the blood pressure cuff and every time he would get a high reading someone would get concerned. He would tell the nurse or tech to come back in a few minutes, then close his eyes and slow his breath and concentrate until the next blood pressure reading. He would consistently lower his blood pressure back to acceptable levels and he would smile every time. He had won that battle. I need to learn that type of control.

So to recap the last eight months, Jacob got cancer and relapsed three times, Shari lost her job and her health insurance benefits and I lost my business. This is why you should never ask, "What else could go wrong," because there is almost always something else. Unfortunately, it seems like everything is going wrong for me at one time.

Day 252, Sunday, October 9, 2011

The second infection that Jacob is dealing with is E-Coli. This was probably brought on by the other bacterial infection. I'm not sure how they are tied together, but from what I understand it is not uncommon for this to happen. Jacob started another antibiotic specifically meant to deal with the E-Coli. Other than having really bad diarrhea every couple of hours, Jacob is feeling slightly better.

Coach Huebert and his family came for a visit shortly before noon. Jacob was smiling and talking for the first time in four days. During their visit my sister Cheryl and her husband Bob showed up. Bob is waiting for a liver and pancreas transplant and has been battling with his own health issues. Due to Jacob's infections he cannot be around anyone with a compromised immune system, so Bob had to stand at the door for the entire visit. During Cheryl and Bob's visit, the Thompson family stopped by. Dana had just had his flu shot, so since he was carrying the live virus, he too had to stand in the doorway the whole time. The flurry of activity made the afternoon go by quickly, which is always good.

Day 253, Monday, October 10, 2011

After Dr. Gordon and Mandy made their rounds this morning I headed back to Aurora. I have a lot of work to do organizing the files and figuring out who is owed and how much. Matt has been very gracious so far and I am astonished at the composure that he has shown. He is a better man than I will ever be.

I stopped to use up the last of our Cenex gas cards in Ashland on the way home. Jessie pulled in for fuel as I was paying. He had come to Ashland to check on one of our new projects. I pulled up behind him at the pump and we had a long talk for the first time since the collapse of the company. He too is extremely gracious in handling this situation. I don't know if anyone else could be put in this situation after having all of the day-to-day construction burden dropped on his shoulders for the past eight months. He is genuinely more concerned about my health and my family than he is about the status of his job. I am amazed by his attitude and willingness to do whatever is necessary.

I picked up Jerod and Dalton from football practice tonight and we spent a nice evening together. After eating supper down the street at the Peterson's, I took Dalton to get a haircut and then we all watched Monday Night Football together. We haven't seen them much lately and I hate the fact that they are basically living alone right now. Glen and Patsy take care of making sure they are fed and they usually have a friend over on the weekend or go to a friend's house. So far they seem to be dealing with everything very well, but I'm sure that they miss us.

Day 254, Tuesday, October 11, 2011

Today I worked in the office all day organizing information and collecting invoices from everyone that I owe money too. I stayed in Aurora all day and went to Dalton's last football game at 4:30pm. His teammates were flat and uninspired and they played badly. It started to rain in the first quarter and it seemed almost perfectly gloomy and depressing. The game was suspended in the 3rd quarter after multiple flashes of lightning. It restarted shortly after 6:00pm, but then was called off at the end of the 3rd quarter because of more lightning. They were behind 12-8 when the game was called. Dalton took this loss extremely hard. He plays hard because that is his nature, but he also has a little extra fire because I believe he is also playing for Jacob's approval. He looks up to his big brother more than he will admit and he also feels more for Jacob than he will admit.

I left the game after the first suspension because I had to be in Omaha to meet with Matt at 7:30pm. This was our first face-to-face meeting since the house of cards collapsed last week. He handled himself with grace and dignity and that probably made it even harder on me. We talked for over an hour before we went our separate ways. The last thing he said to me as I walked away was, "Gary, take care of yourself."

Day 255, Wednesday, October 12, 2011

Jacob had a bone marrow biopsy at 8:30am. We have all made the trip down to the PACU many times for his multiple biopsies and spinal taps, but this one felt more ominous. We know exactly what bed they will take him to. We are acquainted with most of the staff and we definitely know the procedure. The importance of this day added a definite weight to all of our hearts.

Like usual, the procedure went as planned. We actually spent far less time waiting for Jacob to recover. In the past, Jacob has usually slept for about an hour after the procedure, but this time he was awake before we returned from the waiting room. The next few hours were spent anxiously anticipating the results. We tried to carry on like it was a normal day, but we were all on edge. We were told that preliminary results would not come back until tomorrow, but we all knew that we would probably hear something before 5:00pm. At about 4:45pm Mandy came in to tell us that the preliminary results were negative for cancer and final results would be back in a couple of days. Jacob had cleared this hurdle. There was a very good chance that the cancer would not respond to this last treatment, so even though the cancer should respond to chemotherapy, he has shown that the opposite is not only possible, but probable. There was no sense of joy in the room. It was mostly just a sense of relief. We all know that the challenge ahead of him now is to stay in remission for the next two weeks while he is not receiving chemo. So while today's news is fantastic it is tempered by the fact that a much larger obstacle awaits in two weeks. We will embrace this good news and enjoy this time as much as possible focusing our energy on staying positive and praying for another good result after the next biopsy.

Day 256, Thursday, October 13, 2011

This morning Jacob seemed fine until our visit with Dr. Gordon and Mandy. During our visit he had some sort of mental episode. Dr. Gordon was explaining that he would be getting another biopsy in approximately two weeks and would be tentatively scheduled for admission for his stem cell transplant on November 3. Jacob seemed to get very confused and almost panicky. He was lying in his bed trying to enter the dates into his cell phone and kept mentioning dates that were not even close to what we were discussing. He has behaved in a similar way in the past. Sometimes he tries to process too much information and he gets overloaded and confused and begins to get physically hyperactive, but this time was different. After we would explain it to him again he would say, "I got it, I got it, I got it" and keep typing on his phone. Then he would tell us what he was entering and it wasn't even close. At one point he stated that one of the procedures would be starting at 9:00am and no one had ever mentioned an appointment time. We weren't even certain on dates let alone times.

Dr. Gordon and Mandy then stepped out of the room and I followed them. They are concerned that something else might be going on in Jacob's brain. Two weeks ago when he was admitted for this latest round of chemotherapy he had a similar incident with Dr. Beck. That time he was having short term memory lapses along with slurred speech and his eyes were rolling back in his head. At that time we blamed it on the steroids and high blood sugar. This time we thought it was probably due to steroids and lack of sleep, but they were not willing to dismiss it that easily, so they ordered an MRI. The happiness that we felt about the clean biopsy was now tempered by the fear of a possible brain tumor.

Jacob got the MRI around 12:30pm and later that afternoon we were told that it showed nothing out of the ordinary. Again, we are not overjoyed as much as relieved. It's like Mike Larson told me early in this journey. Never let yourself get too high and never let yourself get too low.

Day 259, Sunday, October 16, 2011

Today was the Conference Championship against Crete for my youth football team. Jacob told me a couple days ago that he wanted me at the game. He wants a League Championship and he thinks my presence will help, so last night I drove home, did some paperwork for a couple of hours and then watched TV with Jerod and Dalton until around midnight.

Since I have not been at practice all week, I decided to sit up in the press box during the game and communicate with my assistant coaches using our headsets. I didn't want to change the way the team had prepared all week. I was not around when they prepared for this game and I did not tell anyone that I would be in attendance because everything changes with Jacob so fluidly. My assistants have done a great job with the kids in my absence and I do not want to undermine what they have accomplished or how they have prepared. Jerod and Dalton sat with me in the spot where Jacob would normally be. We beat Crete 30-20 and will play for the League Championship in one week. I was texting updates to Jacob the entire game.

Day 260, Monday, October 17, 2011

Shari and I went to our room around 10:00pm so that Jacob could go to sleep. He called me at 12:15am saying that he couldn't sleep and he was afraid that the Lymphoma had come back. Then he asked me to stay with him in his room. He was very anxious and scared when I got to his room. He told me that he was having some difficulty breathing again. His breathing problems are caused by congestion as a result of his infections. He has a Rhinovirus infection which is causing some Sinusitis. His sinuses are swollen and causing him to have difficulty breathing. It has nothing to do with his lymphoma, but the steroids are probably adding to his paranoia. The lymphoma caused difficulty breathing by restricting his trachea, not by restricting his sinuses. I tried to calm him down and reason with him and he did relax and was asleep before 1:00am.

Day 262, Wednesday, October 19, 2011

Jacob weighed 134lbs this morning as he continues to battle a low grade fever. He has been hovering around 101 degrees since Sunday night. When Dr. Harper stopped in on rounds today, he thought that Jacob's port might be infected. The site is red and slightly swollen and a little tender to the touch. They will monitor the site today and take blood cultures from his port to find out if it is infected and what type of infection.

Shari left for home around 2:15pm today. We agreed that if she was going to get a break she would need to do it while he was admitted instead of out-patient. She is the one who gives him all of his meds including the antibiotic, insulin and Neupogen shots. Since September 26 she has only been home one day. 22 out of the last 23 days she has been with Jacob in the Hospital. She needs to see her other boys.

At 9:30pm the Resident stopped by to look at Jacob's port. She said that the affected area appeared to be smaller than it was earlier. Dr. Harper had drawn some lines around it this morning so that they could accurately track the size and shape of the redness. This evening it appeared to have retracted from its earlier boundaries.

At 10:00pm tonight Jacob's fever spiked to 103.3. Since they have already drawn blood for the cultures, they just gave him some Tylenol and will wait until the results come back before proceeding with any new antibiotics.

At 11:20pm his temperature was 99.1 degrees. When the Tech came in, Jacob was asleep but sweating profusely on top of his covers. She immediately thought that his fever had finally broken. We'll see what happens in the morning.

Jacob's weight loss has been staggering. This once chiseled young athlete has always been out of place in this new environment. He did not look like the typical cancer patient. He may have lost his hair and his face may have gotten puffy but he had always kept his weight up. Even though his muscle definition and mass may have changed, you really couldn't tell much difference in his overall outward appearance. In the last four weeks that has changed. His once powerful legs are now literally just skin and bone. His knees are bigger in circumference than his thighs. He was always very proud of his "squatters butt". To most athletes this is a sign of explosiveness and power. He was proud of the stretch marks on his butt and his thighs—they were a badge of honor earned by many hours of concentrated effort in the weight room.

When he was in 8th grade he decided that he wanted to try for the school record in the squat in the 123lb weight class. The previous record was around 180lbs. and he knew that he could break it. The only problem was that he weighed 135lbs. Shari and I did not like the idea of him forcing himself to lose 12lbs at his age. He really didn't have that weight to lose. After much deliberation and seeing how much it meant to him, we decided to let him try it, but we would have to monitor how he lost the weight. The weekend before the testing he basically ate nothing but jello to try to lose the final few pounds and on Monday morning he had made it to 123. That morning he broke the school record and later that afternoon a sophomore re-broke Jacob's new record. Jacob then went in after school and broke the record set by the sophomore. The next morning the sophomore broke Jacob's record again and the testing was over. He did not end up with the school record, but he did break it twice and was only bested by a kid that was two years older. He found little solace in that fact. To him he had failed. Nothing but the best has ever satisfied him, and even when he is the best he wonders if he just overachieved.

His thighs were also massive. He understood that to play football, especially if you are undersized, you had to be powerful from the waist down. I have seen too many "athletes" that just concentrate on their upper body strength and neglect their lower body. Most sports are actually played from the waist down. The upper body completes the task, but the lower body puts you in position to be successful. Jacob understood this fact and worked diligently on what really mattered. People also commented on the size of his calves. He has done countless ankle raises on our stair case at home developing those calf muscles. Now there is basically nothing left. As he stands next to his bed doing his Physical Therapy exercises it's hard to watch him struggle with these simple exercises.

He holds on to the wall as he steps up onto a step stool. His hands shake with each repetition and his legs start to quiver as he nears the equivalent of one flight of stairs. When he gets done he is completely wiped out and falls asleep quickly once he climbs back into bed.

His upper body has also dwindled to nothing. Jacob never spent a lot of time sculpting his upper body. Every lift he did was for practical purposes. A lot of guys will only do certain lifts because it will make them look better at the pool or on the beach, but Jacob's sole purpose for lifting was to create strength and power that would be utilized on the football field. We have gone back into our stacks of pictures at home and found a few pictures of Jacob before he got sick. His shoulders were broad, he had the "V" look to his torso that every man strives to achieve. Now he is frail-looking and weak. He looks like the stereotypical cancer patient that you can all picture in your mind. He looks like everyone else at the Treatment Center. I don't grieve for this loss because all of that pales in comparison to his survival. I feel badly for Jacob as I know that he sees what his body has become, but I will never spend one second wishing that he would return to his former stature. If he wins this battle he will have proven that his mind and spirit are far stronger than his muscular body ever was.

He can rebuild his body, but he has to win this fight first.

Day 263, Thursday, October 20, 2011

This morning Jacob's fever has gotten better. He was around 101 degrees all night, but has gone down to about 99 degrees this morning. A surgeon came in to look at his port and stated that they would probably have to remove it in order to cure the infection around it. Dr. Harper came in afterward and stated that he thought it looked better than it did yesterday and he suggested that we wait until tomorrow morning to re-evaluate. The surgeons are going to reserve the OR for noon tomorrow just in case. Infectious Disease will also be stopping in to assess the situation. For now, they will increase his Vancomycin and possibly add another antibiotic. Ultimately, Jacob needs to clear this infection and his counts will need to rebound before they will proceed with the transplant. The bone marrow biopsy is still planned for mid-week next week and he is now scheduled for admission on November 4 to begin radiation in preparation for the transplant. We have two weeks to get rid of any infection and get his counts up. The clock is ticking.

Infectious Disease thinks that his port might be infected, but it might not be. They have ordered another CT scan to determine if there is any sign of infection internally. Jacob had the CT scan done at 4:45pm. Anesthesia came in around 5:30pm to gather all of their pre-procedure information. Dr. Harper came in at 6:45pm to tell us that there was a small amount of fluid around his port, but nothing dramatic. However, they did find some nodules on Jacob's lungs that might be another infection. We will proceed tonight as planning on him having the port removed tomorrow, but if he stays the same or improves overnight they will leave the port in for the weekend to give the new antibiotics time to work. If he is worse tomorrow morning they will have to remove his port and take our chances with an open wound and no white blood cells to fight site infection. Tomorrow will be a nerve wracking day. Tonight we pray for the new antibiotics to work and eradicate this new infection in his lungs.

Earlier tonight I ordered Jacob's supper—mashed potatoes with gravy, some bacon, cottage cheese and Ensure to drink. He sat at the edge of his bed and tried to take a spoonful of potatoes and said, "I can't, I'm too bloated." I reminded him that he had gained a pound yesterday and if he didn't eat he would lose that pound that he worked for. His chin dropped to his chest and he fought back the tears and said, "I'm trying to do everything I can, but…" he choked back the words. He has tried so hard to do everything right and yet he can't get ahead of this disease. I see his will starting to fade along with his body and it scares me to death. How much more must he endure? Will he ever get to the transplant? We were eight days away from the transplant when the leukemia popped up. We made it through the last bone marrow biopsy only to be re-admitted with an infection. Now the next bone marrow biopsy is in question because of this infection and if things don't clear up in the next fifteen days they will have to postpone the transplant again. We are in the 11th hour and desperately need things to turn in his favor soon.

We had another talk about God tonight. He met with the psychologist this afternoon and was excited to get a chance to talk with him. Jacob never tells us what they talk about and we don't ask. Today he did tell me that he asked the psychologist about his belief in God and the psychologist said that he wasn't comfortable talking about that. He told Jacob that he would refer him to a chaplain for help with that subject. Jacob and I spoke about having faith in

God and what it takes to get into Heaven. At one point Jacob told me that he did not feel that he had done enough to earn a place in Heaven. I explained to him that one only has to accept Jesus Christ as your Savior and ask for the forgiveness of your sins. There are no other requirements. I also asked him what would change in his life if he accepted Christ. What would he do differently? He agreed that it would not require any radical changes in behavior or lifestyle, just faith. He has come a long way on his spiritual journey and he has helped me recapture my belief in God. At some point you have to admit that one can only do so much, and that ultimately his fate, as well as ours, is in God's hands.

Tonight Jacob listened to the "Soundslide" from after the Hastings game last Friday night. During the interview, Coach Huebert was asked what "JP3" meant to the team and Coach talked about how the team is motivated by Jacobs's perseverance and attitude. We all know that the team is thinking about Jacob, but it was nice to hear the coach talk about him. We feel so isolated and distant. Everyone has heard the cliché, "life goes on," but when it is going on without you and you are aware of what you are missing, it seems cruel. This relatively small item changed Jacob's demeanor completely. He has been depressed and fatigued all day—the lowest I have ever seen him. Shortly after hearing the Soundslide, I left to use the restroom and when I returned he was sitting on a chair in his room. His feet were tapping on the floor and he was planning how he would take in more calories tomorrow, gain weight, and get stronger. He kept repeating, "I can do this, I can do this." His adrenaline was pumping. I think it was because for the first time this year he has been recognized as part of this team outside of the locker room. He missed the team picture and was listed as such in the paper. He will not appear in the school yearbook picture of the team. He has only been able to attend three games out of eight so far this year and he hasn't been to practice in a month or more. Seeing his teammates with "JP3" written on the tape around their wrists, or seeing someone wearing one of his rubber wristbands let him visually confirm what he has heard so many times—that people are thinking and praying for him. In my opinion, though, hearing his coach say a few words about what Jacob means to the team and seeing a picture of himself standing on the sidelines at the McCook game really meant the most to Jacob. He could see and hear himself being included and discussed as an important part of the team. Coach Randy Huebert and the owner of the local newspaper, Kurt Johnson, will probably never comprehend what an impact their efforts made on Jacob tonight. I will contact them both when we get home to convey our appreciation, but words will never do justice to the change that I saw in my son tonight. If things start to swing in our favor over the next few days, I think we can point to this moment as the turning point. I hope that we can.

DAY 264, FRIDAY, OCTOBER 21, 2011

The decision has been made to leave his port in over the weekend and re-assess his condition Monday morning. This is a relief to all of us. I just didn't see what the benefits would be by taking it out today. The new antibiotics have not even been running for 24 hours and one of the doctors said that it usually takes 24-48 hours before they would see any results. With absolutely no immune system, cutting him open seemed like an unnecessary risk today. If the infection does not improve over the weekend, then the port will need to be removed. The doctors also believe that the nodules found on his lung are pneumonia. They will monitor him day-by-day to see how that situation progresses.

At 2:00pm Dr. Law came in specifically to let Jacob know that his ANC was 200 and his white blood cells were at .5. This is the first time this month that his counts have started to rebound. Everything that needs to happen in the next two weeks leading up to, and including, the stem cell transplant hinge upon these numbers rising as his immune system returns. Jacob was very excited to get this news. He pumped his fist a few times and smiled from ear to ear. He needed some good news and he got it.

The plan today was to get Jacob to drink as much "Ensure" and "Super Shakes" as he could to get some calories into his system. He weighed 134lbs. this morning, so he did lose the weight that he had gained the day before. For lunch we ordered two chocolate Ensures and one chocolate Super Shake which added up to 1,200 calories. By the end of the day we had gotten approximately 2,000 calories into his body and we hope to see a small weight gain tomorrow. Eating solid food has gotten more difficult because he is suffering from constipation and bloating from the IV fluids. After his disappointment with the mashed potatoes last night we decided to just try to push the high calorie liquids today. We will see how it worked tomorrow morning.

Shari got back to Omaha around 4:30pm. We spent a quiet evening in Jacob's room listening to the Aurora football game.

Around 11:45pm Jacob asked me if I would say a prayer. I was stunned for a moment as he has never asked me to do this before. I agreed and said a short prayer thanking God for the doctor's decision to wait on removing his port. I thanked God for Jacob's immune system improving today. I thanked him for the time we have together now and to give his brothers and grandparents strength to get through this process also. When I finished I asked, "Was that OK?" He said yes, but that I forgot to ask for forgiveness of my sins. I told him that you don't have to ask for forgiveness every day. If you are living your life the right way you shouldn't have to ask for forgiveness all the time. Even after all of our talks he was still not clear on what was expected of him. I also told him that it doesn't hurt to ask for forgiveness, but if you are continuing to sin and then continually asking for forgiveness, then you haven't truly committed yourself to God. Jacob also said that I thanked God more than he does when he prays. He said that he says please a lot more than I did. My response was that if someone is always asking you for something and never shows appreciation, how willing are you to continue to give? We had a good day today so it's only right to thank God for the blessings that we did receive today. Appreciate the small victories and be thankful for them. We have had enough setbacks and disappointments. We must appreciate the good things when they happen.

Day 265, Saturday, October 22, 2011

(133.5lbs) All three sets of doctors made their rounds this morning and were pleased with what they saw from Jacob. His overall appearance is better, the redness around his port is lighter, his temperatures are going down and his counts continue to rise. Everything was going so well that Dr. Harper ordered that his port be de-accessed today. His port has been accessed since sometime in August. He has been on IV fluids almost continuously for two months. His port site has been irritated for the past few weeks because it has been accessed for so long. We were all glad to hear that the needle would be out of his chest at least for a few days and all medications and fluids would be given by the peripheral IV in his left arm.

As with everything else in this process, though, there were complications. When the nurse removed the needle, the site was extremely red and oozing puss. We learned that your body cannot create puss unless you have Neutrophils. Neutrophils are part of your immune system and they are one component of the blood counts that we were excited to see rising. However, as that count rises so does the amount of puss at the infection site. Our nurse called all of the doctors and they all came back in this morning to re-assess. They all agreed that the port would need to be removed very soon in order to cure this infection. The bacteria that is causing this infection sticks to any foreign matter in your body. The port is made of plastic and it is impossible to kill all of the bacteria attached to the port, so it must be removed. Jacob will undergo surgery tomorrow morning to have it removed. We are disappointed that the antibiotics did not work, but we are happy that they waited a couple of days before cutting him open. When they were first discussing the removal of his port he had no immune system, so the wound would take longer to heal and pose a higher risk of another infection. Now his counts are rebounding nicely and his body will heal better and be more resistant to another infection. His ANC was 700 this morning, up from 200 yesterday and his white blood cell count was 1.0, up from .5 yesterday. By the time he has surgery tomorrow, those should both increase substantially.

We watched the Nebraska – Minnesota game and then went for a short walk for the first time in a long while. We didn't go very far, we just stayed in the hallway walking from one end to the other. When we got done Jacob sat on the side of his bed and said, "129." I said, "What do you mean?" He said, "That was 129 steps." He was counting his steps as we went for our walk. He now has a new benchmark to beat. I wrote "129" on the white board in his room so that he could have a visible goal to work toward. The kid who could not get winded at track practice 18 months ago is now counting his short wobbly steps down the hallway of the Pediatric Unit.

Paul Nauman and Gregg Kremer stopped in for a visit around 6:00pm. Jacob has been looking forward to this visit for quite some time. We all sat together and had a nice visit and shared some of our spiritual experiences and conversations. Jacob has come a long way in his belief in God, but he still struggles with the concept of salvation. After about an hour Shari and I excused ourselves from the room so that he could ask Paul and Gregg any questions that he might not be comfortable asking in front of his parents. Paul and Gregg left around 8:00pm and told us that they would be honored to continue to walk this path with Jacob.

DAY 266, SUNDAY, OCTOBER 23, 2011

Jacob had his port removed this morning. Everything went well. He slept most of the morning and early afternoon. My youth football team is playing in the League Championship today and Jacob told me that he wanted me to be there. This team dedicated their season to Jacob at the very first practice and today they won the League Championship game 6-0 to go undefeated this season. I told the team after the game that what they had done this year was special far beyond just winning seven football games. It is extremely rare when a season is dedicated to someone and then that team goes on to be an undefeated champion. I told them how proud I was that they persevered through my absence and overcame their own adversity to achieve their goal. This has been a season that I will certainly never forget.

Day 267, Monday, October 24, 2011

Everyone came in this morning to inform us that cultures from Jacob's port were positive for bacteria. We already knew there was an obvious infection, but now they can target it with antibiotics. Jacob's counts continue to rise and he feels better. His next bone marrow biopsy is now officially scheduled for tomorrow. He is excited that his last Neupogen shot will be today.

For the first time we said a prayer out loud together before Shari left for the room at the Nebraska House. We have done everything we can to get to this point. The future is in God's hands.

Day 268, Tuesday, October 25, 2011

Jacob left his room at 7:40am for this latest bone marrow biopsy. He will also have a PICC line inserted in his arm to replace the port that was removed. He got back to his room shortly after 10:00am.

Today is another "Mr. Clean" day at Aurora High School—October 12 was the first. Mr. Clean day is when students wear white T-shirts to school to try and look like Mr. Clean. We have posted on Jacob's Care Page that if his bone marrow biopsies were "clean" then we could proceed with the next step in the treatment. So, the kids in Aurora decided to have a "Mr. Clean Day" every time Jacob had another bone marrow biopsy. This was their way of showing support and hoping for a "clean" result.

DAY 269, WEDNESDAY, OCTOBER 26, 2011

We waited in Jacob's room all day for any news regarding yesterday's bone marrow biopsy. Dr. Law stopped in early to check on Jacob and said that Dr. Beck or Dr. Gordon would be in later. Dr. Beck came and visited in the morning, but had no information. Infectious Disease stopped by to update us on

Jacob's infections, but knew nothing about the biopsy. Mandy came in around 3:00pm to give Jacob an invitation to a party in November, but had no information. Finally at 5:15pm Dr. Gordon arrived at Jacob's room. For the past two days I have been anticipating this moment and now that Dr. Gordon is here, I want him to go away. My hands started to sweat and I could feel my heart begin to race as he walked into the room. It was my belief that the reason the results have taken so long was because they were bad and Dr. Gordon was conferring with more colleagues on where we go from here. We have received results from the last couple of bone marrow biopsies the same day. This delay has caused concern. The other cause for concern was who would be giving us the news. Good news has been delivered by other doctors or Mandy, but bad news has always been delivered by Dr. Gordon. In my mind, if someone else was coming in to tell us, that meant the results were good, but if we had to wait for Dr. Gordon then that meant the results were bad. It's amazing what goes through one's mind when given enough time to think.

In the end the results were good. Dr. Gordon was extremely encouraged by what was not found. He said that there were a few lymphoma cells in his blood and some small clusters of leukemia in his bone marrow, but if final results confirm this tomorrow, he will move forward with the transplant next Friday. Adding to the good news was the fact that he is now scheduled to be released tomorrow. This time we get to go home, not the Nebraska House. So, not only are we thrilled with the good news about the biopsy, we are also thrilled to be going home. Jacob has only been home for 1½ days in the past month.

Final results should be available sometime tomorrow afternoon and Dr. Gordon said he would call us when they are complete. The worst case scenario right now is that Jacob would have to go through one more round of this same chemotherapy if they find more cancer cells in the final results. This protocol obviously worked and worked well, so if there are a few stubborn cells left over then one more round should take care of them. After what Jacob has had to endure this past month none of us want to go through that again, but if we have to do it to get him cured then that is what we will do. It has been an agonizing month, but it will all be worth it when he is cured.

DAY 270, THURSDAY, OCTOBER 27, 2011

We found out this afternoon that the final results of the bone marrow biopsy were essentially the same as the preliminary results. Mandy found out and sprinted upstairs to make sure that she caught us before Jacob was released. We anxiously awaited the final documentation and were finally released around 4:30pm. The ride home and the rest of the evening were thankfully uneventful. I did notice that Jacob stayed awake the entire ride home. He usually sleeps the whole time, but this time he was looking out of the window and commenting on things as we drove by. I think he was soaking it all in after basically being locked down for the past month.

Jacob will be sleeping in the master bedroom while he is at home until transplant. We decided that we wanted him upstairs so that we can keep an eye on him in order to avoid another life flight scenario. Shari and I will sleep in the living room on the futon mattress and use Jacob's bathroom in the basement, a small inconvenience to be a whole family again.

Eleven

FIVE DAYS
AT HOME

Day 271, Friday. October 28, 2011

Unpacking and getting organized were the main items on the agenda today. I went to the office for a while and met with my banker to discuss liquidating the company's assets. I also picked up the mail and found a couple of letters from attorneys demanding payment on various items. I also went to the Sheriff's office to pick up a summons to appear in Civil Court from another subcontractor that I owe. My next critical step will be to find legal representation for the impending bankruptcy.

At 6:30pm we left for the Aurora football game against Norris. This is the first round of the playoffs and first game that Jacob will attend in the past seven weeks. He has missed the last six games and is eager to be back on the sidelines.

We arrived just before the players ran onto the field and the plan was for Jacob to stay at the back of the pack and walk out following everyone else. Last year Jacob was always the last one to run onto the field. I'm not sure why he did this, but he must have had his reasons and he never changes tradition. I walked onto the field to videotape Jacob as he stepped back onto the playing field for the first time in almost two months. There was a substantial delay after the last player ran onto the field. Jacob had tried to jog behind the others and tripped. I did not know this until much later. I thought he was just walking really slowly. His friend Bryce told me that Jacob had tried to start jogging and immediately fell to the ground. He looked up at Bryce and said, "I can't run." Bryce helped him to his feet and they walked onto the field together. This is just another example of him trying to push himself further than expectations. A week ago he could barely walk. We were literally counting steps as he walked down the hall. Now he was trying to jog on an uneven surface. Luckily he didn't damage his PICC line or tear open his port site. He walked to the sidelines, encouraged a couple of his teammates then sat in the wheelchair for the rest of the game. Shari and I stayed with him and I pushed him back and forth down the sideline so that he could have the best vantage point. Three of Aurora's touchdowns happened right in front of him. Aurora won a thriller 40-31 and Jacob was given the game ball by his teammates. It was a perfect night.

After every game the team meets in the east endzone. I wheeled Jacob over to the spot and his teammates gathered around him after they got done shaking hands. It was an emotional sight to see him sitting in a wheelchair all bundled up and not able to physically interact with his "brothers". The entire team surrounded Jacob as they listened to their coach address the team. Coach Huebert talked about playing "Aurora Football" and how he was proud of the boys for playing hard and never giving up. The tradition after the game is for the coach and the players to shout out something, or someone, who deserves three cheers. The team then yells, "hooray, hooray, hooray". Coach Huebert announced that there was a special guest with them tonight, and asked for "three cheers for Jacob Peters". We expected this to happen, but it did not make it any less emotional. Every week Coach Huebert has a key word that they emphasize. This week the word was "gratitude". I like that.

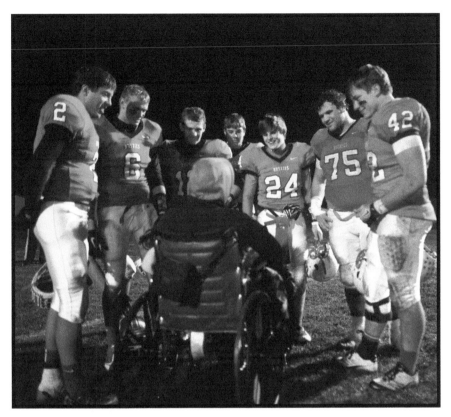

During this whole time there were reporters milling around taking pictures and video. They could all see that obviously there was something wrong with Jacob because of the wheelchair and the mask, but they didn't know his story. After the team meeting one of the photographers came over to Shari and I to ask about Jacob's situation. I tried to say the words, but instead I broke down. The emotions of the past month boiled over and I found it almost impossible to form the words, "he has cancer". Shari spoke to him for a short time while I tried to collect my composure. Meanwhile, some of Jacob's classmates came over to give me a hug and asked if they could wheel him off the field. I hugged them all and used this time to gather my thoughts. The reporter was from the Lincoln Journal-Star and as I pulled myself together I managed to briefly summarize his story. The reporter asked us if it would be OK to do a story about Jacob. Shari and I both said that would be Jacob's decision. Early in this journey the local newspaper had asked to do a story about him and his response was, "I don't want to be known for this". So we deferred to Jacob and the reporter said he would give us the weekend to think about it and someone would call us on Monday. My feeling is that now might be the appropriate time to tell his story. I'm not sure why I feel that way, but that is my gut instinct. We'll see what Jacob decides this weekend.

DAY 272, SATURDAY, OCTOBER 29, 2011

A perfectly quiet day at home. Jacob went to the hospital for labs at 10:30am and then spent the afternoon lying on the loveseat in the living room upstairs watching Nebraska play Michigan State and then took a nap. His lab results were all good and we thoroughly enjoy being home.

A seemingly constant reminder of the cruelty of Jacob's situation is the ESPN series "Year of the Quarterback". This program is a series of widely varying topics with one central theme—Quarterbacks. The following is a description of the program pulled from ESPN's website:

> *The Year of the Quarterback: The Kickoff*, a one-hour show previewing ESPN's year-long examination into the lives and careers of quarterbacks from high school to the NFL, will air Tuesday, Dec. 14, at 10 p.m. on ESPN. Written and hosted by Chris Connelly, the special will introduce the *Year of the Quarterback* (YQB) and its goal to provide an in-depth exploration into one of the most storied, analyzed, and discussed positions in sports. The special will include an unprecedented "quarterback roundtable" drawn from ESPN's own stable of experts, including Super Bowl-winning head coach **Jon Gruden**, former NFL Player of the Year **Ron Jaworski** and Super Bowl champion and Pro Football Hall of Fame quarterback **Steve Young**, as well as current and former NFL quarterbacks **John Elway**, **Troy Aikman**, **Joe Namath**, **Aaron Rogers** and **Vince Young**. The roundtable is designed to delve into America's obsession with the quarterback: the mystique behind the position, the level of athleticism, and the pop culture aspect of quarterback "celebrity status." The special will also include first-person accounts from the "blue chip" high school recruit, the Heisman hopeful and the NFL legend.

Jacob and I watched the first show in the series call "The Kick-off" back in December and now there is a new episode in the series airing every month. I do not know if Jacob has watched any of these episodes. I know we have not watched them together, but I have personally seen bits and pieces of a couple shows. I have found that I can only watch small portions before my emotions overtake my interest and I break down crying. How ironic is it that my son the quarterback is diagnosed with cancer in the same year that ESPN has dedicated an entire season of programming celebrating the quarterback.

We are still maintaining focus on beating this disease and working toward completing a full recovery and athletic comeback, but the reality is that he is missing a great deal of his opportunity for development right now. At times it seems cruel that this highly promoted series is unfolding right before his eyes, yet he is segregated from feeling like a part of the legacy being promoted. It would be different if he wasn't confined to the house or a hospital room so often with few other entertainment options available to him. He loves watching ESPN and this show is promoted heavily most days, so he cannot escape the images. Jacob has not even hinted that this has bothered him, but I know that under normal circumstances we would have watched every episode together and probably each episode more than once. We have not even spoken about the series since that first episode was broadcast, which tells me that it bothers him and he wants to avoid the topic and avoid the pain of the emotions.

Day 273, Sunday, October 30, 2011

Today we officially celebrated Jacob's 17th birthday. One month ago we all got together at the hospital, but today we are having the traditional gathering. My mom and dad came over for lunch and brought Jacob's favorite meal, verenike with sour cream gravy and homemade birthday cake. After lunch Shari's mom and dad came over for cake and ice cream just like we have done for the past 16 birthdays.

This evening Jacob started reading Tim Tebow's book, "Through my eyes". He found a paragraph that he really likes. *All those drills, in addition to physical conditioning, were also great psychological and confidence conditioners for us as a team, even for the guy who ended up in the bathroom stall. Because for the next four years, whenever we took the field, we knew that our opponent hadn't gone through anything at all similar to what we had. Coach Mick's mind-set dovetailed perfectly with my mantra: Somewhere he is out there, training while I am not. One day when we meet, he will win."*

He also told us tonight that he does not want to be interviewed for the Lincoln Journal-Star. He wants to be known for his accomplishments, not his ailments.

Day 275, Tuesday, November 1, 2011

Jacob needed a platelet transfusion today in Grand Island. This process usually does not take that long but today it took a total of six hours. The orders had not gotten through to the medical personnel in Grand Island so Shari and Jacob spent most of the day sitting and waiting for the transfusion to begin. Of course Jacob was frustrated because we are returning to Omaha tomorrow and he wants to enjoy this day at home, not sitting in another hospital. Once they returned from Grand Island, his PICC line would not flush properly, so he had to go to the hospital in Aurora to have it cleared and flushed. At one point Jacob even told Shari that everything that was going wrong today was a bad omen for test results tomorrow in Omaha.

Regardless of the frustrations of the day, being at home for the past five days has been no less than fantastic.

We had another talk about God tonight.

Twelve

4TH DOWN

DAY 276, WEDNESDAY, NOVEMBER 2, 2011

We left for Omaha shortly before 5:00am. Jacob's schedule for the day was:

    7:00am PET scan
    9:30am Clinic appointment with Dr. Gordon
    10:30am Spinal Tap
    1:15pm CT scan

The day was scheduled to end with a final consultation with Dr. Gordon prior to transplant. However, we found out today that the lymphoma in Jacob's neck and chest have grown again. The transplant has been postponed for at least three weeks.

It was around 2:30pm when Dr. Gordon came into the room and immediately stated that Jacob's scans today were "disappointing". All the air left the room with that one word. There was no audible response from Jacob, Shari, or myself. We were all just devastated. We were literally less than 48 hours away from starting the transplant process and now he will have to endure another round of the same chemotherapy that he endured one month ago. None of us were emotional this time. I think tears were replaced by frustration and despair. I felt completely hollow. In the past I have felt pain, anger, and nausea, but this time hollow is the best definition. We are so close to getting the transplant and so many things fell in line just in the nick of time that maybe I felt that we were destined to get the transplant this time and that nothing could set us back now. It's amazing that I could feel so positive about the process at this point when I had concerns in the back of my mind just yesterday about Jacob's current

183

condition. He has developed a slight cough over the past couple of days and his voice has gotten more gravelly. It was concerning to me, but I know that I was denying that it could be a problem. My mind has been in so many places these past few months that I have developed a way to believe in a positive outcome while plainly observing an obvious symptom to the contrary. I wanted to believe so badly that today would be a good day that I minimized the reality. The reality was that he was showing signs of breathing difficulty again and I wanted to dismiss it as a cough due to unrelated circumstances.

This will certainly have an effect on Jacob's faith in God also. I believe that he had turned the corner a couple of weeks ago. Paul and Gregg were encouraged by their last conversation with Jacob and I too felt that he had reached a point of belief and security in his faith. Now this setback. After all that he has been through and to make a commitment to believe in God, to have this news so close to the goal of reaching transplant is monumental.

We know what to expect from the chemotherapy over the next eight days and it won't be pleasant. However, he knows that he has been through it before and can endure it again. What is the most concerning is the chance for infections again. He will definitely become neutropenic again and be just as susceptible to the same infections as he had the last time. This is what has us all concerned the most. The plan will probably be to release him to the Nebraska House in the Lied Center once the chemotherapy is complete. I don't believe that anyone would be comfortable sending him home after what happened the last time.

As we spoke with Dr. Gordon we all believe that in an ideal situation we should have gone to transplant a week earlier. The plan this time is to finish the chemotherapy as planned and then if we get similar results we will move straight to transplant. Hopefully this will be in about three weeks. Jacob has shown that he cannot stay in remission for long so if this has any chance to work we need to strike as soon as he gets in remission again. I stated these concerns to Dr. Gordon when we started the last round of chemo. He said that the transplant will only work if Jacob is in a good, solid remission. My argument was that he has been in remission before, but does not stay in remission for long so we need to move quickly once he reaches remission. I know that the standard protocol has to be followed and that ideally he would get another round of chemotherapy after he gets into remission to ensure that the remission is solid. My opinion, though, is that knowing his past history of relapse, we should move quickly to transplant to try and stay ahead of the relapse which was certain to come. I hope that the cancer has not become too resistant to the drugs at this point. We are now all on the same page moving forward. The goal is to get him into remission, get a negative bone marrow biopsy, CT scan, PET scan, and spinal tap, then move forward with the transplant protocol. No more waiting to see if he stays in remission—it's obvious to everyone now that he won't.

Day 277, Thursday, November 3, 2011

Today was a quiet day. At 2:00pm the nurse brought in his first dose of steroids to start this round of chemotherapy. It was a surreal moment watching him hold those pills in his hand now knowing what to expect over the next few weeks. Jacob paused for a moment and stared silently at the pills in his hand before putting them in his mouth. He knows what's coming and I think he wanted to take a breath and gather himself first. At 3:00pm the nurse hung the first bag of chemo and we were officially back in the grind. At 4:00pm he spiked a fever of 101.5 which stayed until approximately 10:00pm. Jacob was shocked at the initial reading because he felt fine and couldn't even tell that he had a fever. The nurse drew some labs for blood cultures and we will now begin another 24-48 hour wait to see if he has another infection. We are hoping that the fever is just a side effect of the first chemotherapy drug.

Day 278, Friday, November 4, 2011

Jacob was scheduled to have surgery today to place the new port/catheter in his chest that he will need for the stem cell transplant. They came to take him down to the operating room shortly after 8:00am. Shortly after 9:00am the nurse came in to tell us the procedure had been cancelled because his "lab results were off". Mandy came in after we got back to Jacob's room to let us know that the surgeon called off the procedure because of Jacob's fever. However, Jacob has not had a fever since 10:00pm last night, so she was confused as to why they would cancel the procedure. His counts have already begun to drop and they cannot do this procedure once he is neutropenic again. If they wait until his counts come back it might be too late. We are hoping to go to transplant before his counts completely recover this time so that we don't run into the same problem that we just had. We asked if they would reschedule for Monday and Mandy said that his counts would probably be too low by then. He needs to have this procedure done sooner rather than later.

The decision was made that surgery would be delayed until 7:30am Monday if he does not have a fever between now and then. The chemo fog has already set in. Jacob is groggy and his speech has become mumbled again. Concentration is again an issue and we have told him that he will only get to use his phone or his computer, but not both at the same time. It seems that the further into the fog he goes, the more he uses his electronics. This leads to him being distracted from what is going on around him. In an ideal world this would be a good thing, however, when the medical staff is asking him questions and he either does not answer or gets confused, that leads to more concerns. We will monitor his usage this time and try to avoid the mental "episodes" that he had the last time.

The Aurora football team lost its quarterfinal game to Crete tonight 14-13. Aurora held the lead with less than four minutes to play when our quarterback fell in the endzone giving Crete two points on the safety. This was eerily similar to last year's semi-final game that was also played in Crete. Last year Aurora held the lead until the last six minutes of that game. This was a heartbreaker for us all. The boys played the best game of the season defensively. They repeatedly turned Crete away at the goal line, but in the end, Crete ran more than twice as many plays as Aurora and most of those plays were run on the Aurora side of the field. It is really hard to beat a great team if they play most of the game on your side of the field. The boys fought hard, never gave up, and held Jacob close to their hearts all season. We are proud of them all and appreciate all of the support they have given to Jacob this season.

At 10:15pm Jacob turned to ask me a question that I knew was coming. "Would I have made a difference in the outcome tonight?" I knew this would be his reaction to the loss. I tried to explain that the team has to play with the players available and that those kinds of questions just serve to tear him apart emotionally. He broke down and cried as hard as I have seen him cry during this entire process. He knows that he would have been a substantial contributor to this team and his tears were not because of the steroids, they were coming from the competitor inside him. We talked for about half an hour on keeping focused on his current goals for treatment while grieving the loss for his team. Shari and I both told him that he needs to cry after the loss tonight because it is perfectly normal to be upset that the season is over. I want him to feel the loss and cry for the seniors, but I also want him to stay focused on keeping his strength in fighting this disease. He asked about when he would be able to start throwing the football again because if he can't throw he won't maximize his usefulness to the team next year. He asked if I thought he was done growing and I told him truthfully that, yes I think he is done growing and he will have to just make the most out of what he has. If he would not have broken down tonight I would have been more worried about his mental state. He cried heavily last year after the semi-final loss to Crete because he felt so bad for the seniors. We stood together at the North end of the field after that game and as he cried he stated, "It wasn't supposed to end this way." This year he was more heavily invested emotionally because he knew he should have been a contributor on the field and he did do a good job of finding a new way to lead his teammates. I'm glad that we were in the room with him when he broke down. He is not thinking straight now that he is back on the steroids and we need to be here whenever he needs to talk.

At 11:00pm he sat up on the side of his bed and started to do PT. This was the warrior in Jacob coming out. In his mind his senior season started tonight when the last buzzer sounded in Crete. When he stood beside the bed to do his leg raises he was extremely unstable and almost fell several times, but Shari and I helped him and he finished his workout at 11:20pm. He then asked me, "How come I handle disappointment by punishing myself physically?" I told him that he wasn't punishing himself by doing his PT, he was improving himself. This goes back to what I mentioned much earlier in this journal about doing push-ups and sit-ups after losing in the conference championship football game when he was in 6th grade. He has never settled for anything less than perfection and it was reassuring to see that attitude again tonight. I didn't tell him, but this was a "normal" reaction for Jacob after a loss. Remember, "normal" is one of the words that we try not to use around him anymore.

Day 279, Saturday, November 5, 2011

Jacob was really wobbly and incoherent this morning. The steroids and chemotherapy are starting to ravage his body again. Not only is he very weak, but the drugs cause Neuropathy in his feet and hands. He loses feeling in the bottom of his feet so the muscles that help stabilize him when he stands don't work correctly and cause him to be unstable. As the day went along he got better mentally and maybe a little bit physically, but he is still not quite right. I limited his access to his phone and computer and it seemed to really help his overall mental awareness. I think he gets over-stimulated when he is using his phone and computer at the same time.

Shari left for home this afternoon, but before she left she went to the grocery store and bought Jacob some snacks that he had asked for. We have to monitor everything he eats to minimize the amount of insulin he will need. When he eats too many carbs he needs a lot of insulin and he complains that the injection site burns when the dosage is too high. We have become quite good at counting carbs and finding foods he can eat without creating more problems.

Day 280, Sunday, November 6, 2011

Shari came back to Omaha this evening. We had another quiet/boring day. We have all agreed that boring days are good. When things are boring that means there has been no bad news. It seems like the only times that things aren't boring are times that we have gotten bad news. We have learned to adapt to the daily monotony and grind of this round of chemo. Every three hours someone is coming in to check on Jacob, day and night. He has to be poked multiple times a day to check his blood sugar and adjust for his "meals". Once they count his carb intake, he gets an insulin shot. He also has to have a neupogen shot in his abdomen every day to help his white blood cells return faster. He's been poked so many times that they are now poking his toes to draw blood because his finger tips are so black and blue and full of holes. This is what we now call "boring" days. We know what to expect and we appreciate the lack of "action".

At bed time tonight Jacob told me that he did not need me to stay with him overnight. Usually he asks me to get his Tim Tebow book before he gets ready to go to sleep. Tonight I sat it on the chair next to him so that he could reach it on his own. He reads one chapter every night before he goes to sleep. I was apprehensive about leaving him alone since he is still wobbly and weak, but the nurses said that they would help him if he needed it and he promised to ask for help. Tomorrow he is having surgery and I think he wants to stay up later tonight to text his friends and that's important too.

DAY 281, MONDAY, NOVEMBER 7, 2011

As scheduled, Jacob had a double lumen external catheter implanted in his chest this morning. He now has two small tubes sticking out of his chest to make it easier to administer fluids and medicine. The best part of this is that unlike his port, he will not have a needle puncturing his chest all day every day. This will take the place of his port that was removed and is necessary before we proceed to transplant. Everything went well and he even felt good enough to enjoy Chili's for lunch. He hasn't had "real" food for a while and it was great to watch him eat.

DAY 282, TUESDAY, NOVEMBER 8, 2011

Knowing that we are going to be here for a while I decided that it was time for me to make a trip home for a day. I need to do some more paperwork and tonight Jerod and Dalton had a wrestling meet and I wanted to be there to watch them and support them too. We have been apart so long and I feel terrible that they are having to live their lives this way, but Shari and I need to be where we are. Some day this will all be over and we will be together as a family again. If Jacob can persevere with all that he has lost and all that he is going through, then we can all do the same. Jerod and Dalton are being forced to mature quicker than they should. They understand the gravity of this situation and they are doing a great job.

DAY 283, WEDNESDAY, NOVEMBER 9, 2011

Today I met with an attorney in Lincoln before returning to Omaha. My company will have to file for bankruptcy and I will need representation for the pending and impending lawsuits.

DAY 284, THURSDAY, NOVEMBER 10, 2011

We found out today that the stem cells have already been donated, frozen, and on their way to Omaha so that we would have them when we need them.

Today was the last day of Chemotherapy.

Day 286, Saturday, November 12, 2011

This morning we all went down to a Christmas party sponsored by Aflac. Every year they invite the families of cancer patients for breakfast and gifts at the Med Center. Jacob walked the entire way down to the party which was quite a walk considering we had to change elevators several times and cross a skywalk to get to another building. We listened to the Elkhorn South High School Show Choir sing a few songs, then we were given presents for the entire family including Jerod and Dalton. Jacob opened all of the presents just in case his brothers were given something that he wanted. When it was time to go he asked me to get a wheelchair because he was feeling weak again. I found myself looking around the room at all of the families battling cancer and feeling absolute sadness. As I watched the Show Choir sing and dance all that I could think of was that these kids were Jacob's age and they were getting to do what they love. Maybe this was jealousy taking the place of sadness.

Shari went home this afternoon and Jacob and I spent the rest of the weekend watching football and resting. He walked the halls a few times and did his PT workout at least once a day. We are trying to find foods that are low in carbs so that he does not need such a large correction post-meal. When he gets around 20 units of insulin it burns after injected and if his blood sugar continues to run at high levels, they won't lower his dosage. That is his goal for the weekend. Eat smart and demand that they change his insulin dosage tomorrow.

Day 288, Monday, November 14, 2011

Shari returned after two days at home. We were released to the Lied Center around 4:45pm. The Physical Therapist Jacob had worked with saw him walking out of the PICU and commented on how well he was moving. She actually did not recognize him as he walked by, she thought he was a different patient she had worked with instead of Jacob. The last time she had seen him he could barely stand and I was instructed to hold onto him while he was doing his workout. Jacob was now standing tall and looking confident as he walked all the way to our room at the Lied Center with no problems at all. Once we got to the room Jacob laid down on one of the beds in the room and I hooked up his Playstation. He played for a while and then attempted to eat some supper. He has been bloated all day and is suffering from constipation so eating is difficult at best. He ate one piece of string cheese, drank a Glucerna and went to sleep.

He woke up around midnight complaining about stomach pain and not being able to get comfortable. His pain level was increasing so we called the Oncologist on-call. She suggested that we go to the Emergency Room because there was a possibility that Jacob's pain was being caused by an ulcer.

He was checked out at the Emergency Room and given a low dose of morphine to ease his pain and was taken away for an X-ray of his abdomen. He was given a second and third dose of morphine and still his pain would not subside. He was then admitted back into the hospital.

I leaned over the bed and told Jacob
about the plan to "knock him out"
until the infections had passed and that
when he woke up he would feel better.
He could not respond verbally, but as I
spoke he slowly lifted his right thumb
to acknowledge that he understood
and he was on board with the plan.

Thirteen

IT WASN'T SUPPOSED TO
END THIS WAY

DAY 289, TUESDAY, NOVEMBER 15, 2011

We got to the room in the Pediatric Ward around 3:30am and waited for all of the standard admission protocols. Around 4:45am we had completed everything and I asked Shari if she would stay with Jacob for the rest of the night this time so that I might be able to get some sleep. I also needed to get out of the room because he was in a good deal of pain and could not get comfortable. For whatever reason, this was agitating me more than usual. I don't handle watching kids in pain very well and his discomfort was causing me agony. We agreed that we would rotate time with him, so that at least one of us could get some sleep.

After getting a very restful sleep I returned to the room to find that nothing had really changed. Jacob had been in a large amount of pain the entire time and the laxatives had not done their job yet. What startled me the most is that Shari said that Jacob had vomited while I was away. This was new.

Shari left for the room at the Lied Center around 1:30pm to shower and get cleaned up. Around 2:00pm Jacob got up to use the toilet and I stayed in the room to make sure that he would be safe. When he got up from the toilet he stumbled a bit and said that he had blurred vision. I grabbed him under the arms and ushered him to bed, then I went to get the nurse. His blood pressure was 62/49 and his pulse was racing again. She immediately declared this an emergency and called the medical team in. It did not take long for fourteen people to come sprinting into the room. They immediately started dumping in 1000ml of saline solution to try to bring his pressure back up. A few minutes later he started to improve and they were all satisfied that he was stabilized. The core group of Jacob's doctors stayed outside the room for a while to discuss what had just happened and observe in case it happened again. At 3:15pm it did. This time he could not get off the toilet by himself and he was not making any sense. I pulled up his boxers and grabbed him under the arms again. This time he could not move his feet and I literally dragged him over to his bed. His pressure crashed again and this time most of the medical team was on site when it happened. Once he laid back down and relaxed, his pressure started to stabilize again. Dr. Lowas believed that these crashes were being brought on by the strain of trying to push so hard because of the constipation. We left it at that and hoped that the laxatives would kick in and he would not have to push so hard very soon.

The situation escalated from there.

Around 4:00pm Jacob told me that he needed to use the toilet again, but this time before he even got out of bed he began vomiting. Luckily I grabbed a basin for him to throw up in as he sat on the edge of the bed. He was throwing up a reddish brown liquid that was extremely sticky and stringy. He did not have any food left in his stomach, so I figured it was just bile. When he was finished he fell backwards onto the bed and became completely unresponsive. The medical team once again rushed in and tried to bring him back. His breathing was good and his pulse was still strong, but he would not respond at all. They did the sternum rub and rubbed the bottom of his feet repeatedly while Shari and I held his hand and tried to talk him back. Finally, he responded. For a while it was just squeezing my hand or wiggling his toes, but it was at least a response. Now they are moving him to the PICU.

Once he was moved into the PICU they started him on some antibiotics because he obviously had some kind of infection. By now Jacob was having a hard time communicating. He would move in and out of consciousness and his words were slurred, but he could still communicate if he really tried. An arterial line was placed in his left wrist so that they could continually monitor his blood pressure and draw labs from that line. He was still vomiting occasionally so a tube was inserted through his nose into his stomach to eliminate the vomiting. Of course he gagged when they were installing the line and he vomited more of the same liquid onto his left shoulder and pillow. By now he was wearing a hospital gown and nothing else because he would not be able to get out of bed to use the toilet. He was told that they would clean him up afterward so just let it go whenever he felt it coming. By now this was beyond his comprehension. He had been restrained after the arterial line and stomach tube were installed because he kept trying to pull them out. Every time he started feeling the urge he would try to get up and would say "baaroo". That was as close to "bathroom" as he could get. He would fight it for a bit while Shari and I would try to explain that he was not going to be getting out of bed. Finally after several large bowel movements, he was cleaned up and was fitted with an adult diaper and a catheter. As the evening progressed he was fairly stable except for one more small blood pressure episode that was handled rather quickly. The internist on duty was happy with the way Jacob was progressing and thought that he would be in much better shape by tomorrow morning. Shari went back to the room this time around 2:15am. I stayed in the recliner beside Jacob's bed.

Day 290, Wednesday, November 16, 2011

Jacob had been resting fairly comfortably for awhile, but then around 2:30am he became agitated and his speech was incomprehensible. He would pull on one of the restraints and then pull on the other. After that yielded no results he would grab both side rails and try to sit up. He was too weak to sit up on his own so he would flop back onto his pillow. He could not formulate words at this point so it was impossible for him to communicate what was bothering him. This went on until around 10:30am. Shari came back to his room around 7:30am and sat next to his bed and held his hand and tried to calm him down, but it never lasted very long and he would be thrashing around again. This was causing great concern with all of the doctors because he should have responded to the antibiotics by now. His abdomen had also become quite distended which was a new sign of a more serious infection. The Intensivist ordered a head and abdomen CT to be done as soon as possible to see what was happening in his abdomen and try to diagnose any problems that might be in his brain.

In order to do the CT scan, Jacob would have to be sedated and intubated because he was writhing around and was not responding to verbal requests.

This was very scary for Shari and I, but we knew it was necessary to try and diagnose his situation. I leaned over the bed and told Jacob about the plan to "knock him out" until the infections had passed and that when he woke up he would feel better. He could not respond verbally, but as I spoke he slowly lifted his right thumb to acknowledge that he understood and he was on board with the plan. They then asked us to step out of the room while they intubated him and we did. When we came back into the room, he was completely sedated and the ventilator tube was sticking out of his mouth. He was finally calm now, but of course completely unresponsive to us. They wheeled him off to do the CT scan and we elected to stay in the room and rest for the approximate hour that he would be gone.

Shortly after Jacob was wheeled back into the room we heard someone at the nurse's station say, "we need to call Neurosurgery STAT!" Shari and I both heard it, but there are several patients in the PICU, so we were not sure that they were talking about Jacob. Unfortunately they were. The Intensivist came in to let us know that Jacob's abdomen was full of fluid and that the walls of his bowels were inflamed and possibly torn. They also saw that there was fluid on his brain that was probably caused by a different infection. She then informed us that Jacob's chances of survival were decreasing exponentially with every test that they were running. Blood tests showed that there was a large amount of acid being released into his body which led them to believe that his bowels had been perforated. Then Dr. Lowas came in to tell us that there also appeared to be a mass at the base of Jacob's brain. Almost immediately upon hearing that news I stated that we needed to sign a DNR now. The doctors explained that any one of these problems would be extremely difficult for him to overcome, but in his weakened condition, there was no hope at this point. Shari and I spoke briefly and held each other while we cried and agreed that his fight was now fundamentally over. I stepped out of the room and called Shari's dad and asked him to pick up Jerod and Dalton immediately and come to Omaha right away. I then called my parents and asked if they would come also.

We spoke with Dr. Gordon about how this process would unfold and he said that they would keep him comfortable until we requested to stop the medicine and then we could have the breathing tube removed if we chose. I tearfully told him that I had been having two nightmares about Jacob's passing. One was that he would be in excruciating pain as Mandy had described back in

September and the other was that the tumor in his neck would suffocate him and we would have to sit by and watch. He assured me that they would keep the sedation and pain meds intact and that he would feel no pain. At one point I asked about a spot that was developing in his left eye and was told that it was a result of having very few platelets in his bloodstream and that he was probably bleeding internally.

My parents, my sister and brother-in-law arrived around 4:40pm and the medical staff were administering a lot of medicine and fluids just to keep Jacob alive long enough for everyone to say goodbye. We could tell by the body language of the medical staff that they were running out of options and the rest of the family needed to show up soon. Around 5:20pm Jerod and Dalton arrived with Glen and Patsy. I stopped them in the hall to brace them for what they were about to see. Jacob was lying in bed with a tube sticking out of his mouth and one going up his left nostril. His eyes were half open, but his eyeballs were partially rolled back in his head. His pupils were fixed and dilated and there was no movement. They were both caught off guard while I described this in the hall. When they walked into the room they both erupted in tears and were wailing uncontrollably. They had arrived just in the nick of time. Mandy had just told me that we did not have much time and that the only thing keeping him alive was the fluids and the medicine that were being pumped at full speed. Everyone in the room took their turns saying good bye and then I said a short prayer thanking God for the 17 years that we were blessed with Jacob. I then turned to Dr. Gordon and gave him a nod to stop the pumps. Shari was holding his right hand and I was holding his left. Jerod and Dalton were seated beside the bed as we watched every labored breath and his decreasing blood pressures. After about fifteen minutes his blood pressure reached zero and approximately 15-20 minutes later at 6:12pm his heart stopped beating. Dr. Gordon then grabbed his stethoscope and the ventilator was momentarily stopped so that he could confirm that Jacob had died. The ventilator was then turned back on and we were asked if we were ready to turn it off. I looked across the bed at Shari and we both nodded in agreement and the machine was turned off and Jacob was perfectly still.

My son was gone.

My son was gone.

Fourteen

THE DAYS THAT FOLLOWED

Earlier in the week I had considered going home on Monday night after Shari returned so that I could work on some business and get to watch Jerod and Dalton at their wrestling meet. I had done this several times previously, but this time I was very apprehensive and decided to stay in Omaha. If I had left right after he had been released, I would have been at home when he went to the Emergency Room and probably would not have come back until the next morning. As hard as it was to see him decline in that way, I would never have been able to forgive myself for not being there. I had spent a considerable amount of time worrying that I would not be around for some reason when he passed, so now I can at least put that nightmare behind me. It has been replaced by the nightmarish images of the past few days though.

The doctors told us that Jacob could possibly hear us in the room so Shari and I both took time during this process to whisper something privately in his ear. I will not reveal what I said and I never want to know what she said to him.

Afterwards I asked for clarification on everything that had just transpired. It was vaguely reassuring to hear that we were left without any options. We had done everything possible and Jacob had fought valiantly, but ultimately this was a situation with only one outcome. It does not make it any easier, but I wanted to be able to reassure my family that there were no unexplored alternatives.

Mandy asked us to step out of the room for a while so that Jacob could be cleaned up and prepared for transfer to the morgue. We picked up our belongings out of room 5344 and went to our room at the Lied Center. A short while later we were called back to sign some paperwork and were allowed to see

Jacob one last time. He was lying in his bed with none of the tubes and wires connected anymore. The sheets had been replaced and he was lying there in total peace. Shari and I both said our final goodbyes and both Jerod and Dalton placed their head on Jacob's chest and told him that they loved him. I gently stroked the bridge of his nose just like I did when he was a baby when I was trying to get him to sleep. Shari leaned in and kissed his forehead and said, "Just like I have said every other night when I leave the room: good night Jacob, I love you." We then turned away and as we were leaving I turned back for one more look and did not want to leave the room. I wanted to stay and hold him and stare at him and just be with him, but I also did not want to drag this moment out. We had all said the words that we needed to say and now was the time to let him go.

We went back to our room at the Lied Center and I started writing the final post for Jacob's Care Page. I was interrupted by phone calls and text messages and it took longer than I expected to find the right words. I wanted to right a very detailed thank you and eulogize Jacob to a certain extent. I decided that this posting on the Care Page was not the proper forum, so I kept it short and just gave everyone what they needed to know. After I posted the update I went down to the end of the hall and started personally calling some of my closest friends so that they would not hear this second hand from someone else. After the first couple of calls the word was out and I started receiving calls from the people that I had intended to call. I felt bad that I was not able to contact some of these people first so that they could hear it from me, but with all of the communication in the world today the word spread almost instantly.

My sister and brother-in-law took my parents back to Henderson and Glen and Patsy decided to stay in the Lied Center also. Social Work had arranged for another room right across the hall from ours. As we were getting prepared for bed I found myself pacing and wondering if staying in Omaha was the right decision. I couldn't stop thinking that Jacob would be picked up sometime tonight and that he would be in Aurora long before we got up to leave Omaha the next morning. I was confused and did not know what the correct decision was: stay or go home. Shari had basically passed out during this time. She ate a pretzel yesterday and had nothing to eat all day today and the stress was causing her to look woozy. We stopped and got her another pretzel on the way back to the room even though eating was the last thing either one of us had on our mind. After a brief rest she decided that going home was the right thing to do. We quickly packed everything in the room and she went across the hall to tell her parents that we were checking out.

We left the parking garage around 10:30pm and headed towards Interstate 80. As we pulled onto the entrance ramp I was shocked at what I saw. The license plate on the van in front of us read "28-C500". This was our local mortuary's van. Jacob was in the vehicle immediately in front of us. I got a cold shiver down my spine and Shari immediately started to cry. We never said another word, but I followed him all the way back to Aurora. I took comfort in knowing that we were all going home at the same time. After the two-hour drive home the van turned off to go to the mortuary and I thought to myself, "He's just going over to Ben's house." Ben is a close friend of Jacob's and his family lives in and owns the local mortuary. That helped me cope.

Once we got home and unloaded, Jerod and Dalton went straight to their rooms. Shari sat in one of the chairs in the living room and I started to pace again. I was not ready to be left alone. I asked both boys if they would come out into the living room for a while. The futon was still lying in the middle of the living room from our last five day home stay with Jacob, so both boys got on the floor and drifted off to sleep. I do not want to go to sleep because I fear where my thoughts will go. Will I have nightmares about what just transpired or will I wake up thinking that Jacob is fine only to relive the trauma and revisit all of those emotions again? It is 2:52am as I write this and I am scared to go to sleep.

I will miss my son.

I am done counting the days of this ordeal. It is over and now pointless to mark each day with an irrelevant number.

Thursday, November 17, 2011

First thing this morning I started calling the college coaches that Jacob had developed relationships with. I started with Curt Baldus at the University of Nebraska. He had shown a special interest in Jacob a few years ago at football camp in Lincoln. He was one of the first people that Jacob called upon diagnosis and had kept in touch with him periodically. Curt remembered Jacob as someone who stood out in a crowd. He said that Jacob stood out among hundreds of campers. Jacob's passion for the game and the pure joy that he showed being on the field were evident to Curt immediately. Curt said that Jacob was a rare individual who had that much talent and that much passion to go along with a fantastic work ethic. I thanked Curt for also getting the Nebraska coaching staff to sign a card and send it to him the first week of his illness. He has received numerous cards and notes and this one rates right up there at the top.

The second coach that I called was Matt Wheeler at Wartburg College in Waverly, Iowa. He is close friends with Curt Baldus and had also noticed Jacob at football camp in Lincoln. Jacob would occasionally check in with Matt to discuss football. I can remember sitting in the Cancer Center in Grand Island when he decided to call Matt to let him know of his diagnosis. They talked for quite a while and mostly just about Jacob personally. I knew then that Jacob would always have a home at Wartburg College. Matt and I spoke for about fifteen minutes and it was obvious at that point why Jacob liked this coach so much.

Lastly, I called Coach Tarver at Stanford. He did not know Jacob personally but he was Stanford's recruiter for the state of Nebraska and he was the one Jacob called after receiving their letter. I just wanted him to know that Jacob had passed away and how much that recruiting letter meant to Jacob. This may have been the hardest call that I had to make knowing that this letter was the representation of all of Jacob's dreams coming true and he would never get a chance to realize those dreams.

I thanked them all for being such a positive influence on Jacob over the past few years. It is easy for a teenager to listen to his father but not hear him. Jacob always heard what I had to say and he took it to heart. The reinforcement of those ideas by men that he respects, outside of the family, is astronomical. I told them that as a father I would have been at ease sending him to college knowing that men like this would be looking after his best interest. Every one of them was always more interested in Jacob personally more than athletically. They are all good men.

We had a meeting with the mortuary today at 11:00am. As I alluded to earlier the local mortician's son, Ben, is one of Jacob's oldest friends and we knew this was going to be a difficult meeting. As we all fought back the tears we managed to outline the basics and we left with a list of items to accomplish. First on the list was to choose casket bearers. I hadn't even thought about that yet. We also need to select music and pictures for the service. Jerod and Dalton went to the meeting with us because we want them to be a part of this process. They have been on their own for the past couple of months and we need to bond together more now than ever. They both have had good ideas about Jacob's funeral. Dalton suggested that the Varsity Football Team should wear their jerseys to the funeral. When we saw Jacob's casket for the first time he suggested that we put a "3" on the lid, so that once the casket is closed the number will be visible. Jerod has suggested that Jacob should be buried with his black belt from Tae-kwondo and they both agree that while the video is being played during the service that the song "Stronger" by Emphatic be playing in the background. This is the song from Jacob's sophomore highlight video. Hopefully this will help them cope with this loss.

We had a long talk with the boys at lunch today. We asked if they wanted to talk about anything that they saw yesterday or if they had any questions about anything else. They both admitted that they were not aware of how dire the situation had become when they arrived in Omaha last night. They were not expecting to see what they saw and even though I tried to brace them for what they saw it was not enough. Jerod broke down and said that he just could not believe that he watched Jacob die. After Jacob passed, Jerod sat in the chair next to his bed and held Jacob's hand for quite a while. Jacob and Jerod were never visibly very close. After we had Dalton, Jerod was so close in age that they became inseparable for a while and Jacob was old enough to not want to interact with their activities. Jacob was always really hard on Jerod and expected him to be a carbon copy of himself for a long time.

Jerod is his own person with his own strengths and weaknesses, and Jacob learned that as he got older. Jerod is known for his hard work and dedication to the weight room and I know that Jacob was proud of that.

Dalton was the typical annoying youngest brother, but Dalton has something that Jacob and Jerod don't…size. He is 5'-9" and weighs around 170lbs with size 14 feet and he is in 7th grade. Jacob never got to see Dalton in the weight room and did not get to see him play football this year. I think if he had, he would have been very pleased. Dalton craves Jacob's approval and shows a lot of the same personality traits as Jacob. Dalton is an outstanding leader both on and off the field and is also known for his work ethic and dedication to lifting weights. Jacob set a great example for his younger brothers and they are working very hard to meet his expectations.

We also talked about Jacob's spiritual journey over the past few months. We have not had a lot of time to have this discussion with Jerod and Dalton and it is important to know what we discussed with Jacob during those many nights in the hospital.

We have decided to ask the members of his flag football team to be his casket bearers. Jacob always looked to this team as the starting point of some lifelong friendships as well as his athletic career. These are the boys who also did most of the dirty work at his golf benefit this past summer. I know for certain that these young men would be his first choice. We have chosen to also have ten honorary casket bearers as well. These men are adults that Jacob respects and admires and have been mentors to him through different stages of his life. Rod Perry and his sons Brandon and Chase have always been like family to Jacob. Rod was always known as "Uncle Rod" and Jacob loved him. Brandon and Chase have always been like big brothers to Jacob. They would pick on him and knock him around a little and Jacob would always come back for more. He looked up to both of these young men and they were always there for him. Paul Graham is a local police officer who I have known since I was quite young. "Policeman Paul" as he was labeled by Jacob went out of his way to befriend Jacob at an early age and was Jacob's DARE sponsor when he was in 5th grade. Jessie McCoy is my former construction manager and Jacob spent quite a bit of time with him over the past few summers. Jessie was Jacob's boss and taught him to work hard on something besides athletics and do the job right the first time. Jacob hated doing the menial labor of cleaning up the jobsites or spraying weeds, but he would never complain to Jessie. He would do his work and complain to me. I would always tell him to talk to his boss not me. Randy Huebert, Kyle Peterson, Gordon Wilson, Nate Larsen and Scott Jones are the Varsity Football coaches at Aurora High School. Jacob loved and respected each and every one of these men for their unique skill sets and abilities. He liked how each one brought something unique to the table and how they all meshed to make a cohesive staff. He truly felt that he was being coached by the very best staff in the state.

I wrote Jacob's obituary and have included it below:

Jacob Peters, the oldest son of Gary and Shari Peters was born in Lincoln, Nebraska on September 30, 1994 and died in Omaha, Nebraska on November 16, 2011 at the age of 17.

Jacob grew up in Aurora and was fiercely proud of being a Husky. He thrived on the high expectations that accompany the affiliation with his school. He had a burning desire to compete at all times. Whether it was on the field, the court, the track or the classroom, he was always striving to be the best. Jacob was a firm believer in controlling his attitude and his effort. Sometimes things don't go your way, and you can't control all of your surroundings, but you can always control your attitude and your effort.

Jacob was in FBLA, FCA, Student Council, elected to the Varsity Football Unity Council, elected Junior Class Treasurer, inducted into the National Honor Society and a member of the United Methodist Church in Aurora. His future plans included playing football at some level in college then becoming a coach to teach others the right way to play the game that he loved.

Jacob loved meeting new friends and once you were let into his heart his loyalty was unending. He loved his fellow students and especially his classmates. Sometimes he would push too hard instead of giving a nudge in the right direction, but that was only because he saw that everyone has something great to offer, and that greatness just needs to be uncovered.

Those who are left behind to carry forward his legacy are his parents, Gary and Shari Peters, his brothers Jerod and Dalton Peters, Grandparents Glen and Patsy Beran all of Aurora, Grandparents Wilbur and Marian Peters, Aunt Cheryl and Uncle Bob Ratzlaff all of Henderson, Uncle Dave and Aunt Cheryl Beran of Huntington Beach, California, Uncle Pat and Aunt Linda Beran of Omaha and cousins Miles Beran, Grant Beran, Andrew Beran and Brooke Beran and his Great Grandma Angie Beran.

Our house was filled with friends tonight. Around 7:00pm people started showing up and the last of them left at 11:00pm. There were a lot of hugs and a lot of tears, but it was really helpful to talk to all of these people and listen to their memories of Jacob.

FRIDAY, NOVEMBER 18, 2011

Friday marked the end of another cycle of weight lifting at the school. At the end of each cycle each athlete is tested to see how much improvement has been made. These tests are called "max-outs". Jacob loved max-outs. He loved being able to chart his progress and this was a very tangible way of seeing himself getting better. During the weight lifting cycle you can feel yourself getting stronger, but it is hard to quantify that value. It requires patience and perseverance to continue putting all of your efforts into the work without knowing the immediate results. There is no instant gratification which has become the norm in our society today.

Jerod went to max-outs this morning. He and Dalton have been lifting diligently since they were eligible to begin after their 6th grade year. Dalton was really congested this morning and didn't feel he could do his best so he decided to stay home. Jerod really wanted to go for two reasons. Today was the day to find out how much you have improved and those days only come a few times each year so he did not want to miss that opportunity for affirmation. The second reason is because he knew that is where Jacob would want him to be.

I took Jerod up to the school at 6:45am and after he got out of the car and walked into the school I didn't leave. I sat there thinking back to all of the times that I sat in that same spot with Jacob. Then I saw Blake Williams, one of Jacob's best friends and one of the boys that I was told was having an extremely hard time coping with Jacob's death. I got out and we embraced each other in the parking lot. We were both sobbing as we walked into the school holding each other. We went straight into the coaches' office and I told him that I understood his pain. I then told him that Jacob loved him and would want him to keep it together and not do anything foolish. He never spoke a word. He is a quiet young man anyway, but now he was completely silent. I told him that we would spend more time talking and that I wanted him to come over to the house so we could have some privacy.

As Blake was leaving the head football coach walked in and pulled me into his office. I thanked him for all that he had done for my son and let him know that we had used him as a role model many times. Jacob really admired all of the coaches, but the head coach had a special place in his heart. Randy is a good Christian man and set a great example for how to live your life. When Jacob was struggling with his faith and was referring to Christians as hypocrites, we would say "Coach Huebert is not a hypocrite" and that was enough to satisfy Jacob. We stood in his office for an hour talking about Jacob and his journey before Jerod found me after completing his max-outs. As we walked out of the office we found ourselves surrounded by a few of Jacob's friends. There was one young man in particular that I was looking for, but he was not there yet. I stood in the center of this semi-circle of friends and told them how much they meant to Jacob and that I wanted them to all come over to the house so that we could talk. Shortly after our conversation started, Bryce Hewen, the young man I was waiting for, arrived. I had been told by a couple of people that I needed to speak with him soon. People have been worried about what he might do because he was not handling Jacob's death well.

I pulled Bryce off to the side and we sat down facing each other on the bench in the locker room. He would not look me in the eye. His head stayed down and the tears dripped from his face. I told him that I was hurting too and that I needed him for support. I said a few more words of comfort and then told him to look me in the eye as I told him to stay strong during school and then come over to the house tonight so that we could talk and above all don't do anything stupid before then.

Jerod and I then walked to the car and drove home. On the way home I asked Jerod how he did at max-outs. He said that he maxed out at 155lbs on the bench press and 355lbs on the squat. I told him that I was proud of him for even going to max-outs today and that I was proud of the improvement that he had made since the previous max-outs. As we walked into the house, he turned to me and said, "Do you think Jacob would be proud of me?" I told him that absolutely he would be proud. Jacob would never say that to his brother, but he would have been proud. Jacob said few kind words to his brothers. Most of the time you had to interpret his silence as approval. He was hard on his brothers and I believe it was because he didn't want them to ride on his coattails. They needed to uphold the reputation that he had built, but they needed to do it on their own. He was very complimentary of other people but compliments to his brothers were few and far between. There were always repercussions for falling short of his expectations, but I think that came from Jacob's opinion that you should be reprimanded for making a mistake, but you should not be rewarded for just doing what you were supposed to do. Improving each day and living up to the reputation that he had built was what Jerod and Dalton were supposed to do, so he did not feel the need to compliment them on that. That is a pretty tough ideology, but I understand and respect it.

Shortly after 9:00am we got a visit at home from the School Administration. They came over to offer their condolences and we had a nice visit. They all had very kind words for Jacob. I told him that I felt it was very rare for a young man to have affection and appreciation for school faculty AND administration. Often the faculty is admired, but the administration can be seen as the iron fist that enforces policy, but Jacob had a fondness for each of them. He respected their authority and could see that what they were doing was for the benefit of all students and that their hearts were in the right place. They agreed that it was extremely rare.

We had to cut our visit with the administration short because we had an appointment at the cemetery to pick the spot where Jacob would be laid to rest. It was a somber trip to the cemetery as I felt that this was a gigantic decision. When we got to the cemetery, Mike McQuiston was waiting for us and asked if there were any family members that were buried somewhere that we might like to be near. The only ones that I could think of were my grandparents and there was no room near them. I thought of my friend Craig Newlun who had a son that was still born when Jacob was only one year old. I asked about where Peyton had been buried and he was in the Catholic section and there was no room near him anyway. Craig is a close friend and if Peyton had survived I am confident that he and Jacob would have become good friends. I was disappointed that they could not be buried close to one another because that would have given my heart some peace.

We went over to the newest area of the cemetery where only a few people had been buried so far. There was no real point of reference for us as we looked over this open piece of land. I was feeling despair as I could find no inspiration to select one plot over another. I felt that I had to find some significance in the place that he would be laid to rest. The caretaker of the cemetery then pulled out a map of the area and my eyes immediately went to the name "Ron Perry" and then right next to it "Rod Perry". Rod Perry has been one of my closest lifelong friends and Jacob grew up calling him "Uncle Rod". The Perrys were also our first visitors during Jacob's initial stay at the Med Center. I knew that this was the place for him. Then it dawned on me, Shari and I were also picking out our final resting place. This brought an eeriness to the situation because for whatever reason I had not thought about my own death. My heart was calm as we selected plot 26. Each plot is made up of four spots and Jacob would be buried in spot #3 of course. I had found the significance that I was looking for and my heart was at ease.

We spent the rest of the afternoon picking out pictures for the slideshow that would be played at the funeral. This task seemed relatively simple when first assigned, but it proved to be the largest task of all. Shari has taken a lot of pictures of the boys over the years and we had 17 years of memories to sort through. We spent all afternoon and part of the early evening sorting through thousands of photographs. The mortuary needed 40-45 pictures which did not seem like a difficult task, but we were overwhelmed by the sheer volume.

We had heard through the grapevine that sometime this evening some of Jacob's classmates wanted to come over and visit. I was glad to hear that maybe the two boys that I had spoken to had invited some more people to come along. Today we found out that the night Jacob died almost got out of control with some of these kids. We heard stories of kids acting out all over town. It all culminated in about 50 kids spray painting Jacob's name on the south and east side of the school gymnasium. We knew that they had all gathered at McDonald's then the Methodist Church and then at Lauren Schuster's house, but early in the morning they were apparently running unchecked in town and things escalated. The words that I kept hearing from people were "confused" and "angry". I understood those feelings and could identify with those feelings of wanting to lash out. These kids needed me and I needed them—quickly.

We intentionally requested that no other visitors come over tonight in anticipation of the classmates. The FBLA chapter was sponsoring a dodgeball tournament tonight at the high school and most of Jacob's friends would be there. I'm glad that they did not postpone or cancel the dodgeball tournament because that had to be a great escape from the gravity of this ordeal for those kids. Around 10:00pm kids started showing up and by 10:30pm our living room was completely full of kids. I asked them how much they wanted to know about Jacob's death and they said "everything". I'm not sure how long it took to tell the story of his final hours, but I didn't skip any details and they hung on every word. After I finished I asked if any of them had any questions and it was silent. They were probably still processing the images of what I had just laid out for them, so I told another short story of his journey. Slowly the questions started coming. They began to open up and soon the questions turned to "I remember when". Bryce, the young man who had been having such a hard time these past couple of days was leading the way. I have no idea how many times he said, "I remember when", and I could see the pain and tension slowly melting away even if it was just for awhile tonight he was showing some signs of healing. The questions and stories went on for hours and hours. The main group left sometime between midnight and 2:00am, but the last five boys stayed until 5:00am. A couple of them were lying on the floor, one was lying on the love seat and the others were sitting in the chairs or on the floor. Occasionally some would drift off to sleep and occasionally there would be another question and occasionally there would be extended periods of silence as we all stared at the floor or the walls. I don't think those boys wanted that night to end, I know that I didn't. I wanted to stay there with his friends and tell stories forever. They wanted to cling to any memory of Jacob that they could and maybe being in his house felt good. It was a beautiful period of time that I will never forget and I'm sure that it helped those kids and I know that it helped me. Each of those kids holds a piece of Jacob, each of them were a part of Jacob. When I spend time with these kids I can pull a small piece of my son out of each one of them. That is comforting to know. Every friend of his will bring a little bit of my son back to me, if only for a brief period of time.

Saturday, November 19, 2011

We finally finished sorting pictures Saturday morning around lunch time. I took them over to the mortuary when we finished and I got an unexpected surprise. Mike had finished preparing Jacob and he wanted me see him. I wasn't sure that I was ready for this, but I was amazed at what I saw. Jacob was beautiful. We had given Jacob's school picture to Mike so that he could use it to reference the way Jacob looked in his jersey. Jacob was very particular about how he looked in his jersey and Mike nailed it. He looked exactly like the picture. I have been to funerals where the person has either not looked good or not like I remembered them. Jacob looked amazing. Last night when Jacob's classmates were at the house, Ben Grossnicklaus asked if Jacob would look a lot different and I said that I didn't think so. He obviously looked different than he did when he was healthy because he was bald and his face was a little puffy because of the steroids, but for those who had seen him over the past few months he should look the same.

Shari had been having a tough morning with all the stress and tough decisions that needed to be made on the spot. She had made an appointment with her hair stylist this morning, but had to push it back because of the picture project and that also added to her angst. When I returned from the mortuary Shari was preparing to leave for her hair appointment and I grabbed her and told her that I had just seen Jacob in his casket and he was beautiful. I was hoping that hearing that would help to ease some of her tension and give her comfort in knowing that she would not be disappointed when she saw him.

I had forgotten that the Nebraska-Michigan football game had started at 11:00am today. I knew the game was televised, but I didn't know if I could watch it without Jacob. We didn't watch every game together, but lately we had and I was not sure how I would feel without him now. I turned on the game and found Nebraska behind 17-10 and as I watched they fell behind 31-10 and were making a lot of mistakes. It didn't take long before I passed out in my chair waking up briefly to see that they were falling further and further behind. Michigan ended up beating Nebraska 45-17 but I paid little attention if any at all.

We had family visitation at the mortuary tonight around 4:00pm. Tonight was just an informal visitation for the immediate family. We had told the boys earlier that if they wanted to give Jacob something to place in the casket that this would be the time to do it. This was an easy decision for Dalton. He went into his room and got a picture of himself executing a block during a 7th grade football game against Hastings Middle School this past season. This was probably his best game of the season and Jacob never got to see him play. Dalton would always ask how he did and I know that he was seeking Jacob's approval after every game. I thought that this picture was perfect because he understood that Jacob would appreciate the fact that he was doing his job and doing it well. After he placed it in the casket he stood over Jacob and said, "I know that you always said that I have the tools to be very good, and I promise you that I will do the work, I will do the work to get better."

Jerod took a little longer to decide, but I thought he made a great decision. Jacob had earned his 1st degree black belt in Tae Kwon Do a couple of years before Jerod did. When Jerod earned his 1st degree, Jacob had earned his 2nd degree. Jerod ended up getting Jacob's actual belt because it already said "J. Peters" on the belt along with the Roman numeral I, so it fit perfectly for Jerod. I did not remember that had happened, but Jerod did and he wanted Jacob to have his original 1st degree black belt back. I was proud of Jerod wanting to give this up because there is no replacement belt for him. This belt was displayed on Jerod's trophy case and he was proud of it. He has struggled outwardly more than Dalton has and hopefully this gesture will help him cope with this loss. He has always been more emotional than Jacob or Dalton and it's good to see him cry for his brother. Sometimes Jerod has a hard time being decisive, but with this gesture there was no indecision. He too stood over the casket, but his words were only for Jacob and himself. He says that he talks to Jacob through prayer.

Shari gave Jacob a picture of all five of us from this past Christmas. As a mother she wants him to remember that we are still a family and we will all love him forever. I was not at all surprised that this is what she wanted to give him. I cannot describe the feelings that she has had throughout this journey. I can only try to support her and comfort her when I can. A father's love runs deep and is strong and firm, but I know that a mother's love is special. While I don't believe that she loved Jacob more than I do, I have seen that there is a definite difference in a mother's love. When Jacob was incoherent and mumbling on Wednesday morning I tried to hold his hand to comfort him and reassure him that I was there. He would use my hand to try to pull himself out of bed and eventually I had to stop holding his hand. When Shari came back into the room she sat beside the bed. It was obvious that I was frustrated with Jacob not lying still, so she pulled her chair next to his bed and held his hand. He immediately calmed down and relaxed. When he would start to struggle again she would say, "It's OK Jacob, just lie down and try to relax." Her voice was quiet and calm and he would lie back down right away. I believe that she could have stayed there indefinitely holding his hand and calming him down. There is a definite difference in a mother's love.

I had a hard time figuring out what I wanted Jacob to take with him. I searched the house for something of significance to send with him. I wanted to give him something with a meaning that he would appreciate and understand. I went downstairs to the store room and drug out some of the tubs that held memorabilia from my youth. As I looked at old pictures, trophies, yearbooks and clothing nothing spoke to me as being significant. I kept thinking, "how do I show a father's love for eternity?" He had gotten a watch from his mother and me for Christmas this past year, but he never actually wore it. It was too big when he got it and it took some time to get it sized correctly and then he got sick. I thought for a moment about that, but again it did not hold much significance to him because it was just a watch in a box that sat beside his bed. I finally went into our bedroom and looked in the cigar box that I keep beside my bed. In it I have kept small drawings that the boys have made for me and any little item that might hold a special memory. In it I found a card that my sister had given to me for Christmas a few years ago. Inside that card were pictures of Jacob, me, my father, and my paternal grandfather. Four generations of the Peters men. When I showed this card to Jerod he thought that I should keep it, but I knew that this was the right gift to give. Jacob was proud of the Peters name and he loved his Grandpa Peters very much. I knew that he had an appreciation for family heritage and would have treasured this item if he was alive. He has brought so much honor to the family name and would be proud to be pictured with his grandpa and great-grandpa.

He had been such an inspiration to the kids on my youth football team that I gave him one of the gold medals that we ordered for the players. Engraved on the back of the medal were the words, "AYF 2011, League Champs, 4JP3". Because the kids dedicated the season to Jacob and then went undefeated to win a championship, I felt he was a part of the team. He had told me two weeks in a row to leave the hospital and go coach my team. He always said, "I want a championship and you can help your team win." The medal is not only a symbol of the championship, but also the young lives that he touched.

As a family we decided early on that he would be buried with the game ball from the playoff game against Norris. This was the last game that he got to attend and he thoroughly enjoyed being back with his team. Having them give him the game ball was an honor for Jacob and he would have displayed that ball proudly his entire life, so we knew that he would want it forever. It was given to him by those that he also considered to be family.

Jacob was put to rest wearing his red football jersey over a long sleeve white T-shirt along with black sweat pants, red socks (the ones that the team wore at home games) and his favorite new pair of shoes. He had a Team Tyler bracelet on one wrist in honor of Tyler Larson who died fighting cancer last year and a "Keep the Faith" bracelet on the other wrist in honor of Jeff Sutter, his 8th grade football coach who is currently in remission. When Jacob would go to outpatient treatment he would always wear these wristbands. When he was admitted for inpatient treatment he would only take them off because they always interfered with the hospital wristbands. We know that he never forgot either one of these men and their wristbands were important to him.

This red jersey was the one that he wore for home games and now he was home forever. This was not even a decision. There was no question in our minds that he would want to wear #3 forever. He was also wearing a pair of black sweatpants that said "Aurora Football" with the name "Peters" sandwiched in between. Jacob never liked wearing jeans or dress pants so he wore shorts and sweatpants every day. He dressed like an athlete and did not care to wear the latest trends in fashion. He was an athlete and he wanted to look like one.

We had no visitor's tonight and I was uneasy all night long. Earlier in the day my closest friend in my youth, Brian, had mentioned that he would be stopping by sometime. He drove past the house when we were at family visitation and since we weren't home he called to say he would catch up with me later. I tried calling him several times to let him know we were home, but there was no answer. I then called another lifelong friend and classmate, but he was at his wife's Christmas party. I really wanted to be around more people, but there was no one available. Brian and his brother Gregg finally came over around 11:00pm. This might sound late to most people but I told them that I probably would not be sleeping much and they could come over whenever they wanted. I just feel the need to be around people. Loneliness makes my thoughts turn dark and I really don't want to go to that dark place anymore. They stayed for a while and then Shari decided to go to sleep on the futon, which was still on the living room floor, while I sat in my chair and watched TV. Eventually I drifted off to sleep. I have found that it is better to pass out watching television than lay in my bed waiting to fall asleep. That is when my mind races. I have told several people that I am afraid to sleep right now. I am afraid of the nightmares that I might have and I am afraid of waking up thinking everything is fine then being slapped with the realization that he is gone and dealing with those emotions all over again.

The nightmare that I fear involves being back in room 5344 sitting at his bedside while he was irritated and incoherent or after he was sedated and we were waiting for him to die. These are powerful images in my mind and something that I do not want to re-live. I know that sooner or later this will happen and it terrifies me. It was excruciating enough when it happened.

In the fog that sometimes accompanies the first few moments of consciousness is where I fear that I will believe everything is OK. I woke up at some point Thursday night with that exact feeling. I was confused and then I knew something was wrong, but I could not remember what it was. I looked around the room and then my eyes locked on Jacob's picture hanging in the hallway. I was instantly horrified to recall that Jacob was gone forever.

I know that it is not healthy to go sleepless for too long and eventually I will just pass out, but until then I will try to occupy my mind with good thoughts. I actually slept in my bed for a couple of hours early Sunday morning and I didn't have any problems, so I'm sure that I will be able to ease back into it.

Sunday, November 20, 2011

Today I wrote Jacob's eulogy. It took me all morning to complete the main body and then I spent most of the afternoon modifying the text. It was hard to condense what I wanted to say about Jacob. There were so many points that I wanted to make or stories that I wanted to share that I found my mind wandering quite often as I was writing and then I would have to redirect my focus. I hope that someday I will be given the opportunity to tell Jacob's story to inspire and motivate other people.

Visitation was at the church from 6:00-8:30pm Sunday night. We got there shortly after 5:00pm so that we could spend a little time with Jacob before everyone showed up. I'm glad that we went early because people started showing up at 5:40pm. Shari, Jerod, Dalton, and I stood next to the pews at the front of the church right next to Jacob. We greeted every person that came down the aisle. I wanted to thank every person that had come to see my son and say goodbye. We stood there shaking hands until 8:20pm when the last person finally came down the aisle. 2 hours and 40 minutes of continuous people. We were amazed at the turn out. We have no idea how many people came through, but even Shari's brother Dave said, "This was impressive."

At one point a young woman who is a senior this year at Aurora stopped to tell us a "Jacob Story". She told us about a volleyball game that she had played in. She didn't play much, but came off the bench and got limited time on the court. She said there was one set play that was designed for her to score and it worked several times. After the game Jacob walked up to her and crossed his arms in front of his chest in the shape of an X. She asked him what that meant and he said, "You're the X-factor. The other team had no answer for you." She said that she would always remember the feeling that she got from someone appreciating her hard work. She was not the most talented player on the team, but Jacob could appreciate her work ethic and ability to take advantage of every opportunity that she earned.

After each member of the junior class came through they all gathered in one section to wait for everyone else to leave. After the last person had left they all began to gather around him again at the front of the church. Then they sat in the pews directly across from the casket and talked, occasionally gathering back with him again. Then someone walked around to the other side of the casket and noticed the "3" that Dalton had helped me adhere to the casket Friday afternoon. They were all obviously moved and it was a touching moment.

The video slideshow had been running and everyone had seen all of the pictures when Mike McQuiston asked me if I would like the juniors to watch the video with the accompanying music. I thought it was a great idea to share this with them first before anyone else outside the family. By now I was in the midst of all of Jacob's classmates in the pews. I find a lot of comfort being surrounded by the people that he loved so much. We watched the video together and cried together and then sadly we needed to leave. We had stayed almost an hour late and everyone, including the mortuary staff, needed to go home.

Two of my closest friends arrived during the evening and I asked that they both come over after the visitation so that we could talk. Jim Allen was my college roommate and someone that I know will never change. He is steadfast in his love for his family and friends and will be there for me at every turn. Craig Newlun is a high school classmate and we have grown closer over the years. Craig is an outstanding individual of the highest moral character and I have always looked to him as a guide for how to be a good man. They have both experienced losses similar to Jacob. Jim's younger brother Wes was killed in an automobile accident in 1992 when he was just 16 years old. Jacob's funeral will be held in the same church. Craig and his wife Stephanie had a stillborn son, Peyton, in 1995. They got to hold him, but he never lived outside the womb. I was fortunate to have these two men with me tonight to talk about Jacob. They felt the loss of Jacob very deeply as well. They both knew Jacob well and he considered both of them to be good friends with him as well as me.

Jim spent the night at our house and slept on the futon in the living room. I stayed in my chair and tried to watch TV for a while. I could tell that the light from the picture was bothering Jim so I turned the TV off and went to bed to attempt my first real night of sleep. I was apprehensive and scared as I pulled the covers up to my chin, but fell asleep very quickly. I slept all night—no nightmares—no false realizations. Maybe I will find a way through this to carry on the way Jacob would have wanted.

Fifteen

SAYING GOODBYE AND GIVING THANKS

MONDAY, NOVEMBER 21, 2011

I awoke this morning to the sounds of Jerod getting ready to go to lifting. He had asked me yesterday if it would be OK if he went this morning knowing that today was the day of the funeral. I told him that I think it would be a fitting tribute for him to lift this morning. Jacob despised missing the lifting days. He would definitely want the boys to lift this morning and then go to the funeral later. Dalton is still fighting quite a bit of congestion and so he again stated that he couldn't be doing his best so he didn't want to go at all. That was the way Jacob was. Give it everything or don't go at all. Another fitting tribute to Jacob was the fact that we went to pick up one of Jerod's friends on the way to the school. Jacob always tried to eliminate the excuse of not having a ride to lifting. He knew that I would support his leadership and that if he thought we needed to pick someone up, I would agree. We did this on several occasions.

At one point Jacob was obsessed with getting two of his classmates into the weight room. These boys both had something that Jacob did not and would not ever have—size. They were both extremely large kids, but they could also move fairly well. They were not obese, they were not unathletic. They were just unexplored and undeveloped. He knew that they could both help his team and he wanted desperately to get them into the weight room. For months we would leave our house a little bit earlier on Monday, Wednesday, and Friday mornings to pick these boys up. They were both telling Jacob that their parents would not get up that early to take them to school. Jacob knew that we would be up, so he told them that we would be outside their house waiting—no excuses. I am not exaggerating when I say that we did this routine for several months. Not weeks, not days, MONTHS. Not one time did either one of these boys get up and come with us. That day at school they would give him another excuse and he would always say, "We'll be there next time", and we were. Over time, Jacob's persistence worked on one of these young men. Sam started lifting and he started getting better. I don't know why he started coming and Jacob did not care why he started coming. He was just happy that Sam was there.

Jacob also started a program to reward any lineman in his class that attended the morning lifting sessions at least 10 times per month. The coaches already had a program in place that rewarded attendance with a "Survivor" T-shirt, but Jacob thought some people needed a little more motivation. If they would attend at least 10 times out of the normally scheduled 12 times, then he would take them out to eat. He was trying to find a way to motivate these guys to stay in the weight room in the off season and what better way to motivate teenage boys than with a free meal. He started this program immediately after his sophomore season and unfortunately we only got to treat the winners to a meal a couple of times before he got sick. This is just another example of his determination and leadership that he applied towards reaching his goals while improving others.

I felt a lot of pride in Jerod as we drove to the school with his friend in tow.

We left the house around noon for the funeral. We were told to be there by 12:30pm so that they could read the cards on the floral arrangements to the family. Knowing that this was the last time that we would actually get to see Jacob's body we wanted to be plenty early so that we had our chance to talk to him before other family arrived. We all got a chance to give him our love one more time before they closed the casket.

The funeral was beautiful. The service was perfect. The message from the Pastors was perfect. Jerod got up in front of everyone and read a Facebook post that he made in honor of Jacob. I have included it below:

> *The boy named JP3 is gone but the man named Jacob Peters lives forever and so does what he stood for. It took more than four infections and a brain tumor and all of the other cancer in his body to*

take him down, yet after they unplugged the machines it still took over 45 minutes for his heart to stop. If that is not a strong heart, I don't know what is. So for all of you people out there, hold JP3 in your hearts but remember Jacob Peters the man and what that man stood for. I love you Jacob and I will never forget you!

I have never been as proud of Jerod as I was at that time. He spoke clearly and held his head high. He even lifted his head from his text and made eye contact with the crowd. He did an amazing job and at the closing of his remarks he looked at Jacob and spoke to him directly.

I then stepped to the pulpit and asked that the medical staff that was in attendance stand and be recognized for their dedication and commitment to fixing Jacob and their relentlessness in that pursuit. Other people had given up on him weeks earlier, but they stayed the course just like Jacob would have done. I told them that the last page that Jacob had turned on his desktop calendar was October 5, 2011, the day before he was life-flighted to Omaha with his first major infection. The motivational phrase for that day was "desire success— then stick with the job". I thought this would have been the perfect message that Jacob would want for them. It's the way he lived his life and the way that they pursued a cure for him. They will always hold a special place in our hearts and even though we never want to go back to that hospital again I would love to see them again and share their lives. He was not just a patient, he was their friend, and even though he hated treatment, I believe he loved them all.

I then read what I had written for Jacob's eulogy.:

Jacob was a warrior.

As we sat at our home a couple of days ago surrounded by Jacob's classmates I was comforted by the stories that were told. I was most moved when Bryce Hewen told us that when he would ask Jacob how he was doing the standard response was "I'm fine", or "I'm good". Throughout this entire journey that was his standard response to the medical staff in Omaha. Everyone at the Medical Center would always ask, "Is there anything else I can get for you, or do for you?" The response was always the same, "I'm fine." I was comforted by this because now I knew that he was not just trying to be strong for his mother and I. This was really the way that he lived his life.

Jacob only knew one way to take on a challenge and that way was head-on. He never took the easy way out. Several times during his treatment after receiving bad news, we would be given the option to come home for a few days to organize our lives before beginning a new protocol. Every single time he elected to begin treatment immediately. He could have chosen to come home and spend time with friends for a while and then return for treatment, but during that time he would not be getting better and Jacob truly believed that if you are not getting better you're getting worse. This was as true in the weight room as it was in the cancer treatment room. At these times Shari and I left the decision in his hands and there was never any hesitation, he would take the challenge head-on.

He was dedicated to his team and his friends. One of the clearest illustrations of this was the day of the McCook game. Jacob was told early that week by the doctor that he would not be attending the game on Friday night. He decided that he needed to write a letter to the team. This was his way of contributing. I told him that if he wrote it I would deliver it in person to Coach Huebert. I went home later in the week and handed the letter to Coach Huebert and asked him to read it aloud before the game. In a rare moment of good fortune Jacob was actually released the morning of the game after another week long stay in the hospital following yet another relapse. We drove home to unload and reorganize and then left immediately for McCook. On the way out of town we stopped by the school where the coaches were preparing to leave for the game. Jacob ran inside and told a surprised Coach Huebert to throw that letter away because he would be at the game tonight.

He was on IV fluids the entire time that we were on the road. When we got to McCook we disconnected the IV and I taped a plastic box to his chest to protect the needle that was still access- ing his port. He got to stand on the sidelines with his team the entire game. After the game we found that the needle had been bumped and was hanging half-way out of his chest. We went to the

Emergency Room in McCook and they removed the needle and sterilized the site. We then returned to the field so that he could hang out with his teammates as they were finishing the post game meal.

I saved that letter on my computer and I would like to share it with all of you.

To my teammates and brothers,

There is only one place in the world I want to be tonight, and that is right there with you guys, but I can't. If I was there, I would prepare as hard as I can, but I can't. If I was there I would warm-up as hard as I can, but I can't. If I was there I would play every single down as hard as I can, but I can't. I would do every single thing as hard as I can, but I can't. You all have an opportunity tonight that I would do anything to have. Take full advantage of every single second. You should never be able to look back and say "maybe I could have gone harder, then we would have won." Don't allow that to even be a possibility. Give every ounce of energy you have, every play. Leave that field with no regrets. Know that you did everything you possibly could have to help the team. Play every single play like it's your last, because you never know when it will be. You may only have one chance at McCook, don't allow yourself to be beaten. We've worked too hard for too long to lose. Don't do this for me, do it for your teammates, the coaches, and yourself. No regrets. Kick some ass. We are Aurora, now go play like it!

Jacob Peters

After Jacob was told that he also had leukemia, we talked about staying mentally strong through the panic attacks and depression that were sure to be brought on by the steroids he would be taking again and after I got done preaching he said, "I can take anything, but why do I always have to." That is the closest he ever came to complaining. Even after all of the times that he had been ripped away at the last second from his friends or his team, he never complained. In the last few weeks he read Tim Tebow's book titled

"Through my eyes". Even though he was very sick, at the end of the day he would still say, "I feel like I didn't accomplish anything today." Reading this book gave him a sense of accomplishment and gave him peace. He never stopped trying to get better.

I have kept a journal throughout this journey and on September 28 I wrote the following:

If this process leads to Jacob's death at least he will not have to endure anymore of the mental and physical decline. I will be relieved that he will no longer have to fight a battle that he did not choose, but I will miss him more than my mind can imagine. He is my best friend as well as my first born. He and I can talk about anything and we both have the same opinions about almost everything. He is everything that I am not. He is glorious and magnificent, intelligent, motivated, hard working, dedicated, athletic and funny.

I will miss my son.

As a family we were honored by the massive attendance at Jacob's funeral. I was most honored, though, by the attendance of a few individuals. Jacob's former Tae Kwon Do instructor, my high school football coach, the medical staff from Omaha, fraternity brothers that I hadn't seen in 20 years, and some of my high school classmates among others. We are confident in saying that there were well over 1,000 people that attended either the visitation or the funeral. We are blown away at the impact that our son has had on so many people. It does make this process of grieving easier when I know that he was loved by so many at such a young age and he affected people of all ages. We have heard wonderful stories from young children, his peers and his teachers. We found out later that some of his friends had approached the medical staff and thanked them for everything that they had done for Jacob. What a wonderful gesture from a bunch of devastated teenagers. Jacob was surrounded by good friends as well as mentors. They should also be commended for the man that he became because there is a part of each of them in Jacob.

After the service, the football team was dismissed first, followed by the casket bearers. We followed Jacob up the aisle and as we walked through the doorway the team had formed a "tunnel" that led to the hearse. We knew ahead of time about this and I am grateful that we did. This was a wonderful moment, but had it been a surprise I probably would have been sobbing uncontrollably and missed the memory in my mind. I will never forget watching his flag football teammates carry him past his varsity football teammates and coaches.

The players were all loaded onto a bus that was to follow the lead car out to the cemetery. Jacob followed the bus and we were again right behind him. I commented on the way to the cemetery that at no time since his death has he been behind us. Even on the trip home from the hospital the night he died he was leading the way for us.

As we drove north toward the cemetery we came to an intersection where a carload of kids was waiting for the procession to pass. I don't know what made me look at the car, but as the hearse passed by the passenger in the rear seat behind the driver raised their hand out of the open window and raised three fingers. Apparently they did not know Jacob well enough to attend the funeral, but that sign of respect spoke volumes to me.

(We found out a few days later that the bus carrying the football team was bus #3. How fitting.)

It took a long time for everyone to gather around the gravesite. It was a nice day for the end of November but there was still a chill in the air. Jacob's pallbearers were all shivering, especially Blake Williams. Blake does not have an ounce of fat on his body and he was shivering and covered with goose bumps. I asked him a couple of times if he wanted an extra jacket that we had in the car and he refused. He wanted to be strong for Jacob.

I have feared the graveside ceremony for a long time. I thought that I would have an extremely hard time letting go knowing that soon he would be six feet below and covered with dirt. I have some separation anxiety even at more simple times like a weekend with friends or a family trip that is ending. How was I possibly going to make it through this? I found myself strangely calm as I stared at the casket. To me now, this was just a box. Jacob was no longer there. He was with us and he was everywhere. I know that I felt his strength when I got up to speak at the funeral. I know that I feel his peace as we stand beside his grave. I know that now he is larger than we can imagine because he is no longer trapped inside that 5 foot 8 inch body and I can find some peace in that.

As I stated earlier, we were honored by the vast number of people that attended Jacob's funeral, but most honored by the attendance of a few people. This statement was never more true than when we got to the reception after the graveside service. Shortly after we walked through the door a young man came up to me and shook my hand. "My name is Parker Davis," he stated. I almost collapsed. Parker had met Jacob three summers ago at "Top Gun" football camp in Orlando, Florida. They were warm-up partners before camp practices and struck up a friendship immediately. They were together in Florida for only a few days and stayed in touch through Facebook and text messages. The only other time that they were together in person was a random meeting at a Nebraska Football game.

JACOB, MIDDLE LEFT, AND PARKER, MIDDLE RIGHT

Parker and his father, Lloyd, had driven five hours from Dodge City, Kansas, to attend the funeral and were returning home that same night. I could not express enough our appreciation and how honored we were that they came all that distance. I told Parker how Jacob always spoke of him and how Jacob never admitted that anyone else his age at any camp was better than himself, but he never said that he was better than Parker. I told him how much Jacob respected him because I think Jacob saw himself in Parker. Parker was humble and said that he never knew how much that he had meant to Jacob. I replied that that was the reason that he came today. They may not have known it when they left Dodge City in the morning, but Jacob was guiding them to Nebraska so that Parker would know how much he meant to him. We spoke briefly about Parker's future plans and Lloyd had some very kind things to say about Jacob and then we parted. The last thing that I told Parker before we walked away was that we as a family would be following him from now on. We are Parker Davis' biggest fans.

I never moved far from the spot where I met Parker. After our discussion, I was basically stuck in the same spot as people were beginning to leave the reception and wishing us well as they left. I stood there for another two hours as people made their way to the door. I've never hugged so many people in my life and at the end of the night I was so filled with pride that I could not feel sad. There were so many people saying beautiful things about Jacob that I could not feel anything but pride. My son was the man that every parent hopes their child could become. He did it in less than 17 years and the young man that we knew at home was just a small part of the man that engaged the world.

Tonight was also the annual varsity football potluck supper at the school. After the reception we went home to change and then went up to the school to spend the evening with the team and their families. Shari and I were not sure if we should go to the potluck, but thought that Jacob would have wanted to be there and we should support his teammates the way they have supported us. As we had hoped, the night was all about the team and their accomplishments this season. There were a couple of pictures of Jacob in the senior video, but no other special mentions, which is the way that it should be. Jacob was awarded a varsity letter, but his name was read in alphabetical order just like everyone else. Shari and I were both brought to tears as they read his name and we were glad that he was listed just as everyone else—just another member of the team. Jacob was also recognized for selling the most fundraiser cards and again, no special attention was drawn to him or us. The only time that he was given special attention was at the conclusion of the evening. Coach Huebert took the microphone and said that he and the other coaches had each written a tribute to Jacob Peters. As soon as he said the "J" in Jacob the microphone stopped working. As we met with some of his friends later, they were certain that Jacob had shut off the microphone because he did not want the special attention. After a brief delay one of the custodians found a small clip-on microphone and coach read all five tributes. I have included them below.

Coach Wilson

A smile. And does he have a good one. You know it's easy to think football when you think of Jacob. Strong, competitive, intense, driven. But it's that smile. The one you see when he's with his friends joking around. The one you see when you know he's up to something. The one you see when he's pushed himself past a challenge when most would have given up. That smile you see when he's on the football field and that smile you see when he's off of it. The smile you see when he's with his family. It's that smile. And does he have a good one.

Coach Larsen

Jacob Peters was the ultimate Aurora football player. He was a weight room junkie and constantly worked to improve his skill and technique on both sides of the ball. He was an outstanding teammate, always trying to help his brothers on the team reach their full potential and pushing them to give everything they had. He is a perfect example of how to approach the game of football and how to attack adversity in life. His passion, strength and courage are only a few of the many qualities that made him a very special young man. While we are all going to miss him a great deal, the name Jacob Peters will always be synonymous with Aurora Football in my mind.

Coach Jones

I cannot even begin to imagine what you are feeling and I know that these words are of little comfort right now but hopefully as time goes by they will mean more to you.

I am so very sorry that Jacob is gone, he will be missed very much by a lot of people for a long time. Always remember that the short time that Jacob was with us was very well spent. He was a very focused young man. He listened to people he trusted and respected and tried to do everything in his power to live by the guidelines those people gave him. His work ethic and passion was second to none. Running, lifting, throwing, coming to team camp at Hastings last summer and helping with practices and scrimmages. Making the trip to McCook to help inspire his teammates on the sidelines. Being at practices and games when NOBODY would have expected him to be there, but he wanted to be there to support his teammates. He was obviously very weak and not feeling well, but when I shook his hand after the Norris game and he said, "Good job Coach", it was very hard for me to keep it all together. Jacob was a great example for young and old with his spirit, his passion, his effort, his attitude and his loyalty right up to the day he died. So, please don't ever forget the tremendous positive effect he had on people during the short time that we had with him with us!

Coach Peterson

When reflecting back on all the time I have spent with Jacob, two characteristics keep jumping out at me. First of all, Jacob worked hard. It did not matter if it was in the weight room, in the classroom or on the field, no one was going to outwork Jacob. His weight room work ethic was second to none. Jacob had high goals and expectations for himself and his team. He understood that accomplishing those goals was going to take a great deal of time and effort and it all started in the weight room. Secondly, Jacob saw things in others that they themselves could not see. I remember Jacob coming to me as an 8th grader, telling me about this huge kid that just moved here from Colorado. He saw potential in Sam Pickrell when others might not have, including Sam. He convinced Sam to come to the weight room and even "rewarded" him and others by taking them out to eat for good attendance. Now that is a QB that knew how to take care of his linemen. I will miss having Jacob around. His positive attitude was infectious, but his spirit will remain for all who ever knew him.

Head Coach Randy Huebert
Jacob Peters: I will miss your presence. You were always in the mix,
in the weight room, option drill, 90 series, agilities, you were there,
working hard, soaking up information, getting better. Your deter-
mination was remarkable – why? You were dedicated. You knew
what you wanted and what you needed to do to get it. You enjoyed
every minute of the journey. Your passion for life was written all
over your face. The sparkle in your eye, your smile and the confi-
dence in your walk I know I will miss. You left it all on the field, no
regrets. You played like a champion because you are one. Now keep
your arm loose, your faith has set you free. God Bless.

After the potluck was over we returned home—alone. Now is the time that I have feared the most lately. All ceremonies are done and everyone will return to their normal lives and we will be alone to deal with the catastrophic void that is left in our lives. Thankfully, Brian Kremer, Gregg Kremer and Craig Newlun came over around 9:30pm to talk. This was very comforting to me because I had been around hundreds of people all day and now there were none. This was a nice way of winding down from the craziness and allowing us to decompress.

Tonight was the Class B State Championship football game. We only watched the very end of the game, but Elkhorn beat Crete for the title. I know that Jacob was smiling. Crete had ended Aurora's season the past two years and that left a hole in Jacob's heart. Crete won last year's state title and Aurora had won the previous two. Crete had won the previous two before that, so to Jacob that meant that Crete had the number one program in the state. If Crete had won tonight that would have given them four titles in the last six years and Jacob's senior season would not have been able to overcome those numbers. As it is, if the class of 2013 can win a state title next season that would mean in the past seven years Crete would have three, Aurora would have three and our latest championship would give us the title of best football program in Class B. This was one of Jacob's dreams—to take this program on his back and leave it on top when he was done. How beautiful and bittersweet it would be if his dreams come true next year.

Also tonight was a Monday Night Football game with Jacob's beloved New England Patriots facing the Kansas City Chiefs. The Patriots defense has been struggling all year and has been a point of concern for Jacob. Tonight New England won handily. Their much maligned defense gave up 3 points, had 3 interceptions and 3 sacks. Spooky.

TUESDAY, NOVEMBER 22, 2011

This morning we spent over two hours opening cards and memorials then took a break and went to Jacob's grave to place a floral arrangement from his grandparents. I had woken up this morning promising myself that I would not go to his grave today. I am afraid that if I start a streak of continuous days visiting the grave that I will not be able to stop. I always gave Jacob a hard time about having Obsessive Compulsive Disorder because when it came to certain things, he did. I have similar problems like that. He would always have to have the volume of any audio device set to a number that was divisible by five, just small things like that. I was concerned that I would develop OCD about visiting his grave and I wanted to stop it before it got started, but we needed to place this arrangement on his grave so I relented.

When we got home, Shari found another sizable stack of cards in our mailbox and we spent another 45 minutes opening and cataloging all of those and reading the emails that were sent to the mortuary. I was particularly touched by an email that we received from a mother of a student in the sophomore class. I have included it below.

> *Our fondest memory of Jacob would be two years ago at the Aurora track meet. Jacob and our son Zachary both ran in the 400 meter dash. Jacob ran an awesome race that day. After he ran he came up into the stands where Zachary was sitting with his father and I. Jacob handed Zach his track shoes. He told Zach "I just beat my personal record wearing these shoes put them on and go for it". There was a small issue in size, they were a 10 and at the time Zach wore a size 11. Zach put the shoes on and did an amazing job. He beat his personal record that day to. He continued wearing those shoes through the rest of the season. They became known as his "magic shoes". I am sure that Jacob never knew this but Zach*

still has those shoes. All of his other shoes that he has out grown we have given to charity but he has never let those go and I imagine it will be a VERY long time before he will part with them.

We are sorry for your loss. Jacob will be missed!!

The Scheil Family

I remember the day that this happened. This was the day that I referred to earlier when I wrote about the Middle School track meet that was starting as Jacob was finishing his extra track workouts. Zach is a great runner, but his times had been sub-par all year. Zach was not using spikes when he ran the 400, he was just wearing regular running shoes. Jacob knew that Zach would be varsity in a couple of years and he was counting on Zach being on the 1600 meter relay with him. He asked me if he could give Zach his spikes to see if that would help. I told him that would be a great example of selfless leadership and if he felt compelled he should do it. I remember Zach running well from that point on. Jacob and I never spoke about it again. When I look back on it now that was an amazing day. He wore himself out trying to improve his body and then used his heart and his mind to try and make someone else better. His passion to be the best and be surrounded by the best was limitless.

Jim Allen had earlier spoken to me about the ripple effect that Jacob's life would have and this was one ripple in the water.

Shane Thorell was Jacob's 8th grade football coach. He had sent hand written notes to Jacob throughout his battle with cancer and even visited Jacob in the hospital in October. Shane was the last head coach of the University of Nebraska freshman football team. He developed a relationship with former Nebraska head coach and current athletic director Tom Osborne. After Jacob died, Shane called Coach Osborne and told him about Jacob. Today we received a personally signed letter in the mail from Coach Osborne offering his condolences. Ironically, we always told Jacob that he had met Tom Osborne a long time ago. We were members of the St. Marks United Methodist Church in Lincoln when Jacob was born and the day of his baptism Coach Osborne and his family were in the congregation. Life can be funny about things like that. A Nebraska football great watches Jacob be baptized and then 17 years later unknowingly sends a letter of condolences to his parents after his death.

Today we got our copy of the local newspaper in the mail. We were interviewed last Saturday evening and we knew that the article would be in this week's paper. Along with the news article and the obituary there was a nice article in the "Husky Bark" which is the student published portion of the paper.

The only problem that I have with the article was the headline "Peters loses battle with cancer at 17". Jacob didn't lose the battle. He fought every minute of every day as every week and month trudged along. He could have given up when the group of doctors did, but he chose to fight on. The cancer did not win. This may be just a question of semantics because either way my son is gone forever, but I know to him it would be important to recognize that he did not lose—he died fighting. The chemotherapy caused the infections that led to his death. That would be an important distinction to Jacob.

Another article that appeared in the paper was a wrap up of this year's football season. Eventually the question was raised regarding the status of the quarterback situation for next season. The paper listed Jacob's classmate Troy and a young man named Luke in the class below as candidates for the job. What did not appear was the quote from Head Coach Randy Huebert stating that he had not given up on Jacob making a return to the field next year. The paper was published the day after Jacob's funeral so the editor wisely chose to leave out that portion of the interview. The interview had actually taken place on the same day that Jacob died. Coach Huebert was making his comments that day at approximately the same time that the medical staff was telling us that Jacob was not going to make it. Regardless of the timing, it meant a great deal to all of us that Jacob's coach had not quit on him either.

Around suppertime we got a visit from another classmate of Jacob's. I won't include his name at this time because I'm not certain that he wants people to know. He was feeling bad because he had not realized that when Jacob was pushing him a few years ago he was trying to make him better. At the time this young man just thought Jacob was being a jerk and blew him off. He felt so bad now that he realized that Jacob saw something special in him and was only trying to help him improve. He could barely say the words as he broke down with almost each syllable. I told him that we understood that sometimes Jacob would push too hard and that not everybody's personalities are going to mesh. It was OK for this young man to reject what Jacob was selling. Not everyone has to live their life the way he did. This young man has a laid back, easy going personality, but he loves wrestling. His passion for wrestling is just manifested in different ways than Jacob's passion. It's easy to look back now and say that "I should have seen," but that is not how life works. Jacob was not a saint by any means, but sometimes when people die they can be treated as one. I told this young man that if he wanted to honor Jacob now, then he should do those things that Jacob wanted him to do. I have told many people over the past few days that what Jacob wanted was not hard to do. Just give everything you have in everything you do at all times. It's purely about attitude and effort.

Around 7:30pm we were visited by about 10 classmates again. I have told them repeatedly to stop by anytime to talk or just hang out. These kids find comfort in being here and I probably find more comfort in them being here. It's wonderful to hear them share their stories. Thankfully one of their stories led me to find out the true story about a framed poem that I had been given by a young lady at Jacob's visitation. At some point during the evening visitation a young woman walked up and handed me a frame with a poem that she would like us to have and then ran away in tears. I read the poem and thought it was very nice and moved on to the next person in line. The title of the poem is "The Fallen Soldier". I thought that she had found this poem on the internet and had printed it on nice paper and framed it. During our discussion tonight I learned that she had written this poem for Jacob a couple days after he died. I felt horrible for not knowing what she had done. I had never heard this girl's name before so I did not even know how she knew Jacob. What a wonderful gift to give a family after the loss of a loved one. I told Jacob's friend Bryce that we had to meet this girl again to express our gratitude and hear her Jacob story.

Shari also got a message on Facebook that night from another young woman that had a Jacob story. She told us of a time at the County Fair this past year when she walked by Jacob and a group of his friends. One of the boys called her a rude name. Jacob called her back over to the group and made the boy apologize to her and then told her to never let anyone call her that name. This girl was not one of Jacob's close friends. She was a year younger and hung out with a completely different crowd. Once again I was filled with pride as I knew that my son would stand up for other people who either couldn't or wouldn't stand up for themselves.

The last two boys left our house at 2:40am.

WEDNESDAY, NOVEMBER 23, 2011

We all slept in this morning. I have been sleeping in bed and so far I have had no problems. Not only have I not had any nightmares, I cannot remember having any dreams. I am still tired, but I am getting more sleep now.

My lifelong friend Rod Perry called this morning to check on us. We had a nice talk that led me to two realizations about what Jacob was telling me in the hours before he died. This whole time I was confused at some of the things that he was mumbling and I have been telling people that at the time he was sedated he thought they were just treating his infections and he would wake up feeling better. Now I have a different opinion. Late Tuesday evening, the night before he died, he kept saying, "I wanna leave." He repeatedly tried to sit up in bed and leave. At no time during this entire process had he ever said that. There were times when he would say, "I'm sick of this hospital" or "I can't wait to go home," but never did he say he wanted to leave. He knew that even though he hated the hospital, this was the place he needed to be to get better. He knew that he had to put in his time and do what he was told and that eventually he would be free. Looking back now I think he was telling me that he was ready to leave this earth. I sat there for months watching him endure physical and mental torture and deterioration while keeping a positive outlook and strong spirit. How much more could we expect him to endure? I don't understand the process of how your soul passes on after leaving the body or at what point he could see heaven and want to be released from this torturous prison of cancer, but I now feel that he was telling us that this was the end, hours before the doctors realized it.

Early Wednesday morning he was mumbling badly and as the nurse stood next to his bed I thought I heard him say, "Take the floor." I asked him several times if that is indeed what he said and he always replied with an affirmative nod and a faint, "ya". I asked him if he meant a basketball floor and he would shake his head, "no". I asked him if he meant the floor like the one that I was standing on and he would nod and say, "ya". I was frustrated because I felt he knew what he was saying and that I just couldn't understand. Then I thought that he was just delirious and the medications were making him babble. Now I think I know what he was saying.

When we met with Mike, the funeral director, he asked me if anyone was going to speak for the family and I said that I would like to say a few words. He immediately cautioned me against that telling me that it would be harder than I thought to stand in front of those people and speak about my son. I told him that I felt that I had to try. Mike told me to make sure that I had my comments written down and have someone to back me up in case I could not finish. Over the next couple of days I had several people tell me that they didn't think it was a good idea. When we met with Pastor Fowler I told Shari that I had to try. I felt that I owed it to Jacob to say what I felt and to honor him by speaking on his behalf at his funeral.

I was not confident that I would be able to get through it. I called Paul Naumann and asked him to be prepared to take over if I could not finish. After I finished writing I read what I had written to Shari, Jerod, and Dalton. I broke down several times just reading it to them. How was I going to do it in front of all those people and Jacob? I continued to edit and re-read the pages in the hours leading up to the funeral trying to numb myself to the emotions that accompanied. As we walked through the crowd on the way into the Sanctuary I felt myself getting almost angry. I thought that I would be bawling all the way down the aisle, but instead I felt adrenaline. I sat in the first pew and felt my body rocking slightly back and forth. I stared at the casket almost aggressively. I barely heard the words that were spoken at the beginning of the service. I was locked in and focused on speaking. When Pastor Fowler called me up to the pulpit I was ready to go. Now listening to Jerod speak and standing behind him as he delivered his speech so well almost brought me out of my focus. I still was not confident in my ability to finish as I started to speak, but I felt myself getting stronger as I went. I have no doubt in my mind now that I was feeling the strength of Jacob at that time. He had told me to "Take the floor" and now he was giving me the strength to do it. He knew that the only person in this world that could say the things he wanted to say was me and he was making sure that I did it right.

Shari went out to the mailbox early this afternoon and retrieved another sizable stack of cards. I told her we needed to open them immediately because we will have to start writing thank you cards soon and we needed to stay on top of things. Right as we were preparing to start we got a visit from Paige and Anna Fox. Anna is a close friend of Jacob's. He had a few female friends, but Anna is special. She shared a lot of Jacob's feelings and opinions and she understood and embraced his sense of humor. Anna also told us that she did not think that she would be able to sit through the entire service. When she came to visitation Sunday night she was the most emotional of all the high school students. When she got to the end of the aisle she buried her head in her dad's chest and sobbed. She physically froze in that spot for a few minutes before finally finding the strength to walk by. She never stopped at the casket. She passed by quickly continuing to sob the whole time. She told us that as she sat in the pews at the funeral she felt a calm come over her as if Jacob had put his hand on her shoulder. She believes that Jacob was with her and brought her peace so that she could stay and be a part of the service. We spoke at length about the realizations that I had just had and how we were continuing to hear "Jacob stories" about how he had affected other people's lives when Paige told us another one.

There was a new student in the junior class this year at Aurora. Paige did not want to label him in a negative way, but said he was one of those students that was on the fringe. Everyone tries to find a place to fit in when they are in high school and she thought that this boy had a hard time with that. This boy was having a really hard time with Jacob's death. He didn't show up for school the day of Jacob's funeral. The next day one of the counselors pulled him aside and asked why he felt so strongly about Jacob. Jacob was an athlete and a straight A student. He had grown up in this town and had found his place in the society of high school. What could the connection possibly be? This young man proceeded to say that when he moved here and started attending school, no one would speak to him. He felt alone and unwanted. Jacob walked up to him one day and shook his hand. "I'm Jacob Peters, welcome to Aurora." This one kind gesture affected this young man deeply. Our hearts are filled with pride every time we hear a story like this. Jacob was known as a tough, relentless, hard-nosed fighter and driven to achieve excellence, yet he had the kindest heart that I know. In my eyes it is rare when those two extremes can exist in one person. That beautiful wonder was my son.

Around suppertime, Kirk and Missy Reichardt came over to talk and we ended up ordering pizza. I am glad that they came over because I still find it easier to be around people instead of being alone, especially at night. Shari and I have spent so much time together over the past few months we really need to have our friends around us to make us feel at home again. Another good thing that came out of their visit was the fact that we did not watch the clock. It is hard to believe that Jacob died one week ago today. Earlier in the day I had been marking the time as things had unfolded a week ago. With all the visitors today there was no time to sit here and watch the clock. The only time I remember looking at the clock was 8:30pm. We had made it past the time when we were told Jacob's death was imminent. We had made it past the time when the boys arrived. We had made it past the time when they stopped the medicine, when his blood pressure went to 0, and when his heart stopped. What a blessing it was to have friends here sharing stories with us to distract us from re-living those horrible moments. If they had not been here I know for a fact I would have sat in my chair marking every one of those milestones and that would have been very destructive. After they left we spent the next half hour opening the cards that we had started on eight hours earlier. What a wonderful distraction today was.

Thursday, November 24, 2011

Today is Thanksgiving. This will be our first big test on how we move forward without Jacob physically in our lives. I have tried to rationalize the situation by thinking that sooner or later, he was not going to be with us on Thanksgiving anyway. At some point he was going to find a girl and he would have to start rotating holidays, so we would gather as a family without him. This thought process may get me by, but the reality is never far away. We will not set a plate for him at the table and we will not have an empty chair where he used to sit. He will be with us in our hearts and I don't think it is healthy to have that solemn physical reminder staring me in the face. It will be hard, but Jacob never liked Thanksgiving that much anyway. He was always bored and always wanted to go home and watch football in the basement. This year he can be anywhere he pleases.

Sixteen

IN THE MONTHS
THAT FOLLOWED

Over the Thanksgiving break some guys from the class of 2011 stopped over to pay their respects. Sam, Kyle, Austin, and Taylor were seniors when Jacob was a sophomore. He looked up to these young men and strongly desired their approval. After they left I really regretted not asking them one specific question, so I waited until the Christmas break and asked them to come back again. They all came back and we sat downstairs and had another nice conversation, but my question was eating at me the whole time. It was hard to finally verbalize what I needed to ask and I paused, choking up, as I asked the simple question, "Did he earn your respect?" There was no hesitation as all four of them answered, "yes". I thought that I knew the answer to this question before I asked, but I was still anxious in asking. All four then proceeded to tell me instances where Jacob had earned their respect. The one that touched me the most was a story that Jacob had already shared with me. During one practice Kyle and Austin were purposely trying to knock Jacob out of practice. These were two of the most violent players our coaches had ever seen and they were targeting the "cocky" sophomore quarterback for punishment. On one particular play they both hit Jacob at the same time, sending him sailing out of bounds in front of the coaches. Immediately one of the coaches told them to ease up before somebody (Jacob) got hurt. Just then Jacob sprung to his feet and said, "No coach, I can take it" and ran back to the scout team's huddle. It was at that moment that he truly earned the upperclassmen's respect. He came home from practice that night and told me about that hit. He said "Austin and Kyle wrecked my life on one play." I then asked him, "What did you do?" Jacob stated, "I got up and ran back to the huddle." He had no idea that he had just accomplished one of his goals for the season and school hadn't even started yet. It was still pre-season two-a-days.

I felt much better having the burden of that question off of my shoulders. I needed to hear those words spoken out loud. Kyle went on to play linebacker at Chadron State College, he is known as one of the most hard-nosed players to ever go through our program. He later posted on Facebook that Jacob was "The toughest kid I ever knew."

Things will only get harder from here. Every day there will be a reminder of what Jacob will miss. Football, basketball, parent's night, track, FCA, FBLA, Homecoming, Prom, Graduation and more will proceed without him and people will move on with their lives. I don't want to be that guy who breaks down and cries at every event, but I can't control the emotions anymore. The pain is overwhelming.

Besides all of the events listed above, I also think about losing out on watching him become a man. I will miss sending him to college and witnessing his college career and graduation. I will miss him falling in love with a beautiful and talented young woman. I will miss his wedding. I will miss seeing his pride in landing his first coaching job. I will miss his children…my grandchildren. I will miss watching him become a fantastic husband and father and seeing him play with his kids. I will miss watching him interact with his brothers as men, not as boys. I will miss all of the holidays and family gatherings when I should see his face as he walks through the door. At every step along the path for the rest of my life, I will miss him.

It wasn't supposed to end this way.

REST IN PEACE

DECEMBER 2010

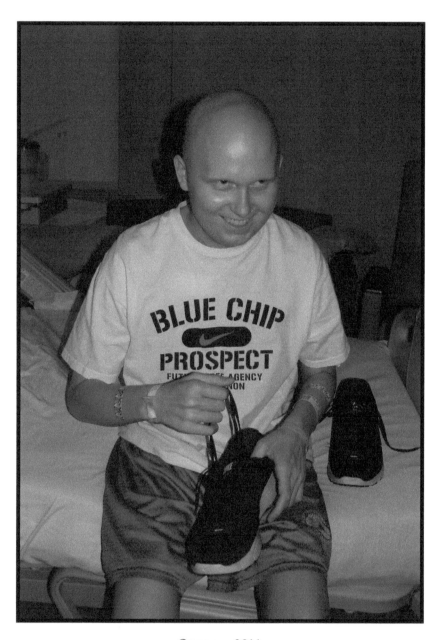

OCTOBER 2011

AFTERWORD

As the years pass by we have learned to cope with the pain, but it is always present, never too far from the surface, and it is unrelenting. Jerod and Dalton have both found their own successes over the years and have honored Jacob's legacy in countless ways. Watching them grow and compete has, at times, been the only thing that has kept me going. I can't imagine the difficulty growing up with the shadow of Jacob Peters being cast over everything they did, but they both wore that burden like a badge of honor. I am profoundly proud of them.

This journal was intended to be documentation of Jacob's journey through a successful treatment so that he could always go back and reflect on the worst time of his life. The hope was that he could lean on this in times of despair to know that he could persevere through anything. Sadly, it has turned into the documentation of his demise. Publishing this journal is an attempt to honor his memory and raise awareness of the plight of pediatric cancer patients and families. I hope it also honors the memory of the other pediatric cancer warriors that we have lost in our hometown.

Tyler Larson
Alyssa Sandmeier
Sydnee Owens
Maddy Spellman

They are all just as special, unique, fantastic and strong as Jacob, and we are honored to have known them and their families.

In 2014 I became the Vice President of the Pediatric Cancer Action Network (PCAN). This organization offers $2,000.00 grants to families of pediatric cancer patients in Nebraska to help with just about any financial hardship they might have. Our organization handles mostly emergency needs like rent, mortgage payments, car payments, utilities, etc. In certain instances we have even helped pay for prescriptions to keep the child on schedule during treatments. Unfortunately, over the past few years we have also had to earmark funds to help families with final planning as well. A sober reminder that the fight to find a cure continues.

PCAN is an all-volunteer organization so that we ensure the maximum benefit to the families from each donation. We are a 501(c)3 organization, so all donations are tax deductible. Our mission is to relieve as much unnecessary stress on parents as possible so that they can focus on the only thing that really matters: the care of their child. All proceeds from the sale of this journal will go directly to PCAN to further assist families in need. After reading this journal, if you find yourself moved to help in any way, you can find us at **pcanaction.org**.

You don't have to get sick
to get better

JACOB'S PERSONAL MANTRA

Somewhere he is out there, training while I am not.
One day when we meet, he will win.

~TIM TEBOW

Pediatric Cancer Action Network

One diagnosis is not rare enough

www.pcanaction.org

CPSIA information can be obtained
at www.ICGtesting.com
Printed in the USA
BVHW020828060522
635597BV00005B/3